Americans for Democratic Action
Its Role In National Politics

Americans for Democratic Action

Its Role In National Politics

By CLIFTON BROCK

Introduction by Max Lerner

Public Affairs Press, Washington, D. C.

FOR EUNICE

INTRODUCTION

This book is more than the history of a liberal organization. It provides an angle of vision—that of an idea-in-action—from which to watch the unfolding of American liberalism in our era. It is written factually, without sentiment or adornment, which is one of its merits, for we feel in it the rough touch of authenticity: this is how it happened, these were the shaping men, and these the shaping events.

There can be no doubt that without the ADA American political thought and action would have become more extremist at both ends, Left and Right. The example of European nations, where Communism penetrated the intellectual and professional groups after the war, is an index of what might have happened in America. With this additional note: the extreme Right would have taken panic at the first signs of a strong trend toward the extreme Left, and America might have witnessed not a McCarthyism which made a bid for power and failed, but one which made its bid come through. I believe that McCarthyism was defeated in the end mainly by responsible American conservatism but such a conservatism could not have functioned in a political climate where the pull was away from the center toward the extremes.

By countering the post-war Communist drive in America to capture the liberal intellectuals, the ADA kept the centrifugal pull from taking over. But it did more. It also undertook to provide some affirmative direction to creative energies in both major parties, especially the Democratic. Although it was itself, in the political spectrum, to the Left of Center, it helped provide a dynamic center between the totalitarian positions, to which men of diverse democratic beliefs could repair.

It was not wholly successful. Given the pluralism of American life and the inevitable fragmentation of thought, what movement could have been? But by supporting the Marshall plan at a critical moment in world history, it gave renewed strength to the drive toward a liberal internationalism which linked it with Woodrow Wilson's appeal for self-determination, Franklin D. Roosevelt's Good Neighbor policy, and also Roosevelt's willingness to use American power in the struggle against world chaos and world tyranny. By throwing its strength toward a welfare society and a bold program for economic growth, the ADA linked itself with the imaginative forces in American history from

Populism and Progressivism through the New Deal. By taking a vanguard position in the civil rights struggle, and fighting it out in committee rooms and on the floor of political conventions, it committed itself to finishing the unfinished business of access. For the heart of American civilization as a dynamic world force is the idea not of a narrow egalitarianism but of equal access to equal opportunity for all. This means that, whatever the individual differences in endowment and talent, each child can have a chance to develop his potential and become a person in a society of richly diverse persons.

For those of us who took part in these battles, whether inside the ADA or (as in my own case) outside but working in the same directions, this book evokes memories of stir and excitement when (like Ulysses in Tennyson's poem) we had a chance to

> *Drink delight of battle with our peers*
> *Far on the ringing plains of windy Troy.*

For the new political generations coming up it will, I hope, serve to show that effective political action is still possible in America even for those who are not professional politicians; that the political system has not rigidified beyond the reach of reason and energy; that the belittling of the political life and career, which corroded the will of so many of my own generation, need not be part of the liberal creed; that the best form of radicalism in America is not that of the absurd and fanatic Right or of the straitjacket Left, but of a radical humanism which makes man's humanity the root as it makes man's welfare the goal of social action.

You will find in this book the names of the men and women who exerted themselves to keep this idea-in-action alive. Foremost, of course, is that of James Loeb, who fathered the ADA movement. But I think also of Joseph Rauh, of Robert Nathan, of Wilson Wyatt, of Arthur Schlesinger, Jr., of James Wechsler, of Hubert Humphrey, of Samuel Beer, of John Roche, of Violet Gunther, and of many others who worked with a quiet commitment. The atmosphere they worked in had its difficulties and ironies. The ADA was not the Svengali which its enemies depicted, seducing innocent political maidens; nor was it the millstone around the neck of the practical politicians which others portrayed it. In a crisis period of history its leaders knew there was a task to be done, neither as a pressure group nor as a political party, but as a leverage group to set in motion forces stronger than itself, and to channel energies that might otherwise go unused or be used destructively. Clifton Brock has told this story admirably, straightforwardly, and with absorptive interest.

One final word. American liberals share the general American sense that size is a mark of success. Since ADA's membership never has been large, does it follow that it has not been a success in American politics? Not at all. The episode of the third-party movement in 1948 around Henry Wallace, and its tragic dissipation of good talents and generous energies, was the great turning point for the ADA and its self image. Not only did this episode show the ADA's effectiveness: it also ruled out a third-party mass movement for the ADA itself. It remained an idea-in-action, and its power remains a leverage power.

But leverage for what? Not for mass opinion in a mass culture, which is the function of the major parties themselves, but for the attitudes of the creative minorities in a creative America. For it is true in politics, as in the arts, that the mass seeks direction from the experience and judgment of the relatively few. If the liberal intellectual and professional group in America had become alienated from the mainstream of political life—as they did in the England of the 1920's and 1930's and in France and Italy in the 1950's—the American situation today would be very different from what it is. The number of ADA leaders working in the Kennedy administration is no "treason of the intellectuals" despite the charge to that effect by many who still belittle political action. It is a healthy sign that some of the best American energies are being kept in the mainstream of American life.

MAX LERNER

New York City

CONTENTS

ABOUT THE AUTHOR

Clifton Brock attended Clemson College in South Carolina, graduating in 1951. A former U.S. Navy journalist, he holds graduate degrees in political science and library science from Florida State University and the University of Michigan. At present he is a librarian and faculty member at the University of North Carolina.

FOREWORD

"Let us not fool ourselves in this hour of appraisal. The progressive forces in America have been routed." —*Nation*, 1946

"Reaction is repudiated. The New Deal is again empowered to carry forward the promise of American life. Nothing less than a new era of reform has been demanded by America." —*New Republic*, 1948

"The night Stevenson conceded the election, most liberals conceded a good deal more. Shaken and forlorn, they lost their last confidence that long-range trends necessarily guaranteed liberals anything." —*Reporter*, 1953

"The next four months will answer some of the questions and resolve at least a few of the doubts of those who voted for Senator John F. Kennedy with hopeful hearts and troubled minds. It will take much longer than that, of course, to form a considered judgment about the Kennedy Administration . . . For our part, we intend to maintain a critical vigilance, but there is no doubt that our chronic crankiness of the past decade is melting away rapidly in the glow of the fine words and good deeds of President Kennedy and his associates." —*Progressive*, 1961

These four quotations serve as verbal vignettes marking the high and low points in the history of political liberalism in the postwar United States. That history, as the words indicate, has not been smooth. Judging by the agonizing self-appraisals which are a staple feature of their journals, American liberals have been riding on a roller coaster, hurtling through the postwar years from exhilarating heights to gloomy depths. Many have found the ride too rough and have abandoned politics for other pursuits. Others have hung on grimly, alternately searching for brake and accelerator to control the momemtum of the liberal movement. For only a very few has the trip been all that was expected. For most the passage through postwar America has been, until recently, a journey of frustration.

From 1945 to 1960 many liberals indulged heavily in nostalgic reminiscence about the glories of the New Deal, waiting for the second coming of Franklin Delano Roosevelt. Those who did not believe in political resurrection were hard put to fill the void left by FDR's death. Few found what they were looking for in Harry S. Truman. Some thought they saw it in Adlai Stevenson but were denied the opportunity to test their belief by placing him at the nation's helm.

Today some liberals see in John Fitzgerald Kennedy much of the greatness of Franklin Delano Roosevelt. Some, while willing and eager to see signs of a second coming, think present political conditions so different from those of the 1930's that even Roosevelt would be of little help to their cause in the 1960's. Others wonder uneasily if they are experiencing just another high point in the political roller coaster ride and if another downward swoop may not lie ahead. A few are remaining quiet for a change, neither exuberant nor despondent. In effect the liberal movement in the United States is today undergoing one of its periodic agonizing reappraisals. This book may be considered a part of that reappraisal.

There are various ways of tracing the uneven progress of American liberalism during the postwar period. The method employed here is to focus on the activities of a conspicuous liberal organization, the Americans for Democratic Action, from its birth immediately following the election of 1946 to the present.

Liberal political groups in the United States have not been noted for longevity. While the reasons for the high incidence of early deaths among such groups are not entirely clear, it is possible to discern at least two contributory factors. One factor is the amoeba-like tendency of liberal organizations to split apart, re-form, and split again. It has been said that the liberals are "like Stephen Leacock's horseman, dashing madly off in all directions." Granville Hicks, attempting during the 1930's to set up a movement to be known as the "Independent Left," gave up after discovering that "American radicalism had been split a dozen different ways."

Another factor responsible for the high mortality rate among liberal groups has been the problem of what attitude to take toward domestic Communists. Those liberals who have attempted to cooperate with the Communists and sometimes unite with them usually have found their ranks disorganized and eventually destroyed by Communist strategy. Yet even those liberal groups which maintained a policy of opposition to Communists have generally been short-lived and ineffective. During the Popular Front days of the 1930's, and later during the World War II rapprochement between the United States and Russia, the anti-Communist policy of liberal groups often led to bitter internal warfare that left little time for positive activities.

By and large, the political climate of the postwar years has not been conducive to the health of liberal, anti-Communist organizations.

Committed by ideology and circumstance to be critical of the status quo, they have found themselves in an era in which few Americans draw fine distinctions between Communists and those who view critically many aspects of current political, social, and economic arrangements. Moreover, some liberal elements, while remaining militantly anti-Communist, have been forced by their deep-rooted civil libertarian commitments into the reluctant role of anti-anti-Communists. Thus they have had to use their usually meager resources to fight a two-front battle.

Subject to these conflicting and contradictory pressures, few non-Communist liberal organizations have survived long enough to make more than a small impression upon their times. Of the several progressive or liberal groups which emerged from World War II, only one —the Americans for Democratic Action—is today anything more than a forgotten set of initials.

Generally recognized as a major voice of organized liberalism, exclusive of purely labor groups, ADA is now in its sixteenth year of political activity. Its record, marked by a few major successes in the early years, followed by serious reverses which forced it into a rearguard holding action, and culminating today in a new position of influence, serves as an appropriate focus for the study of liberal political power in postwar America.

The principal objective of this book is to present a descriptive and analytical account of the role ADA has played in contemporary American affairs. In the initial chapters particular attention is given to the early efforts of this newly-formed group to eliminate the Communists as a significant force in domestic politics. No sooner was this accomplished than ADA found itself engaged in a long drawn out battle against powerful forces on the right symbolized by the late Senator McCarthy. The story of this still ongoing fight—now led by Senator Barry Goldwater, the John Birch Society, and other ultra rightwingers—is covered herein in some detail. Included also is an account of ADA's varying relationships with the Democratic party, as well as an analysis of ADA failure to effectuate liberal policies through Congress. Finally, an effort is made to assess ADA's role and influence within the Kennedy Administration and to appraise the effects of this relationship on ADA, the Administration, and public policy.

PREFACE

Perhaps a word of warning is in order at the beginning. Americans for Democratic Action has been and is a controversial organization; during the course of its existence few objective words have been written about it. Although I am not now and never have been a member of ADA, I am in general agreement with its political, social, and economic objectives.

Complete acknowledgement of all who helped me while writing this book is impossible. Those few who are mentioned represent only the top of the iceberg; many others who contributed much must remain below the surface in anonymity.

Particular thanks must go to three people: Marian Irish, James Prothro, and Elston Roady. Much of whatever merit lies within these pages stems originally from their influence.

Several ADA officials spent many hours adding the flesh of memory to certain bare bones of fact the author amassed in the course of his research. I am especially indebted to national director Vi Gunther, former national chairman Samuel Beer, vice-chairman Joseph Rauh, and to Richard Lambert, Olga Tabaka, William Taylor, David Williams, Page Wilson, and other ADA staff members. Arthur M. Schlesinger, Jr., ADA vice-chairman and now Special Assistant to President Kennedy, and James Loeb, former executive secretary and now U.S. Ambassador to Peru, were also very helpful.

Senator Hubert Humphrey, Tony Smith of Senator Goldwater's staff, Irving Swanson of the Senate Republican Campaign Committee, columnist Marquis Childs, and *New York Post* editor James Wechsler contributed very divergent but useful information and opinions on the political role of ADA.

Mrs. John B. Adams read the initial draft and prevented many inconsistencies. M. B. Schnapper, Editor of Public Affairs Press, pulled the book and its author through some doubtful moments.

To my wife, who kept my study clear of three delightful but boisterous children, I probably owe my sanity.

Much of the material for this book was gathered through interviews with ADA leaders and members and through use of the voluminous files of the organization's national office in Washington. The author had full access to these files, and no restriction was placed upon the use of any material. Such sources will be evident in the text and are

4

not specifically cited except where deemed necessary. Academic documentation in the form of footnotes has been avoided throughout the book, but a comprehensive bibliography of all significant material is appended. For those who wish full and precise documentation, however, a microfilm copy of an earlier draft is available in the Library of Congress.

Whatever errors of fact or interpretation which may be found within are the author's responsibility.

CLIFTON BROCK

Chapel Hill, North Carolina

"ADA's most fundamental tenet is faith in the democratic process. Faith in its capacity to find solutions to the problems that challenge twentieth century society.

"We have faith that—

with major efforts, we can find solutions to the old but continuing problems of civil rights and civil liberties for all Americans; we can develop a more imaginative foreign policy and more creative and robust approaches to disarmament; we can provide a better education for all American children and adequate medical care for the aged.

"We have faith that—

with caution and well-thought-out planning, solutions can be found to unemployment, to the sprawl of urban centers, and to the problems growing out of automation.

"Because ADA is the only independent liberal political organization operating on a nationwide scale, ADA is especially equipped to fight for these values. We are in a position of special advantage to raise the crucial issues of the times for public discussion, and to bring them into the arena of democratic politics for action."

An ADA statement, 1962

Part One

INTRODUCTION

Chapter I

KENNEDY AND THE ADA

On February 10, 1961, four top officials of Americans for Democratic Action were invited to a White House conference with President John F. Kennedy. This event, a minor incident in a busy President's day, sent a small ripple of speculation running through the U.S. political spectrum from left to right, particularly on the right.

Of all measures of influence in Washington, a conference with the President is one of the most difficult to assess. The visitor may be the British Prime Minister or the latest winner of an award from the Future Farmers of America. The conference may portend anything, ranging from preparations for a new summit meeting to a ceremonial endorsement of the Heart Fund Drive. The significance of this particular conference lay somewhere between these two extremes, obviously far below the first but how far above the second no one could say. At its conclusion the President made no comment, and the ADA officials were hardly more enlightening, remarking only that they had enjoyed a "very warm and friendly chat" with Mr. Kennedy.

Political initiates, however, noted one fact. This was the first time official representatives of the Americans for Democratic Action had been invited to the White House since the Truman Administration, and during most of the Truman period they had not been particularly welcome. If ADA officials saw the inside of the White House during Eisenhower's tenure it was along with the thousands of other anonymous tourists who trooped through each day.

Speculation about the implications of this conference and about the nature of the relationship between the new President and ADA increased in subsequent weeks as a surprising number of important executive appointments went to men who were closely associated with Americans for Democratic Action.

The Kennedy cabinet, when completed, contained one ADA member, Orville Freeman, Secretary of Agriculture, and two ex-members, Arthur Goldberg, Secretary of Labor; and Abraham Ribicoff, Secretary of Health, Education, and Welfare.

In the Executive Office of the President was Arthur M. Schlesinger, Jr., one of the original founders of ADA, a past national chairman, and one of the group's leading spokesmen since its formation. Ted Sorensen, long-time legislative aide to Senator Kennedy and now one of the President's closest advisers, had been an ADA member.

In the State Department, Under Secretary Chester Bowles (now Special Adviser to the President for African, Asian, and Latin American affairs) also was an ADA founder and past vice-chairman. G. Mennen Williams, Assistant Secretary for African Affairs, was a member, as was Ambassador-at-Large Averill Harriman. Thomas K. Finletter, Ambassador to NATO, had been a prominent ADA leader in New York. James K. Galbraith, Ambassador to India, was one of the group's top economic experts. Mrs. Eleanor Roosevelt, U.S. Representative to the United Nations General Assembly, has been ADA's first lady and honorary chairman since 1947.

Frank McCulloch, Chairman of the National Labor Relations Board, is a former chairman of the ADA executive committee. Other ADA leaders or former members holding top posts in the Kennedy administration are Jonathan Bingham, United States Representative to the United Nations Trusteeship Council; Howard Morgan, member of the Federal Power Commission; George Docking, Director of the Export-Import Bank; Charles Murphy, Under Secretary of Agriculture; Ivan Nestingen, Under Secretary of Health, Education, and Welfare; Wilbur Cohen, Assistant Secretary for Legislative Matters, HEW; George Weaver, Assistant Secretary of Labor for International Affairs; and Robert Weaver, Administrator, Housing and Home Finance Agency.

Robert Hartmann, Washington bureau chief of the *Los Angeles Times,* has listed 37 ADA members in prominent administration posts. Others have given figures ranging from 35 to 41 through 45. Mrs. Violet Gunther, present ADA national director, complains: "The present situation is almost as bad as the 'numbers game' during the McCarthy days. We no longer answer inquiries about our people in the Administration."

Long closely associated with ADA, James Loeb, Ambassador to Peru, served as its full-time executive secretary from 1947 through 1951. ADA leaders single him out as the man most responsible for the formation and survival of their group, referring to him as their "organizational genius." During his youth Loeb had for a short period been a socialist. The presence of so many ADA members in the Kennedy Administration has been commended by such liberal newspapers as the *Washington Post* and the *New York Post.* While impressed by the President's audacity, some Administration supporters feel he has been much too friendly toward ADA. Not a few G.O.P. members of Congress are of the conviction that Kennedy has opened

Warren in Cincinnati Enquirer

"I bet you would never know I play by ear!"

Holyoke (Mass.) Transcript Telegram

Gunsmoke

the door wide to leftists. A Capitol Hill Republican recently said privately: "Business people who consider Kennedy a conservative are in for a surprise. Kennedy personally may not be such a red-hot radical, but all these ADA-type advisers are going to get to him eventually. Give them a couple more years, maybe a second Administration, and they'll swing this country so far to the left it'll never straighten up." The *National Review*, an organ of the extreme conservatives, fears a socialist takeover of the government: "The ADA is so happy it can't bear it. Not since Ramsay MacDonald's Socialist government in England in 1924 has an ideological pressure outfit had such a rumble. They are quite literally all over the place, and if there is one conspicuous member of Americans for Democratic Action who has been left out, name him, and an assistant secretaryship, or an embassy, is his for the asking."

Regardless of other considerations, Kennedy's reliance on ADA leaders is definitely noteworthy, especially when viewed against the background of previous relations with the President and the public image of the ADA during the past decade.

For eleven years prior to 1961 Americans for Democratic Action had been almost a pariah of American politics, assailed by Republicans as un-American and socialistic (if not communistic) and regarded by many Democrats as a kiss of death. During the Eisenhower Administration some of its members had been denied security clearance for minor federal jobs. Its exclusion from 1600 Pennsylvania Avenue and from any part in guiding the affairs of state was indicative of its status during most of the 1950's.

As a Representative and Senator, Kennedy was well aware of ADA's reputation. Whether because of this or other reasons, he long kept a cool distance between himself and this outspoken organization. "I never joined the Americans for Democratic Action," he told a *Saturday Evening Post* reporter in 1953. "I'm not comfortable with those people." On ADA's part, the coolness was reciprocated. Less than ten percent of the group's members favored Kennedy as the Democratic Presidential nominee. An ADA vice-chairman, speaking from the floor of the 1960 Democratic National Convention, accused Kennedy of "double crossing the liberals of the country" by picking Lyndon Johnson as his running-mate. And while ADA's national board finally endorsed Kennedy for President, a vocal minority of its members voted against supporting what they called the "lesser of two evils."

In this setting the prominent role of ADA leaders in the Kennedy administration is subject to conflicting interpretations. Should their appointments be considered merely routine payoffs for campaign support? Or do these appointments reflect ADA accession to a position of substantial governmental influence? Does their conspicuousness in the executive branch of government signify that the liberal policies ADA espouses carry strategic weight in the Kennedy administration?

Such questions are, of course, related to the general question which has puzzled many since January, 1961. Just how far to the left of the Eisenhower middle road is Kennedy? Elected on the most liberal platform the Democratic party has ever written, what policies is he likely to pursue in the years ahead?

By the spring of 1962 many thought they had the answers. Those ADA leaders who remained outside the government were criticizing the Kennedy administration for its caution, and some were referring to a "third Eisenhower Administration." On the other hand, Senator Barry Goldwater—along with various leaders of the resurgent right-wing groups which had sprung into prominence since 1958—apparently sees the President as a mere figurehead for ADA advisers who are running the country.

What is Americans for Democratic Action? Prior to further consideration of the role of ADA and the liberalism it represents—within the Kennedy administration and in its broader aspects—must come an answer to this question. And an adequate answer must take into consideration the nature of ADA itself, its objectives, its stormy history, and its peculiar position in American politics.

Chapter II

WHAT IS ADA?

In a sense this whole book is an attempt to explain what ADA is. There is no single and simple answer. ADA members themselves give different replies, some of them contradictory.

Every exploration of so controversial a subject is, of course, conditioned to some extent by the political philosophy and political needs of the explorer. Borrowing Walter Lippmann's phrase, each answer depends upon the "pictures of the world" in the mind of each person.

Senator Joseph McCarthy considered the ADA a dangerous, subversive organization which stood with "razor poised" over the "jugular vein" of American security. Senator Joseph Clark sees ADA as an organization of dedicated liberals working for a better America and a better world and, incidentally, wielding a certain amount of political power in his native Philadelphia. ADA's own official explanation of what ADA is appears on its membership cards: "Americans for Democratic Action is an organization of progressives, dedicated to the achievement of freedom and economic security for all people everywhere, through education and democratic political action."

While ADA's definition injects some high-sounding phrases, plus additional elements which will be dealt with later, Senators McCarthy, Clark and ADA itself would appear to agree on at least two points: that ADA is an "organization" and that ADA is "political."

ADA's Political Role. Taking these points in reverse order, in what sense is ADA political? "In every sense" would be a reasonably accurate but not very specific answer. The incident with which Chapter I begins, a Presidential conference with ADA leaders, offers two avenues of explanation. From this conference it might be inferred that ADA operates on the highest levels of national politics and that it is closely related to the Democratic party. Both inferences have validity but are subject to many qualifications.

One of ADA's primary goals, first stated at its founding convention and reiterated by every succeeding convention, is to work for the nomination and election of liberal candidates for public office, regardless of their party label. The official political stance of the organization is nonpartisan. Although the precise language has varied from

17

year to year, the statement adopted by the 1953 convention illustrates the policy which has defined ADA's political role since 1947:

"Americans for Democratic Action is a national liberal organization. Neither a political party nor part of any political party, ADA encourages the active participation of its members in the party of their choice . . . ADA maintains its independence of either party. ADA will seek out, propose and support candidates who stand for rigorous liberal programs."

There is no mention here of the Democratic or the Republican party. Rather, there is—on the surface—an unequivocal statement of absolute independence of any political party. Despite this, ADA has supported every Democratic Presidential candidate from Truman through Kennedy and opposed every Republican Presidential candidate from Dewey through Nixon. In Congressional elections, ADA has supported, on the average, about twenty Democratic Senatorial candidates for every one Republican. The ratio for House candidates is approximately the same. ADA support on local political levels is less one-sided but still predominately Democratic. All this implies a complex relationship between ADA and both major parties, on national and local levels. It also implies a reality at variance with the group's stated principles.

Before endorsing and supporting a candidate for public office, ADA examines the candidate's record and public utterances. This examination consists of judging each candidate's degree of liberalism, of rating him against some yardstick which distinguishes "liberals" from "conservatives," as ADA defines the two terms. For Presidential candidates, the national board conducts this examination and reaches a decision. For lesser candidates, the power of decision rests with state and local chapters, with advice—sometimes solicited and sometimes unsolicited, sometimes taken and sometimes ignored—from the national office in Washington. This brief description grossly oversimplifies and dehumanizes the ADA endorsement process. However, the point of interest here is that few Republicans survive it.

ADA often has been criticized for proclaiming a pious, above-the-battle policy on one hand and plunging deeply into partisan politics on the other. While admitting its embarrassment on this score, ADA claims that it simply cannot find many liberal Republicans to support. When the issue was raised in a television interview some years ago Joseph Rauh, then serving as national chairman, insisted: "We are independent and non-partisan . . . We look for Republicans to support."

Newspaper clippings about some 1961 activities

ADA OFFERS A PRACTICAL PROGRAM FOR PRACTICAL LIBERALS

THIS IS WHAT ADA

seeks . . .

- Effective American mobilization for the security of the free world against Communism.

- Free enterprise coupled with government responsibility for full employment and rising standards of living.

- Protection of our civil liberties against the attacks of demagogues.

- Enforceable civil rights legislation.

- A dynamic program of aid to the peoples of under-developed countries.

- Comprehensive development of our natural resources for the benefit of all—and the further application of the TVA pattern.

- Integrity at all levels of government—local, state, and national.

THIS IS WHAT ADA

HAS done . . .

- Led the fight against McCarthy and mccarthyism, by putting the facts before the American people—through the press and through the circulation of reprints of a Senate subcommittee's virtually suppressed report on McCarthy's financial affairs.

- Led the fight for economic security plus freedom, and for responsible American participation in world affairs.

- Sparked the drive which put a strong civil rights plank in the Democratic Party platform.

- In Philadelphia, ousted a long-entrenched city machine and replaced it with ADA leaders—and turned a 7000-vote margin for Truman in 1948 into a 160,000 majority for Stevenson.

- In Chicago, helped elect such liberals as Senator Paul Douglas—and sparked the pre-convention drive for Stevenson's nomination.

- In New York, helped elect such ADAers as Senator Lehman, Congressman Javits, and Mayor Wagner.

- In New Jersey, played a leading role in the upset victories of Governor Meyner and Congressman Williams.

THIS IS HOW ADA

works . . .

- ADA works with the established political parties, but maintains its own independence. Our non-partisan tools are political education and political ACTION.

- ADA welcomes as members only those whose devotion to democracy is genuine. That means no Communists or fascists.

- ADA brings into political life, and helps to elect to public office, progressive citizens of both parties.

- ADA is on the firing line, not only during campaigns, but throughout the year—and not only in Washington, but on grass-roots issues in communities like yours throughout the country.

You can help!

- whether you are a business man, trade unionist, doctor, or housewife, by joining ADA and helping it to be EVEN MORE EFFECTIVE!

Act for yourself - not by yourself - through Americans for Democratic Action

Extracts from a circular issued during Eisenhower's administration.

ADA has indeed gone out of its way to find suitable GOP candidates. In 1948 it endorsed and campaigned for Illinois Republican Congressional nominee Richard Hoffman. Hoffman was elected by a 30,000-vote majority in a district which cast almost 190,000 votes, thus enabling ADA to claim that it had supplied the margin of victory. During 1949 and 1950 Hoffman voted against the ADA position on 20 of 22 roll call votes selected by the group as the most significant of the 81st Congress. Not having found what it was looking for, ADA switched its support to Hoffman's Democratic opponent in 1950 and saw its man beaten by 58,000 votes.

Also in 1950, ADA supported Republican Archibald Carey against incumbent Congressman William Dawson. In the 81st Congress Dawson had voted for the ADA position 24 out of 25 times he cast a vote. Dawson won, but by a startlingly low margin for a Chicago Democrat.

In two of these three cases, ADA displayed potent political power on a local level. In all three it emerged empty-handed, largely because it had looked too zealously and too blindly for Republicans to support.

In most instances a decision between two candidates is easy for ADA, although some of the choices may seem odd. Contrary to frequent journalistic assertions that American political parties are quite similar, ADA normally has little difficulty distinguishing between them and the candidates they nominate. Occasionally, however, it suffers from an embarrassment of riches and has to choose between two equally attractive candidates. On these occasions the group's attempt to carry water on both shoulders has failed, usually resulting in conflict within the ADA itself.

In the New York mayoralty election of 1950 the Democrats nominated State Supreme Court Justice Ferdinand Pecora. The Republicans nominated Edward Corsi, a prominent social welfare worker and close associate of former reform mayor Fiorello LaGuardia. Delegates to ADA's New York City convention met in September to decide which man they would endorse. Pecora supporters claimed that "for the first time in this century" the Democratic machine in New York had been persuaded to choose a liberal candidate. "What do you want," asked one delegate, "the Democratic party is damned if it doesn't listen to us, and damned if it does." Corsi supporters, finding themselves in a minority, sought to obtain endorsement of both candidates or neither. "We are confronted with two candidates who have long records of liberal and humanitarian action. We cannot go to the voters and say, unequivocally, that one is a better qualified man than the other."

After a heated two-hour debate, the convention voted 189 to 40 for an endorsement of Pecora. A statement issued to the press explained that while Corsi was "personally a fine man," he was the "hand-picked candidate of Governor Dewey."

On November 7th Vincent Impellitteri, running as an independent backed by no organized political party, was elected mayor of New York by a 219,000-vote plurality, getting almost as many votes as Pecora and Corsi combined.

ADA's "nonpartisan" image has become blurred on several other occasions. In 1954 Republican Congressman Jacob Javits resigned his seat to run against Franklin Roosevelt, Jr., for New York state attorney general. ADA had endorsed and worked for Javits in previous campaigns. During seven years in Congress from 1948 through 1954, Javits had voted "right" by ADA standards on 82 of 87 roll calls. This long record of ADA support earned him no more than a tie with the magic name of Roosevelt; the state convention voted "no endorsement" of either candidate. ADA leaders could point out that Roosevelt had voted 100% "right" during his five years in Congress to Javits' 94%. But for an organization which went to such lengths to find Republicans it could back in Illinois only to ignore a Javits in New York, this explanation sounded hollow. Javits, moreover, survived a national and state Democratic tide to beat Roosevelt by 176,000 votes.

In 1956 Javits again arose to embarrass ADA by announcing against New York Mayor Robert Wagner for the Senate seat left vacant by Herbert Lehman's retirement. During another tumultuous convention session several delegates charged that Javits "had become a little worried" about McCarthy's attacks on ADA and had resigned his membership. The final vote on endorsement was 102 for Wagner, 63 for "no endorsement," and only 2 for Javits.

The decision caused an exodus of the few Republican members from city and state ADA organizations. City Councilman Stanley Issacs, a charter member who had maintained that he saw no inconsistency in being both a Republican and an ADA member, resigned with the explanation that "there is no room for a Republican in ADA." Writing in ADA's national house organ, the chairman of the New York City ADA Campaign Committee boasted: "We are particularly proud to have had the opportunity to endorse our dues-paying member, Mayor Robert Wagner."

Javits defeated Wagner by almost half-a-million votes. As a Senator, Javits has continued to vote "right" by ADA standards. As Mayor, Wagner has not given ADA much reason to be overly proud of its dues-paying member.

These brief case histories of ADA political activity, focused on its relationship with Republicans in New York, imply that ADA is a bumbling, inept "political" organization. If, as in Illinois, the group has wasted its support on Republicans who have failed to support it, in New York it has failed to support Republicans who had earned its backing and has endorsed, instead, Democrats who—whether or not they were deserving Democrats—invariably were losing Democrats.

These cases are somewhat atypical; ADA is not quite as amateurish as they imply. However, these cases do help explain the reciprocal wariness which exists between ADA and the Republicans. They also go far toward explaining why ADA often has been the despair—and laughing stock—of professional politicians of both parties.

As its overall endorsement record indicates, it is with the Democrats that ADA has been most closely involved. The reason for this has been summed up in one comment by a prominent ADA leader: "On a national scale, the Democratic party offers the best hope as a vehicle for liberalism." Despite frequent doubts about this "best hope," and occasional fear that there was no hope at all for liberalism in postwar America, ADA's role in politics has been shaped by this outlook.

Details of ADA activity within and upon the Democratic party, especially on the national level, appear in later chapters. At this point it is necessary to examine ADA's policy toward the party as a whole and to outline its objectives vis-à-vis the Democrats.

ADA's overall objective is to "advance the cause of liberalism in the United States and elsewhere." What is meant by the term "liberalism" is by no means agreed upon within the group itself. There is, for instance, intermittent argument between "economic" liberals, who place primary emphasis upon economic security, and "civil liberties" liberals, who stress individual rights and freedoms. Fiorello LaGuardia once complained that liberals, like soup, came in fifty-seven varieties. With a slight discount, this would be true of ADA today. A definition of ADA's brand of liberalism would require a book on its political philosophy, an undertaking which will not be attempted here. There should be enough in the pages that follow, however, to give a concrete idea of what "ADA liberalism" means.

Regardless of some differences over what it wants to advance, ADA sees the Democratic party as the primary political means of advancing it. In terms of official policy, the party is a means to other ends. In practical terms, one of ADA's major internal problems has been to prevent the party from becoming an end in itself for some of its members and to prevent others from repudiating the Democrats altogether, or even striking out after that old liberal mirage, a third party.

A favorite Republican game has been to picture the Democratic party, its Presidential candidates, its present and past Presidents, and lesser party figures as "captives" of ADA. John T. Flynn once asserted that "the Democratic party is a helpless captive. It is a mere agency of what is known as Americans for Democratic Action. ADA is the socialist holding company. The Democratic party is a mere satellite." So far as is known, few Democratic politicians have lost sleep worrying about being bound hand and foot by so minuscule an organization as ADA. But many ADA leaders and members have experienced the reverse of Mr. Flynn's nightmare, the fear that their group was being swallowed up by the sprawling Democratic party organization.

The question of "how close we should get to the Democrats" has been debated at every ADA convention. This issue has divided those who place emphasis on ADA's long-range ideological and educational aspects from those who are more concerned with the politically immediate problems of legislation and elections. Generalizations are difficult, but on the leadership level the division is largely between academic intellectuals who see ADA as something of an American counterpart to the British Fabian Society and the more politically oriented "activists." On the rank and file level, the division seems to come between those located in areas where the Democratic party is controlled by big-city machine elements and those located in areas where liberal, reform groups control or strongly influence the party.

These patterns of division, in which policy initiative has shifted from one faction to the other, occasionally break into open view. In 1949 the annual convention's political policy commission, dominated by activists, proposed a platform plank which cited the Democratic party as the instrument with which ADA, "maintaining complete independence, might best cooperate in carrying out the Fair Deal program." A minority proposal to delete all reference to the Democratic party was defeated on the floor only after a plea by Senator Hubert Humphrey, ADA's leading political figure. The final plank which emerged from debate was amended to advocate cooperation only with the "Fair Deal elements of the Democratic party."

By 1950, following increasing disillusionment with the performance of the Truman administration and fear of rising Southern influence within the party, the activists had begun to have second thoughts, and the intellectuals had become more insistent upon putting a greater distance between ADA and the Democrats. In that year the convention wrote a 700-word political policy plank which did not once mention either the Democratic or Republican party. ADA was "neither a political party nor part of any political party . . . ADA reaffirms its political independence."

Two months after this was written, however, the Philadelphia ADA chapter adopted a political policy statement asserting that "Cooperation with the Fair Deal elements of the Democratic party in Philadelphia and Pennsylvania affords the best opportunity for the achievement of liberal policy purposes at this time."

Whatever the language of convention platforms, over the years the national and local activists have governed ADA's political policy. In practice, ADA has continued to cooperate as best it can with the Northern liberal elements of the Democratic party and with other liberal Democrats wherever they can be found. Protestations of nonpartisan independence, never taken too seriously, have become ritualistic. As one delegate to the 1961 ADA convention put it, "We're all Democrats here. Dissident Democrats, maybe, but still Democrats."

ADA's curious relationship with the Democrats stems primarily from the fact that there is not one Democratic party, but many. Political scientists describe the structure of American political parties as a "loose association of state and local parties," with power dispersed almost feudalistically among various factions, levels, and individuals and with little central control from the national level. Of the two major parties, this description perhaps fits the Democrats better than the Republicans. Consequently, it is misleading to speak of ADA's relationship with the Democratic party as a whole, since the nature of that relationship varies from level to level and place to place.

On the national level, at least two Democratic parties are in evidence, the "Presidential party" and the "Congressional party." There is no distinct line of division between the two, and various factions and individuals are not so obliging as to wear badges proclaiming their membership in one or the other. Some Democratic politicians probably would deny their existence; the Democratic party is just one big happy family, especially now that it controls the White House and Congress. The facts are otherwise, and ADA has always made a distinction between these two Democratic parties.

In general, ADA ties with the Presidential party—and with the quasi-Presidential party out of power during the Eisenhower years— have been far closer than its ties with the Congressional party. This does not mean that ADA has always been happy about the Presidential candidates nominated by the Democrats. In 1948 it spearheaded an attempt to deny Truman renomination. In 1952 and 1956 a few of its members were uneasy about Stevenson. In 1960 most of them had doubts about Kennedy. Yet once these men were formally nominated ADA found no major obstacle in supporting them.

This is not the place to go into an analysis of the nature of the Presidential constituency and the forces operating on a candidate which seem to cause him to lean in a more liberal direction than the balance of his party. An oversimplified generalization must suffice. Because of the structure of our electoral system, Presidential candidates must appeal first of all to the urban masses of the large and doubtful states. This is especially true of Democratic candidates, particularly if they are to be successful candidates. Every election since 1932—the election of 1960 more so than any other—offers evidence to buttress this generalization.

ADA's short term political goals—such as public housing, civil rights, social security, increased unemployment compensation, aid to depressed areas, federal aid to education and other welfare measures —are generally the same policy objectives apparently desired by the majority of urban voters. Thus a Democratic candidate is likely to pitch his campaign appeal along lines fairly close to ADA's line, leading to a certain similarity of policy and program. It is no accident that conservative charges of ADA domination of the Democratic party are heard most frequently in Presidential election years, usually after the Democratic candidate has come out for some welfare measure which looks as if it might cost money. This analysis exaggerates the affinity which springs up every four years between ADA and Democratic Presidential nominees, but there is enough substance behind it to explain ADA's unbroken record of support for these nominees.

What happens to this similarity of program and policy once a Democratic President is elected may be a different matter. With Truman it was a very different matter indeed. With Kennedy the issue is still in doubt at this writing. Some indications of what seems to be happening and what appears likely to happen in the future are discussed in Chapter XIII.

ADA's relationship with the Congressional Democratic party has been far less cordial. With some Senators and Representatives from the North and West, it has maintained close political and ideological ties, even enrolling a few as members. But for various reasons which are analyzed in Chapter IX, liberal influence in postwar Congresses has not been significant. Since the Democrats have controlled Congress during most of these years, ADA has tended to hold their Congressional party responsible for what it views as sixteen years of liberal stagnation or retreat. During Eisenhower's Presidency ADA was—if anything—more critical of the Johnson-Rayburn leadership in Congress than of the Republican Administration itself. Conservatism on the part of Republicans was only to be expected, but ADA ideology —and its practical political operations—required that Democrats be liberal. Today many in ADA seemingly cannot make up their minds whether to be relieved at Lyndon Johnson's removal from official leadership of the Congressional party or to be fearful of his influence within the Kennedy Administration.

Generalizations are difficult about ADA's relationship with the many state and local Democratic parties. With the great majority— all in the South and most in the West and Midwest—it has no contact at all. With those few state and local parties of the North with which it has some contact or influence, the pattern varies from continual intra-party warfare to close cooperation. The pattern is set in most cases by the nature of the local or state Democratic organization.

In Chicago the ADA chapter remains outside what it considers a corrupt Democratic machine and tries to act as a reform group by entering the primary contests of both parties. Known as the Independent Voters of Illinois, the Chicago chapter has pursued a free-wheeling, independent policy which occasionally embarrasses the national ADA. Despite an efficient ward and precinct operation which has earned the grudging respect of Cook County professionals, IVI's influence is concentrated largely in the area surrounding the University of Chicago, and it has made little impression on Chicago or Illinois politics as a whole.

In Philadelphia, the prize exhibit of ADA influence, the local chapter—sometimes working as an unofficial adjunct to the Democratic organization and sometimes independently or even against it—is a potent political machine in itself. Senator Joseph Clark attributes the heavy Democratic majorities which have come out of Philadelphia in the last decade in large part to ADA's work in organizing the city's independent voters and ousting what had been one of the most corrupt Republican machines in existence. The remark of one of Clark's campaign aides—that "the Senator runs as a Democrat in sixty-six counties in Pennsylvania but as an independent in Philadelphia"—is testimony to ADA's power in this area. The Philadelphia story is a model example of the success of ADA's tactical objective of constructing an independent liberal balance of power between the two major parties. Unfortunately, from ADA's viewpoint, it has not been duplicated in any other city.

The New York ADA, which tries to maintain a separate identity apart from the Liberal party and the local reform club movement, is less effective on the local level. This is due in part to the national interests and outlook of its leaders but primarily to the confusions of state and local politics. Bitter opposition to corrupt Democratic machines might be expected—as in Chicago—to lead the New York ADA to be more convincingly nonpartisan. But its desire to support Republicans on the local level often is thwarted by what ADA considers the stone-age character of the state Republican party and its dominance over the weaker urban liberal faction. As one member remarked, "A few liberal Republicans do exist in the city, but who ever heard of a liberal Republican upstate?" Nelson Rockefeller's appearance on the New York scene, though causing a tentative flutter in the New York ADA at first, has not led to any basic reassessment of this image. These factors, plus a strong national tie to the Democrats, have tended to immobilize one of ADA's largest chapters.

In at least two cases, ADA has played a significant role in infiltrating and rebuilding state Democratic parties. Senator Hubert Humphrey says that his success in reviving a moribund Minnesota Democratic organization, driving the Communists out of the Farmer-Labor party, and creating a strong Democratic-Farmer-Labor combine would have been impossible without ADA as an independent liberal base from which to operate. In Michigan the ADA, while remaining outside the party, joined with the political action forces of labor to create the powerful Democratic machine which carried G. Mennen Williams to six straight terms as governor.

But in both these states, ironically, success was fatal to ADA's own organization. Once a liberal party was in safe control in Minnesota, ADA's members either lost interest or disappeared into the party organization itself. While some of its leaders question Humphrey's assertion that there is no need for ADA in Minnesota now, ADA has not been able to maintain a separate identity in the state. Although a chapter still exists in Detroit, it has been weakened to such an extent that ADA no longer exerts much influence in state politics.

In other cities and states where ADA has an organization its role is primarily one of acting as a liberal, issue-oriented gadfly in the side of patronage-centered Democratic machines.

Looked at from the outside, ADA's overall relationship with the Democratic party resembles a French farce, with ADA jumping coyly in and out on the left side of the big Democratic bed and peering jealously at the Southerners and big-city bosses resting on the right. From inside ADA, however, this relationship has been a frustrating courtship of a party—attractive and repellent at the same time—which ADA suspects might resort to marriage, then leave it at home while consorting with other mistresses.

Early in ADA's history, one of its membership advertisements proclaimed forcefully: "ADA has been built To FUNCTION AT THE POLLS." Much of the organization's energy, especially its chapter activity, has been directed toward the visible and immediate operations of campaigns and elections. But to leave an account of ADA's role in politics at this level would be misrepresentative. Its actual role has encompassed something more—and less—than is implied by examples of an antiseptic, quasi-Democratic reformist group operating somewhat ineffectively in ward and precinct politics.

Beyond the electoral level, however, ADA's role becomes even more complex. Many observers have found it difficult to comprehend and categorize ADA among the many private groups which have always operated in American political life. A Republican gubernatorial candidate in Michigan once complained about "this strange thing called ADA" which was opposing him. "I call it a 'thing' because I don't believe there is any other way to describe it. There has never been anything like it in the history of this country."

During the 1952 Presidential campaign, a *Business Week* writer also was puzzled but a bit more precise: "ADA is too well organized to be called merely a group, too loose to be called a real organization. It is not a political party but has backed men in political elections . . . It isn't a hard-driving outfit bent on promoting its own interests; nor is it merely an intellectual discussion society. About the only way you can describe it is to call it a lobbying agency with political interests but no political attachments."

Difficulty in placing this "thing" and understanding its larger political role is due primarily to the fact that ADA itself has never precisely defined that role. And ADA's own indecision stems originally from the broad nature of its overall objectives and the means it has employed in trying to reach these objectives.

Although expressed in varying language over the years, ADA's objectives add up to something like " achieving freedom and economic security for all people everywhere" or "promotion of peace, prosperity, and democracy at home and abroad." Its publicity is full of such phrases as "the liberals' task," "the liberals' assignment," "the liberals' duty" to do this or that to make a better world. The image of ADA evoked by much of its literature is almost one of a liberal Atlas holding the world on his shoulders with one hand and fighting off the reactionaries with the other.

All this is a rather large order of business. ADA's efforts to achieve such sweeping goals have led it to adopt at least two general lines of strategy and to engage in many different tactical maneuvers. One line of strategy, as we have seen, is to operate as a political action group upon or within the Democratic party, to try to influence that party—even to control it in certain areas—and to use its massive political power to further liberal policies and programs. As the self-appointed guardian of liberalism, however, ADA has never been willing to entrust its objectives—or itself—entirely to the tender mercies of the Democratic party.

Along with its role as a "political action" organization, ADA's other line of strategy has been to operate as a "political idea" organization, an intellectual educational and propaganda group striving to formulate comprehensive liberal positions on national issues and to translate these positions into public policy. The many tactical activities in which ADA has engaged in pursuing this strategy can only be outlined here. At the risk of imposing too much order upon what is actually a piecemeal and loosely-integrated operation, these activities may be categorized as the formulation, dissemination, and implementation of liberal programs and policies.

In its policy formulation efforts ADA tries to act as a stimulator and coordinator of liberal thinking. The national conferences it has convened on civil rights, inflation, full employment, and other problems are examples of these efforts. The purpose of these conferences, usually held in Washington while Congress is considering one of these issues, is to provide a forum for experts—chosen for their newsworthiness as well as for their expertise—whose views and conclusions on such questions are likely to attract attention and command respect. Although its national staff frequently sets the agenda and prepares background papers for these conferences, ADA as an organization remains largely in the wings, preferring that its own political reputation not rub off on the conference itself. Occasionally, ADA has subsidized the research and publication of books and pamphlets, intended for general distribution, which in effect have been liberal policy papers on foreign economic assistance, unemployment, and other issues. ADA also draws upon its own membership, liberally sprinkled with leading academic figures, for analyses and statements on particular issues.

ADA's means of policy dissemination are much like those used by any group trying to attract public attention and mold or affect public opinion. The national office operates an informal speakers' bureau, securing lecture engagements for its members who carry the word to any group willing to listen. A particular effort is made to place members or sympathizers on national television and radio public affairs programs. The national office also publishes a monthly newspaper, the *ADA World,* which does double duty as a house organ and as a propaganda outlet to the general public. Another activity, which serves a propaganda as well as a fund-raising function, is the series of annual Roosevelt Day dinners held each January in many major cities. These dinners, designed to honor Franklin Roosevelt and to call attention to ADA as the ideological heir of the New Deal, have been one of the group's most successful ventures. There is some concern within ADA about what might happen if the Democratic National Committee should decide it would be safe and profitable to add Roosevelt to Jefferson and Jackson on its own dinner circuit.

When and if an issue once raised and publicized reaches the legislative stage, ADA attempts to implement the liberal position on that issue by a more or less typical lobbying operation. Here the organization's own varied membership is probably its greatest asset. No matter what the issue, ADA usually is able to call upon some well-known authority to represent it before Congressional committees. At times this phase of ADA lobbying seems to consist simply of running an underground railroad from Harvard, M.I.T., and other universities through the ADA office and up to Capitol Hill. Once an issue reaches the floor of Congress, ADA does what it can, usually in cooperation with other groups, to see that the liberal position becomes public policy. Normally, however, it indulges in none of those devious activities often evoked by the word "lobbying." ADA seldom can and seldom tries to "apply pressure" or "put the heat" on Congressmen. Its lobbying is a low-pressure operation, designed more to inform and convince friends than to coerce or convert enemies.

In all of these "educational" activities, most of which ADA considers nonpolitical, it consciously strives to act as a conductor or transmission belt between liberal "thinkers" on one end and liberal "doers" on the other. By conferences and research, it tries to originate coherent liberal programs. Its publicity operations are intended to popularize these programs and "fertilize the stream of national thought and discussion" with an infusion of liberal ideas. By lobbying, it tries to bring the whole process from thought to action to a successful conclusion.

One ADA official, Edward Hollander, describes this chain of policy formulation, dissemination, and implementation as an effort to get ideas and issues up into the political marketplace: "What we are really trying to do is raise and publicize problems and issues which others might like to ignore. Then we yell as loud as we can to keep the politicians from sweeping these problems under the rug. Sometimes we can convince some liberal politicians that our position on these issues—say civil rights, for instance—is not only morally right but also good politics. Once the issue is up into the political consciousness of the public we try to keep it moving, but about all we can do is hope that the normal democratic processes will take it to a successful end. Our unique function, I suppose, is to raise embarrassing issues in public places, in as many public places as possible."

It is this aspect of ADA's role, its functioning as a sort of liberal intellectual idea factory, which has caused it to be compared with the British Fabian Society and which has puzzled most American observers. Political machines, research bureaus, educational associations, public relations firms, fund-raising organizations, lobbies, and do-good groups of all varieties are common and understandable features of our complex society. But an outfit which combines all these elements really is something new in this country. One can almost sympathize with those politicians who describe it as a "strange thing" and wish it would go away.

ADA Organization. What kind of an "organization" is it which engages in all these diverse political activities? Given ADA's objectives and its strategy and tactics, one might expect it to be a combination of a grass-roots political army and the Chase National Bank and to possess a command staff comparable to the Pentagon's. The reality is far different. Of the three most important elements of organizational strength—membership, money, and leadership—ADA is rich only in leadership.

Membership in ADA is open, according to its constitution, to "any person of any race, religion, color or national origin who accepts in

good faith the basic principles of Americans for Democratic Action."
ADA believes, however, that "all forms of totalitarianism" are incompatible with its principles, and it specifically excludes any person "who
is a member or follower of any totalitarian organization or who subscribes to totalitarian political beliefs." In plain language, this
means that no Communists or Fascists need apply. While Fascists
have been no problem, ADA has been understandably wary of Communist infiltration, and it has used this constitutional provision on a
number of occasions to exclude individuals whom it suspected of
being Communists or fellow travelers.

Keeping out Communists, however, has been far less a problem
than attracting and holding other members. Originally, ADA saw
possibilities of enrolling enough members in various parts of the
country to make it the potent political action force its founders envisioned. An early ADA internal memorandum exulted: "Starting
from scratch little more than a year ago, ADA now has 109 local
chapters in 41 states. ADA's genuine, unpadded membership of
25,000 is a genuine accomplishment." By 1950, in an appearance
before the House Select Committee on Lobbying Activities, ADA's
national chairman could testify: "At present, ADA has 123 local
chapters in 30 states, and a membership of almost 35,000." *The
Story of ADA,* a publicity brochure issued in 1953, claimed that the
organization had "almost 40,000 members who pay dues of three
dollars or more to 125 chapters and organizing committees in 40
states."

In recent years ADA has made no vociferous membership claims.
While various sources have mentioned figures as high as 45,000, and the
New York Times of December 30, 1960, reported 40,000 members in 80
chapters, it is obvious that such figures are exaggerated. Actually, by
the end of 1959 ADA's organization had contracted to 43 chapters in
14 states, and it could count only 18,000 paid-up members in these
chapters. However, by including at-large members unaffiliated with
any chapter, inactives who have not paid dues but consider themselves
ADAers, and a large number of people who contribute money and
work but do not bother to take out membership cards, it might be
possible to swell ADA's total to something approaching 40,000.

But even this method of counting—in effect, voting the graveyard
shift—does not bring ADA close to the 100,000 figure set in 1955 as a
"realistic goal." Although its leaders claim that ADA was never intended to be a mass organization, one suspects that this contention
reflects more a recognition of hard facts than a statement of deliberate

policy. ADA obviously is concerned that so few Americans have accepted its principles with enough good faith to pay five dollars.

ADA's inability to maintain its original impetus is even more evident in the decline and final expiration of its campus affiliate, Students for Democratic Action. In 1948 SDA was the largest student political group in the nation, with 3,500 members on 200 campuses in 36 states. By 1956 its membership had plummeted to 600. Following further losses and some embarrassing and well-publicized political disagreements with its junior members, ADA abolished Students for Democratic Action in 1959. A recent attempt to revive it as the Campus Division of ADA has met with little success. As of January, 1961, the Campus Division had only eight active chapters, five others in a "highly disorganized state," and a total membership of "no more than 250."

Unlike many small conservative political groups, moreover, what ADA lacks in membership it cannot make up with money. In 1947 the national ADA's income from membership dues, chapter quotas, voluntary contributions and other sources totaled approximately $250,-000. Its local chapters had an additional estimated income of $150,-000. While this was inadequate in relation to ADA's grandiose objectives, it was not a bad start for an organization which had been in operation less than a year. Although ADA was running a deficit of $16,000 by mid-1948, it had begun to receive substantial support from labor. This, coupled with its spiraling membership, seemed to promise financial solvency, if not affluence.

This promise was not to be fulfilled in subsequent years. Although ADA has survived somehow, it has led a hand-to-mouth existence, with financial reports showing decreasing revenues and rising deficits. By the end of 1960 ADA's annual income was down to $126,000, and it was in the red $21,000. Contributions from labor unions, never higher than $66,000 in any one year, were down to $14,000. Total income from local chapters, including the national ADA's share of chapter membership dues plus quotas levied on its stronger chapters, was only $17,000. Voluntary contributions from individuals and organizations amounted to $30,000. Promotional mailings brought in five and ten dollar donations which finally totaled $39,000. Proceeds from Roosevelt Day Dinners, the annual convention, and other minor-fund-raising ventures constituted the balance of 1960 revenue.

This brief organizational survey, when contrasted with ADA's objectives, is sufficient to point up the disparity which exists between the group's aspirations and the numerical and financial resources at its command. It should be sufficient also to show that the picture frequently evoked of ADA—that of a swarming army of doorbell ringers with an inexhaustible pipeline into the pockets of wealthy liberals and the overflowing coffers of labor unions—is a grossly overdrawn caricature. Such an ADA has existed only in the inventive minds of right-wing publicists and politicians and—perhaps—in the dreams of ADA's founders.

This unembellished picture of ADA as it is today, however, raises more questions than it answers. How did such a "thing" come into being at all? Was it ever—even in its early and more vigorous years— a force of any significance in American politics? If so, what happened to it during the decade of the 1950's? If ADA excludes Communists from membership, why has it so often been tagged as a "subversive" or "Communist-front" group? Moreover, why should a President of the United States turn to the members of such a small, impecunious, and suspect organization for counsel and advice? For the answers to these questions, it is necessary to go back to the beginning of ADA and to trace its development in the context of the history of American liberalism during the postwar years.

Part Two

THE BATTLE FOR LIBERAL SUPREMACY

Chapter III

FROM REFORM TO REACTION

If a seismograph could record the fortunes of political movements, the graph showing the course of liberalism in the United States would almost certainly contain a very jagged line. Perhaps more than any other political force, American liberalism has been characterized by ups and downs, zigs and zags. If, moreover, we could examine such a graph closely we would note two particular disturbances in the fourth decade of the twentieth century.

In the mid-1940's two events occurred which rocked U.S. liberalism to its foundations and rearranged the landscape of the American left to an extent not yet fully realized. One of these events was the death of Franklin D. Roosevelt and the succession to the Presidency of Harry S. Truman. The other was the election of 1946.

Rightly or wrongly, for at least one generation of Americans, FDR, the New Deal, and liberalism were almost synonymous terms. Roosevelt was the political instrument through which many of the ideas and plans of the liberal intellectuals of the 1930's and 1940's became social realities. "As long as Franklin Roosevelt was President," as Norman Mackenzie observed in the *New Statesman* in March 1948, "life was politically simple for American liberals. Locally, they supported the Democratic ticket or, sometimes, a liberal Republican candidate. There was a place for them on the New Deal bandwagon, and, until the driver died, some of them were permitted to sit on the front seat and scan the countryside for lurking economic royalists."

Unfortunately, the continued availability of a champion driver meant that the liberal passengers who went along for the ride saw no need for alternative means of transportation. The man with the reins always found room for a goodly number of their kind, and he always got the buggy home in front. When he died, American liberals suddenly found themselves stranded by the side of the road. As one of them, James Loeb, Jr., said, "From March, 1933, until mid-April, 1945, American liberals clung to the illusion that they had 'achieved power' . . . Throughout this long and significant era of the ascendancy of progressive ideas in government, however, there never existed an authentic liberal coalition which could survive the loss of Roosevelt."

39

Even before realizing fully the implications of the loss of Roosevelt, the liberals were forced to examine the man who climbed somewhat reluctantly into the driver's seat. Harry S. Truman was not one of their own. A graduate of the Kansas City Pendergast organization, he represented a big-city machine element with which the liberals lived uneasily inside the wide coalition of forces which comprised the Democratic party. In 1944, moreover, he had replaced Henry Wallace—the man many liberals at the time considered the legitimate heir to Roosevelt—as FDR's running mate. Truman was an unknown quantity; liberals waited uneasily to weigh and judge him.

By late 1946 their verdict was hearty condemnation of President Truman. Not unrepresentative were the sentiments attributed by Eric Goldman to one highly placed liberal: "I look at him, and I say to myself, 'Yes, he is in Roosevelt's chair, yes he is, yes he is.' And then I say, 'Oh, no, no, my God, it's impossible.' "

The evidence leading to this harsh verdict varied with the primary interests of each liberal juror. Those concerned with foreign affairs viewed with alarm what they felt to be the unnecessary deterioration of our wartime alliance with Russia and the threats to world peace stemming from this situation. Said *New Republic* editor Michael Straight: "The all-important issue is world peace . . . Great leadership is demanded of America now in securing peace. It is not within Truman's power to give."

Those liberals concerned with inflation watched Truman struggle vainly with Congress to save the OPA in the summer of 1946. Labor leaders listened incredulously as a Democratic President called for the peacetime drafting of striking railroad workers.

These things, plus many others, the liberals did not like, and "a whole liberal literature rapidly appeared bewailing the loss of Roosevelt and decrying his successor."

The most vociferous liberal quarrel with Truman came over the matter of appointments to prominent posts in the Administration. Under Roosevelt many liberals and progressives had held high offices in the federal bureaucracy, positions from which they originated, nurtured, and protected many of the reforms of the New Deal. Henry Wallace in Agriculture, Harold Ickes in Interior, Frances Perkins in Labor, Henry Morgenthau in the Treasury, Francis Biddle as Attoney-General—all of the Cabinet level—plus Chester Bowles and Leon Henderson in the OPA and Wilson Wyatt as Housing Expediter —these headed on the highest levels a strong corps of liberals whose

ADA World

PUBLISHED EVERY TWO WEEKS · BY AMERICANS FOR DEMOCRATIC ACTION · ADA

VOLUME I, NUMBER 6   WASHINGTON,. D. C.   JUNE 18, 1947

Tax-Labor-Rent-Bills Called 'Triple-Threat' To Nation

As the deadline for White House action on the labor, tax and rent control bills approached, Americans for Democratic Action sent a strong message to President Truman describing the triple-threat legislation as a "design for depression."

With the tax veto now out of the way, it still remains for the Chief Executive to veto or sign the Taft-Hartley labor measure by Friday. (See Congressional Letter, Page 3). The emasculated rent 'control' bill also awaits the President's approval or veto.

Ask Votes

The ADA letter urged a veto of both tax and labor measures. It asked President Truman to call on Congress to extend the existing rent control law, rather than the emasculated bill which was still before both Houses.

Wilson W. Wyatt, ADA national chairman; Leon Henderson, Chairman of the Executive Committee; Vice-Chairman Hubert Humphrey, Mayor of Minneapolis, and Frank-lin D. Roosevelt, Jr, acting in behalf of the national organization, declared that the three bills "constitute a triple-threat to the national welfare."

They added that the legislation taken as a whole "relieves financial responsibilities on those in the upper brackets and imposes a heavy burden on those least able to pay."

Relief For Rich

Although President Truman's subsequent refusal to sign the tax bill was hailed by the nation's press as a veto of a $4,000,000,000 tax cut for the American people, the measure offered relatively little relief to the low and middle-income groups.

Emphasizing this, ADA asserted that "the measure affords only token relief to those in the lower and middle income brackets and allows disproportionate tax reductions for the wealthy."

False Front

Describing the Taft-Hartley bill as one which "penalizes 20 million workers behind the false front of attempted labor reforms," the letter warned the Chief Executive:

"In our opinion, Congress has confused you with a labor bill which so seriously weakens bargaining rights while strengthening the employer that increased industrial strife is inevitable."

On the issue of genuine rent control legislation, ADA held that the measure would further distort the distribution of national income by "virtually imposing a 15 per cent rent increase on 16,000,000 American families."

When Democrat Bites Republican It Isn't News

Back in the days of Democratic majorities in the House and Senate, the traditional formula for an "overnight" follow-up on the Congressional news of the day was this: Corner a GOP Congressman or Senator and get him to blast the latest piece of Democratic legislation which was driving the country to ruin.

Since January, Washington newsmen, who know a good trick when they see one, have tried to apply the same formula in reverse.

A news service bureau reporter admitted last week there might be something to this business about the "venal capitalist press."

The evidence: A list of "overnights" with Democrats blasting Republicans that never got past the desk.

ADA Economic Program Wins Hearing Before Congress

Chapters Sell ADA Program To Halt 'Bust'

City and neighborhood groups in some 20 states are plugging away to get public support for ADA's "Stop Depression" program, due for a hearing before the joint Senate-House Economic Committee next month.

In New York, neighborhood meetings have been held on the East Side, the Village and Chelsea districts of Manhattan, as well as an over-all meeting in Queens. The East Side Branch of ADA has scheduled a public meeting June 24 at the Hotel Shelton.

In Minneapolis and St. Paul, a local Committee on Economic Stability headed by Dorothy Jacobson is at work on a full program of support for ADA's Economic program. It includes radio broadcasts,

(Continued on Page 4)

Joint Senate-House Committee Sets ADA Testimony For July 16

ADA's 9-point program for avoiding a serious economic recession will get a full airing before the U. S. Congress next month in hearings before the joint Senate-House Economic Committee.

Responding to the request of National Chairman Wilson W. Wyatt made May 15 when the report was released, the Senate Committee Chairman Robert A. Taft invited the ADA-sponsored Economic Stability group to present its case at hearings which begin June 23.

Wyatt's request for hearings on the ADA report was underscored two weeks ago when a group of 52 Congressmen petitioned Co-Chairman Rep. Jesse P. Wolcott asking for prompt consideration of ADA's program by this session of Congress.

Ask Committee Time For Bowles, Henderson, Porter

Present schedule calls for appearance of the ADA Committee on Economic Stability before the joint Senate - House committee July 16.

ADA has asked for sufficient time before the committee to allow for the appearance of former OPA Chiefs Chester Bowles, Leon Henderson and Paul Porter, and other sponsors of the organization's Economic Stability report.

Industry, labor, finance and farm organizations will also be given a hearing, Senator Taft announced.

Release of ADA's report in May focused attention on the Taft-Wolcott committee, already more than four months behind its deadline for reporting, as required by the Maximum Employment Act of 1946.

Criticism of the committee's dalliance mounted after release of a report prepared for the group by Dun and Bradstreet, and based on what were charged to be "loaded questions."

Wide publicity and editorial comment on the ADA program was credited in Congressional circles with having forced the joint committee to schedule hearings. Earlier this month, President Truman took open issue with Senator Taft and said the GOP leader's philosophy follows the "old idea of boom and bust."

"Under this philosophy," the President said, "when demand is high, those who have it within their power to administer prices charge every penny that they can get. After a while, purchasing power is unable to keep up with the excessive price level. Then unemployment, business failures, cuts in production, and price reductions follow in rapid succession."

Henderson Addresses NAACP

Leon Henderson will address the 38th Annual Conference of the NAACP in Washington June 24. Henderson will discuss the ADA's domestic program, drafted by the Committee on Economic Stability.

ADA Hits Wallace Views, But Affirms His Right To Air Them

When Henry Wallace returned to Washington this week to make another speech, he found some ready and helpful dumb-bellers in the House Un-American Activities Committee and the 'American Anti-Communist Association.'

The latter group, headed by Congressman Alvin E. O'Konski of Wisconsin, sought a court order to prevent Wallace from using the federally-owned Watergate Theatre for his speech. The U. S. District Court refused to grant the injunction.

ADA smacked both the O'Konski group and Mr. Wallace's foreign policy views, insisting that Wallace is entitled to the rights of free speech even though "he has dangerously confused and misrepresented important international issues at a time when it is more urgent than ever that these issues be the subject of sober, clarifying debate."

ADA Executive Committee Chairman, Leon Henderson, sent the following wire to O'Konski:

"As an organization vigorously opposing many of Henry Wallace's policies and actions, Americans for Democratic Action strongly condemns the position taken by your group in seeking a court order to deny Henry Wallace use of the Watergate theater for a speech.

"Americans for Democratic Action includes among its members Mark Ethridge, Mrs. Eleanor Roosevelt, Dr. Frank Graham, Wilson W. Wyatt, Paul A. Porter, Lillian Smith, Barry Bingham, William H. Davis, Palmer Hoyt, Elmer Davis, Marquis Childs, William Evjue, Melvyn Douglas, Bishop William Scarlett, Mayor Hubert Humphrey, Franklin Roosevelt, Jr., Arthur M. Schlesinger, Jr., and many hundreds of other prominent Americans

genuinely devoted to democratic ideals.

"We do not agree with Mr. Wallace's views on foreign policy and we have repeatedly made this clear.

"We do not agree with Mr. Wallace's view that liberals can cooperate with American Communists and the ADA Constitution expressly excludes Communists from our membership.

"We believe Mr. Wallace has dangerously confused and misrepresented important international issues at a time when it is more urgent than ever before that these issues should be the subject of sober clarifying debate.

"Henry Wallace does not speak for us.

"But freedom of speech and freedom of assembly are first among the 'glories of our democracy.

"We believe any person, including Henry Wallace, is entitled to

(Continued on Page 4)

'We Must Stop Mob Violence In America'

By Lillian Smith

I am thinking today of the sad and tragic events that have piled up to tall a monument to racial hate this past year.

Most of them have occurred close to my home here in Georgia, Walton County with its four lynched. . . Greenville, S. C., where a jury set 23 men free who had confessed to a lynching. . . Now the attempted lynching in Jackson, N. C.

Three events that cast a long shadow across the world.

They were sick men who lynched that Negro at Greenville. Sick men composed that jury who threw justice away like a cheap

Lillian Smith
Author of "Strange Fruit"

thing. Sick men lynched, and sick men protected the lynchers in Walton County. Men made sick by hate and fear and ignorance, and by a culture that too often and too long has given the green light to mob violence and mob hate. Every man, on that jury, every lyncher, every potential lyncher, will tell you: "Keep the rest of the country out of this; this is our business."

Are we too, going to chalk a circle around each racial crime and tell the rest of the world to "Keep out"? Or are we ready now to

take over this emergency and handle it in a mature and sane manner?

There comes a turning point in men's affairs when new decisions must be made to avoid profound disaster. What we do next about lynching and mob violence may well be the test case that will decide our capacity for cooperating with the world in this time of desperate need.

A state, a region, can no more handle racial emergencies alone than it can handle alone the results of a flood or tornado. Our people's prejudice has overflowed the bounds of reason. Increased by world tension, whipped on by a loose-floating hate that is sweeping across the minds of men everywhere, it has reached proportions so destructive of law and order and facile and human values that only the fool, or the sick, can now

say, "Leave us alone and we'll handle it."

For 65 years we have had 4,982 lynchings. Only 1 percent of these lynchings has received a sentence, even of the mildest nature. And nearly every sentence has been suspended.

And now? Four men and women lynched last summer in Georgia. NO ONE PUNISHED. A lynching in South Carolina by jurors who confessed their guilt. NO ONE PUNISHED. Despite the personal courage of judge and prosecuting attorney and the jury refused to punish. Now a new lynching in North Carolina.

There is one right thing to do and we must do it. WE MUST STOP MOB VIOLENCE IN THIS COUNTRY. But we in the South are not strong enough to swing this job alone and we must face

(Continued on Page 3)

First page of the June 18, 1947 issue of ADA World

Reproduction of a circular widely distributed in 1960

ranks spread through all the many gradations of the administrative hierarchy.

By the fall of 1946 all of those named (plus many others) were gone, their places taken by men from outside the ranks of liberalism. The liberals and progressives were leaving Washington as they had come in 1933—by the trainloads. "The New Deal era of political power is ending," *U.S. News and World Report noted.* "The New Dealers are scattering . . . Bereft of the major, unifying touch of the late Franklin D. Roosevelt, they are scattering to all points of the nation."

Not all liberals were willing to lay the entire blame for the decline of their fortunes upon Harry Truman. "One need not write in defense of Mr. Truman," James Wechsler contended, "to realize that many of his woes are politically hereditary . . . His floundering reflects the weakness and irresolution of the liberal forces in the country as much as any personal inadequacy."

But many liberals, contemplating their fall from power and decrying the performance of this accidental heir to Roosevelt, found a scapegoat in the man from Missouri. In Eric Goldman's pungent words: "For each hellish period, its devil, and with every passing month more liberals were placing the horns squarely on Harry Truman's head."

The election of 1946, coming in the midst of such disenchantment with the new President, demonstrated to American liberals that they were in the middle of a major political upheaval. For the first time in sixteen years Republicans would outnumber Democrats in both houses of Congress, and, said Goldman, "a considerable percentage of the new majority were the kind of Republicans who saw dark premonitions of socialism in a bill for free school lunches." As the *New Republic* glumly noted, "Victories fought and won years ago were suddenly in doubt. Everything was debatable again."

The 1946 earthquake, in addition to the damage done to the liberal movement as a whole, also opened up a fault line which threatened to split that movement down the middle. Although never noted for its unanimity of opinion, the American left had been more or less united since the beginning of World War II. The New Deal reforms had gradually won over most of the members of the agrarian and other radical sects of the 1930's, and the wartime alliance with Russia had made even the American Communists ardent backers of FDR. By the end of the war the American left was an indiscriminate grouping of individuals and organizations ranging all the way from non-Communist liberals through socialists and ex-socialists to undisguised Communists.

In 1946 the Republican campaign orators hit this unwieldly coalition at its most vulnerable point. Capitalizing upon growing public apprehension over the postwar intransigence of Russia, they painted a picture of a liberal movement darkly shadowed with overtones of communism or pro-communism.

The Republican charges were directed in particular at two organizations operating on the left in 1946 and rendering campaign assistance to the Democratic party as they attempted to "ride herd on four or five million radical, socialist, liberal, progressive or merely disgusted voters." These were the National Citizens Political Action Committee and the Independent Citizens Committee of the Arts, Sciences and Professions. These two, along with the CIO Political Action Committee, were called the "big three of progressive political action."

The NCPAC, a nonlabor offshoot of the CIO-PAC, had been set up by Sidney Hillman before the 1944 election in an attempt to influence those voters who could not be reached by a purely labor organization; by 1946 the NCPAC could boast a membership of 50,000. The ICCASP, growing out of the 1944 Independent Voters Committee of the Arts and Sciences for Roosevelt and featuring such big Hollywood names as Frank Sinatra, Orson Welles, James Cagney, and Howard Fast, had 18,000 members.

The leaders of both these organizations vehemently denied the Republican charges of Communist domination. Hannah Dorner, publicity agent for the ICCASP, when asked about Communist influence within the organization, replied: "Says who and so what? If the ICC program is like the Communist line, that is purely coincidental."

Despite these denials, the coincidences were becoming a bit too glaring for some liberals. In July Harold Urey and several other prominent scientists pulled out of the Independent Citizens Committee, branding it as a Communist front. In October Harold Ickes, who had accepted the chairmanship of the ICCASP after leaving Truman's cabinet, rumbled out with a similar blast.

The liberals, remembering bitter experiences with popular front groups of prewar years, were beginning to wonder. From the early 1930's until the war they had seen many promising progressive organizations wrecked by Communist infiltration. Among them were the American League Against War and Fascism, the National Negro Congress, and the American Youth Congress. One who watched this wreckage, Robert Bendiner, has described it well:

"For lack of alternatives, Americans with decent social instincts have been joining front organizations, on and off, over the past two decades, and always with the same result. Whether or not they achieved this or that immediate purpose, they inevitably found themselves, in a matter of months, in an unenviable position. They could defend the Communists who invariably ran such groups, strictly for their own purposes and with a program subject to change without notice; they could avert their eyes from such stark reality and, having been fooled into joining in the first place, go on deceiving themselves indefinitely; or they could get out, embittered and with no place to go."

A bizarre but not too atypical example of how the Communists manipulated such front groups occurred in mid-1941. For months during the early part of the year an organization called the American Peace Mobilization attracted national publicity by staging a "perpetual peace vigil" in front of the White House. This was during the period of the Hitler-Stalin Pact, and the APM was agitating against American entrance into the war in aid of Britain and France. On June 21, 1941, the American Peace Mobilization called for the observance of a National Peace Week. On June 22nd Hitler invaded Russia. The "perpetual peace vigil" disappeared overnight, and in July it was announced that the American Peace Mobilization would now be known as the American People's Mobilization, with a program demanding aid to Russia, Britain and France.

Once the United States entered the war, however, American Communists—finding that their primary aim of aid to Russia had become official U.S. policy—began to dissolve their own remaining organizations, to modify their extremist views, and to find acceptance in many liberal groups which had previously been on guard against them.

Thus by the end of 1946 the liberal movement in America, minus the strong leadership of Roosevelt, in acrimonious revolt against his successor, and demoralized by the election setback, also found itself open to at least partially justified attack on grounds of Communist domination.

In the words of James Wechsler: "In America, so it seemed, there was rising Republican reaction, a pro-Communist left, and nothing in between but the still inept, bumbling Presidency of a man who wished he wasn't there."

The American left was ripe for change.

Chapter IV

THE LIBERAL RANKS DIVIDE

From mid-1946 to November of 1948 American liberals were spectators of and parties to a political civil war which raged across the entire front of the American left. In the course of this battle liberals were to attack liberals with more venom than they had ever directed at any economic royalist, the labor movement was to divide and choose sides between the two protagonists, and a political party was to arise and die in a matter of months. In the end a decision would come only at the ballot box, and by the time it came many felt that upon it hung the fate of liberalism as a political force in America.

On the Right: *Americans for Democratic Action.* In May, 1946, there appeared in the pages of the *New Republic* a letter which demonstrated that the war-bred unity of the left was beginning to disintegrate. This letter proved to be the opening shot in a political battle which within two years was to alter radically the topography of the American left.

The immediate target of this verbal missile was a New York gathering known as the Win-the-Peace Conference. Chaired by Paul Robeson and sponsored by the National Citizens Political Action Committee and the Independent Citizens Committee of the Arts, Sciences and Professions, the conference had just concluded with a manifesto which called for unrestricted American aid to Russia while opposing a loan to Britain "until sufficient guarantees have been made that these materials and funds will not be used for the exploitation and oppression of the colonial peoples." The *New Republic* letter denounced the conference and, without mentioning Russia specifically, declared that American liberals must decide now "whether they believe the present critical tension in international affairs is due *exclusively* to the imperialistic, capitalistic, power-mad warmongering of the Western democracies and whether it is their conviction that the *sole* objective of the progressive movement is economic security or whether human freedom is a co-equal good."

Going further, the letter declared that liberals had to make several basic policy and organizational decisions, all of which must lead them

46

FREE SPEECH

vs.

THE COMMUNISTS

Let's get Back into Balance

Americans nowadays have to balance carefully the lasting values of free speech and the immediate dangers of Communist subversion. The Smith Act, and the prosecutions of Communist leaders under it, have put us badly off balance. Let's get back into balance—and save free speech from becoming the first victim of the Communist conspiracy.

Title page of a pamphlet critical of the Smith Act

SO YOU'RE WILLING TO WORK A PRECINCT

This job you're undertaking is the most important one in American politics. Without Precinct Work, political action is like an automobile without a motor. Speeches, billboards, broadcasts and newspaper ads are a good imitation of the body, the wheels and the windshield of an automobile. But Precinct Work is the ENGINE that makes political action GO.

Since Jefferson's day professional politicians have known the importance of Precinct Work. It has been no secret. Nearly every American citizen has been visited by a Republican or Democratic precinct captain. Yet, somehow, we "liberals" and "independents" have never realized how significant these gentlemen are. We've taken them rather for granted. Only recently has it begun to dawn on us that we need to investigate them more closely. We need to learn the answer to several questions:

1. Exactly *what* does a precinct captain do?
2. What are the techniques—the "tricks" of his trade?
3. Why is he so important?
4. What has a professional got that YOU haven't got?
5. What have YOU got that the professional doesn't have?

EXACTLY *WHAT* DOES A PRECINCT CAPTAIN DO?

The work of a precinct captain can be reduced to two simple principles—and one qualification.

THE PRINCIPLES: (1) you *locate your votes*
(2) You *get 'em to the polls.*

THE QUALIFICATION: You do it SYSTEMATICALLY.

Like all summaries, that one is over-simplified. There are many complexities in the background which you need to know about—which you'll learn very shortly. But, they'll all distill to these two main principles. A precinct captain *locates* votes, and gets

3

---

them to the polls. He does it *systematically.* When you multiply one precinct captain by several thousand, you have *THE* factor that wins elections.

Our two principles are also the second and third in order among the four steps of ACTION which go to make up the complete pattern of work for a captain.

(From here on, let's drop this anonymous "captain" we're talking about. Instead, let's talk in terms of "YOU". Picture YOURSELF as the person carrying out the techniques in the rest of this pamphlet.)

STEP-BY-STEP PATTERN OF PRECINCT WORK:

1. *YOU CHECK REGISTRATION.* Check the PEOPLE in your precinct against the Precinct Registration List, which has been given to you by your local chairman. You get newcomers to register. You remove from the list those names which are ineligible.

2. YOU LOCATE YOUR VOTES. After registration, you start canvassing your precinct, door to door, apartment to apartment, even room to room. You *learn the attitudes* of the voters. You *keep a record* of what you learn. The record indicates which voters are inclined to vote for your candidates.

3. YOU GET YOUR VOTES TO THE POLLS. On election day, you make sure that every vote on your side *gets to the polls* and actually *gets voted.*

4. YOU WATCH THE COUNT. On election night, you watch the clerks and judges count the ballots in your polling place so that you

4

WHAT'S THE PROFESSIONAL PRECINCT CAPTAIN GOT THAT YOU HAVEN'T?

The Republican and Democratic captains do have certain advantages. They give full time to canvassing. They have more experience (though they had a first time, too). They have money to spend and jobs to give. They maintain a continuing relation with the voters.

WHAT HAVE YOU GOT THAT THE PRO'S DON'T HAVE?

You have convictions about what you're presenting. You have a more acceptable story to tell. Many people who reject (or eject) the professionals will be perfectly receptive to you, because you're "independent". In many homes you'll find that the ADA name is known and carries considerable weight. In others where it is not known, you'll find respect and hospitality (new members, too, sometimes) when you explain how ADA works for better government and liberal ideals. Finally, you have a special advantage. The Republican and Democratic parties are like two men on a scale—about equally balanced. By throwing your weight to one side or the other you exert force. By aiding one or the other of two contending forces, you hold *a strategic balance of power.*

CHECK LIST FOR ADA PRECINCT LEADERS REGISTRATION—30 DAYS BEFORE ELECTION

1. Canvass house to house. Learn who the new voters are. Learn who has moved away.

2. Urge new voters to register. Tell them when, where, how. Turn in removals to your local chairman.

3. The night before registration, and on registration day, remind voters to register. You CAN'T remind them too often.

12

CANVASSING—THREE WEEKS TO ONE DAY BEFORE THE ELECTION

1. Canvass house to house. Talk to at least one member of every family. Remember your first objective is to LOCATE VOTES. In every case:

   a. Learn their attitude.
   b. Give them any information they want, or get it to them later.
   c. Give them literature.
   d. Mark your list with a plus, minus or zero.

2. After the full round of your precinct, go back to those doubtfuls and unknowns you think you have a chance of converting.

BRINGING IN THE VOTE

1. The night before election, remind all your voters marked with plus.
2. Election Day, get out early; get men to vote before they leave for work; check all day to keep your plus marks coming to vote. Use every possible means to get your voters in. After the polls close it will be too late.

WATCHING THE COUNT

1. Be in the polls before they close. Stay for the count.
2. Watch the ballots. Watch the tally.
AT ALL TIMES—Stay busy and alert. Don't wait to be invited to work. Keep in touch with your Political Action chairman. His job is to furnish you with literature, the Precinct List, a poll watcher's certificate, and if possible, the hard card information. He should help you with information, guidance, counsel. He wants your ideas and suggestions.

TIPS, QUESTIONS, CAUTIONS

TIP: *Don't be discouraged because* your precinct list looks so long. In a 400-voter precinct, there won't be more than 200 households—probably less. Some households will have 6

13

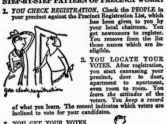

Extracts from "A Precinct Manual For Independents"

"to oppose the admission of Communists to progressive organizations . . . because any united-front movement tends inevitably to become less united and more front."

The writer of this barbed salvo was James Loeb, Jr., executive secretary of a small liberal organization called the Union for Democratic Action. The UDA had been started in 1941 by a group of dissident socialists who split from Norman Thomas' Socialist party after unsuccessfully opposing its isolationist tendencies. Centering primarily in New York, the UDA had limped along through the war years on a small membership and a smaller budget, attempting as best it could to accomplish its stated aims of "fighting a two-front war for democracy" by "protecting democracy at home from reactionaries who desire to destroy social gains under cover of the defense effort and by insisting that democratic terms of peace be made a part of the fight."

By 1946 the UDA, which could never claim over 10,000 members, was a "small but purposeful" organization which was clearly overshadowed by such progressive political action groups as the NCPAC and the ICCASP. Besides its comparative insignificance, the major factor which distinguished the Union for Democratic Action from other liberal groups of the war and immediate postwar years was that it had always excluded Communists from membership. Loeb was once quoted as saying: "During those years we became almost the pariahs of the liberal movement. We were sometimes called 'the hang-back boys' because we refused to participate in so many 'worthy causes' that we knew were run by Communists."

Prior to 1946 the UDA's non-Communist policy had met with only a negative response within progressive ranks. Loeb's letter to the *New Republic,* however, set off a full-throated debate in the liberal press over the question of Communist participation in progressive organizations.

For years it had been an axiom in liberal circles that the dedicated Communists could be depended upon to do the heavy organizational work which no one else wanted. A Chicago correspondent reflected this viewpoint when he answered Loeb: "The old-time liberals, with whom Mr. Loeb identifies himself, are thinkers, not doers. Their idea of action is a semi-annual mass meeting (featuring a Senator or cabinet member with whom they can appear on the platform and be photographed), letters to Congressmen and distribution of tons of literature . . . The real split in the ranks of American liberals is not between Communists and progressives . . . Rather, it is between competents and incompetents."

From the West Coast, however, came a letter blaming liberal defeats in the recent California primaries on the maneuvering of Communists within liberal organizations: "The Communists have demonstrated again and again that they simply cannot be trusted to work for the agreed aims of any non-Marxist organization."

The debate raged within the Union for Democratic Action itself, showing that not all its members were of one mind on the group's non-Communist policy. A UDA leader from Texas pleaded: "We are living in a nervous, worried world, living in the shadow of the atomic bomb. Every ounce of liberal energy should be consecrated to the task of solving the great basic problems of our age, and we simply cannot afford to waste valuable time peering into dark corners and looking under chairs for elusive Reds."

Stanley Issacs, an active UDA leader from New York and a Republican, answered Loeb: "I am not afraid of Communist infiltration and certainly will not abandon a just cause because I object to some who have joined in its support."

Despite some opposition in liberal circles generally and rumblings within the organization itself, Loeb and other leaders of the Union for Democratic Action decided to go ahead with plans for a reorganization of this group which, if successful, would bring to a head the growing split in progressive ranks over the issue of Communist participation. Back in 1943 the UDA leaders had suceeded in interesting ex-Senator George Norris of Nebraska in leading an expansion of their tiny group which would transform it into a national organization able to "serve as a rallying point for all progressives." This effort had failed when CIO president Philip Murray had withdrawn his backing out of fear of antagonizing the AFL and further splitting the labor movement.

Now the UDA national board, sensing the pessimism within the organization due to the postwar reaction and to the group's sad financial state, authorized Loeb to put all the UDA's resources into a "final effort" at expansion. A planning committee headed by Loeb set to work with a target date of November, 1946, at which time it was hoped that a small group of selected liberal leaders could be brought together in Washington to launch an expanded UDA. Following Loeb's May 13th letter the UDA remained quiet about its plans except for a significant announcement that it intended to "set out a solid position between those who regard Russia as the fixed point of international virtue and those who hate and fear Russia to the point of supporting every policy which widens the gulf between Russia and the West."

This time the UDA leaders attempted to make sure that the CIO, the largest progressive organization in the country, would not again pull the rug out from under their efforts. With the help of Eleanor Roosevelt, Loeb finally convinced Philip Murray to give his blessing to the expansion attempt. Despite successive postponements which pushed the conference back two months, final arrangements were set for the first weekend of the new year.

On January 3, 1947, more than four hundred persons met in Washington's Willard Hotel in answer to the UDA call for a conference to reorganize the liberal forces of the country. With Reinhold Niebuhr, noted theologian and chairman of the UDA presiding, they heard Chester Bowles call upon liberals to "organize a progressive front, divorced from Communist influence." Denouncing the "reactionary, tub-thumping leadership of the Republican Party," Bowles went on to outline the political role such an organization should play. Declaring that "we should not harbor any illusions about a third party," he bluntly stated: "We cannot blink the fact that the party of Roosevelt is also the party of Bilbo and Rankin. But the fact remains that we have no practical alternative. All our efforts, all our ingenuity must be thrown into the struggle to establish liberal control of the Democratic party . . . "

On the following day a smaller group of leaders—including Walter Reuther, Mrs. Roosevelt, Joseph Rauh, columnist Marquis Childs, and David Dubinsky, president of the anti-Communist International Ladies Garment Workers Union—met to formulate organizational and policy plans for the proposed new group. When Mrs. Roosevelt reported that the UDA was prepared to disband, the conferees, after some disagreement, decided to call the new organization the Americans for Democratic Action. The planning group, mindful of the severe setbacks suffered by the liberal movement in the last two years, agreed that their immediate objective was "a reconstruction of the liberal movement free of totalitarian influence from either the Left or the Right."

Leon Henderson, a former OPA head, and Wilson Wyatt, erstwhile Housing Expediter, were named co-chairmen of the organization committee, which was charged with perfecting detailed machinery for the national organization and setting up local affiliates. Loeb, who had done the day-to-day work of the UDA, was named secretary-treasurer of the committee.

The conference ended when Barry Bingham, editor of the *Louisville Courier-Journal,* released to the press the following statement of principles and policies of the fledgling ADA:

"1. The New Deal programs must be expanded to insure decent levels of health, nutrition, shelter and education.

"2. Civil liberties must be protected from concentrated wealth and overcentralized government. They must be extended to all Americans regardless of race, color, creed, or sex.

"3. Any sound foreign policy requires a healthy and prosperous domestic economy.

"4. The United States must continue to give full support to the United Nations. The conference endorses the American plan for international control of atomic energy.

"5. Because the interests of the United States are the interests of free men everywhere, America must furnish political and economic support to democratic and freedom-loving peoples the world over.

"6. Within the general framework of present American foreign policy steps must be taken to raise standards of living and support civil and political freedoms everywhere. These policies are in the great democratic tradition of Jefferson, Jackson, Lincoln, Wilson, and Franklin D. Roosevelt. We reject any association with Communists or sympathizers with communism in the United States as completely as we reject any association with fascists or their sympathizers. Both are hostile to the principles of freedom and democracy on which this Republic has grown great."

In his closing words to newsmen covering the conference, Bingham noted that points five and six in particular distinguished the ADA from another organization founded only the week before to compete for the allegiance of American liberals and known as the Progressive Citizens of America.

On the Left: Progressive Citizens of America. In the same issue of the *New Republic* which carried Jim Loeb's controversial letter there appeared a report that the CIO-PAC, the National Citizens Political Action Committee, and the Independent Citizens Committee of the Arts, Sciences and Professions had met on May 11th to coordinate their plans for the coming elections. A week later it was reported that at this meeting a nine-man committee had been set up to "make policy decisions" for all three organizations. By June 3rd the three groups were "hard at work on the details of the plans to coordinate their campaign activities more closely this year." The *New Republic* expressed hope that by 1948 these and other progressive organizations would merge.

The Congress of Industrial Organizations was a major progressive force on the U.S. political scene. Without its cooperation and support no liberal organization could hope to exert any significant influence in American politics. Despite the green light Philip Murray had given Loeb on his expansion efforts, the UDA apparently was only a minor factor in CIO political planning.

In September, 1946, moreover, the CIO-PAC, NCPAC, and ICCASP sponsored a "Conference of Progressives" at Chicago which was one of the largest and most enthusiastic gatherings on the left in years. Its range was indicated by the fact that the conference call was signed by such prominent liberal leaders as James Patton, president of the National Farmers Union; Walter White, secretary of the NAACP; and A. F. Whitney, president of the Brotherhood of Railroad Trainmen. Two former members of Roosevelt's cabinet, Harold Ickes and Henry Morgenthau, Jr., participated in the conference.

The primary action of the Chicago conference was to issue a manifesto calling upon the United States to halt atomic bomb testing and to back Henry Wallace, recently ousted as Secretary of Commerce, in his controversy with the Truman Administration over American foreign policy. A continuations committee was set up to make plans for another conference to be held in January. The *New Republic* proclaimed that "American progressives have grown up . . . No one who attended the Chicago conference can doubt that the political action movement is already mature enough for the party big leagues."

Despite the apparent success of the Chicago conference, all was not harmony within the coalition of the "big three." Harold Ickes, who was shortly to resign as chairman of the ICCASP, lashed out at communism in his speech to the delegates. Some CIO leaders, painfully aware of Republican campaign attacks on the NCPAC and the ICCASP and alert to rumors of Communist domination, were beginning to question the utility of an alliance with these two groups. Philip Murray informed the delegates that he had recently told the Russian foreign minister that "We've got no more use for any damn Communist coming over here meddling in our affairs than you would welcome our meddling in your affairs." The CIO president added: "And so far as I'm concerned, the same thing goes for any damn Communist meddling in the affairs of the independent progressive movement in America."

Despite Murray's rough talk, CIO leaders were unwilling to force an open break with the pro-Communist elements in the liberal and labor movements. On October 15th Murray himself announced plans for the upcoming January conference to be sponsored by the same "big three."

By November word was circulating throughout progressive circles that the NCPAC and the ICCASP would merge. On the last week-end in December—one week before the ADA founding conference—over three hundred delegates from twenty-one states met in New York and voted to merge these two groups and eight other smaller progressive organizations into a new political action group to be called the Progressive Citizens of America. Dr. Frank Kingdon, former chairman of the NCPAC, and sculptor Jo Davidson, former head of the ICCASP, were named co-chairmen of the PCA.

However, the conference made clear that—whoever the formal leaders might be—the real force behind the PCA would be the personality of Henry A. Wallace. This development, not wholly unexpected in liberal circles, brought out into the open the relationship which had been growing in recent months between the former Vice-President and various left-wing elements. As early as the previous summer, Wallace had begun to appear at rallies sponsored by the NCPAC and ICCASP. By the time of the Chicago Conference of Progressives, Wallace had been ousted from his post as Secretary of Commerce after publicly airing his disagreement with Administration policy toward Russia. The Chicago conference approved a militant statement backing Wallace in this controversy, and the delegates enthusiastically made it clear that he was their "man of the hour."

Following the Chicago conference the liberal press began to speculate that Wallace might attempt to build a political movement which, if successful, could evolve into a third party by 1948. Talk of a third party increased in December when Wallace became editor of the *New Republic,* thereby gaining a wide liberal audience for his views. "The primary effort of progressives," he announced, "may be to rebuild the Democratic Party as a liberal party. But we are the captives of no party. If the Democratic Party is incapable of change, we shall strike out along other lines."

Now, in late December, Wallace was the featured speaker at the founding conference of the PCA, which was already being spoken of as "Wallace's group." In his address to the delegates Wallace made no mention of any third party plans. Instead, his appeal—obviously aimed at the upcoming ADA conference—was for unity among all progressives. "The fundamental progressive faith" said Wallace, "is so broad that we should not allow ourselves to be divided on any minor issues."

Despite this, when the conference ended speculation continued that the PCA might prove in the long run to be the vehicle for a Wallace-led third party.

Unlike the ADA, the newly-formed PCA issued no formal statement of policy. Conference speakers indicated, however, that one major objective of the new group would be to work for a broadening and continuation of New Deal domestic policies. In this respect, the PCA would be no different from the ADA. Both would be carrying the ball which Roosevelt had dropped and—so both groups believed—Truman had failed to pick up. This might lead to an occasional fumble, but at least they would be heading toward the same goal.

It was clear immediately, however, that the two groups would clash directly over the question which had recently begun to agitate the whole liberal front—what attitude liberals should take toward Russia and domestic Communists. The ADA had made it known that it did not consider Russia the fixed point of international virtue; critical references to Russia at the PCA convention had met with a chorus of boos. The ADA specifically and pointedly excluded Communists from membership; the PCA made no move to change the policy of its predecessor organizations of welcoming Communists.

The liberal movement, under Roosevelt an essentially united political force, was now divided. And the division was not, as so often in the past, over esoteric points of liberal doctrine. It was over a question which world events were fast making the paramount issue in American politics.

The leaders of the liberal movement had chosen sides, and "the battle for supremacy in that movement" was on.

Chapter V

1947: YEAR OF DOUBT

To one looking back from the perspective of more than a decade, the battle for liberal supremacy in 1947 appears to have been a curious war indeed.

Today the political attitudes of Americans toward Russia and domestic Communism are frozen into an almost monolithic pattern. The question of Communist participation in American political groups is of great significance only to the members of the House Un-American Activities Committee and others who have a vested interest in such matters. The question of Russian motives and actions on the international scene, while of acute concern, is not a topic of partisan debate. Today it is most unlikely that any serious political group will appear and announce that it welcomes Communists as members and that it entertains grave doubts about American policy vis-à-vis Russia. If such a group did arise it would find itself isolated and impotent.

In 1947 the Progressive Citizens of America constituted just such a group as that described. And, far from being impotent, for many months it appeared that the PCA would drive the rival Americans for Democratic Action from the field and take over the leadership of the American left.

The Clash Over Communism. During the early weeks of 1947 the political press—like American liberals themselves—was appraising and taking sides between the newly-formed PCA and ADA. These initial journalistic efforts focused almost exclusively on one of the two areas of conflict between the two groups which were the rationale behind their formation and which were to carry through the entire battle between them. This was their directly opposing policies toward participation of Communists in the liberal movement.

One of the first corners heard from was the extreme left. The danger posed to the Communists by the ADA was evident, and their reaction was immediate. Delegates to the ADA founding conference had scarcely started for home before the *Daily Worker* denounced the new organization as a "Dubinsky plot" instigated by "Wall Street" to prepare the way for "fascism." But ADA leaders had not expected plaudits from this quarter; the PCA was welcome to whatever advantage it could find in open support by the Communists.

If, however, the PCA found these early recruits of dubious value, the ADA was similarly embarrassed by the cordial reception given it in the conservative press. *Time*, after reviewing the founding conference of the PCA, remarked that "not all members of the U.S. political left were impressed by the glowing pink facade of Henry Wallace's Progressive Citizens of America." The ADA, *Time* reported, had "issued a manifesto which distinctly set it apart from the PCA and other left-wingers who fear the tag of Red-baiting more than they fear the Reds themselves." *Newsweek* noted that "the principal difference between the two groups is that the ADA excludes Communists while the PCA attracts them." *U.S. News and World Report* observed that although the ADA called for an expansion of New Deal programs in the domestic field, "it backs American foreign policy, and it rejects any association with Communists in the United States."

Choosing up of sides by the far left and right, while significant in that it identified possible friends and foes on the flanks, left the main body of liberal opinion untouched. Here the liberal press could be a crucial factor in giving an edge to one or the other of the contestants in the early stages of the struggle for liberal supremacy.

The liberal press—like the movement itself—was divided. Robert Bendiner in the *Nation* favored the ADA: "I think we have here something new in the history of American politics—a movement on the Left that is free of the orthodoxies of Marxism, . . . a movement that is neither the projection of one man's personality nor the organized promotion of an economic cure-all." To Bendiner the newly-formed PCA was "a traditional popular front organization . . . It is in the tradition of a fast-fading era, and with or without the support of Henry A. Wallace, I believe it is already anchored in a political backwater."

The majority reaction of the primary organs of progressive journalism was one of irritation that the liberal movement should be split at precisely the time it most needed to be a united political force; the burden of blame for this split was placed upon the ADA. Freda Kirchwey of the *Nation*, noting that the only real issue which divided the two groups was Communism and taking the ADA to task for equating Communism and Fascism, contended that "the primary job of both is to fight Taft-Hartley reaction. It is unfortunate that they cannot tackle the job under one name." Helen Fuller of the *New Republic*, also critical of ADA's anti-Communist stand, asked: "Why don't you folks get together?"

The ADA, it appeared, was off to a slow start. Its militant non-Communist stand, which was reinforcing the fear of many on the left that such a policy would only play into the hands of the reactionaries, was also bringing it unexpected and unwanted support from the right. The ADA was experiencing difficulties recruiting members among liberals "who don't want positive American liberalism defined in a phrase beginning with a negative." Walter Reuther had warned the ADA founding conference that its explicit policy of excluding Communists would bring down upon its head the epithet of "Red-baiters." But now the epithets seemed to be coming not only from Communists and fellow travelers but also from many quarters which had been deemed friendly.

Despite these developments, the ADA refused to modify its non-Communist policy. Its answer to the critics came in the form of a Loeb letter to the *New Republic,* and it was to the point. The founding of ADA, said Loeb, was "a declaration of liberal independence from the stifling and paralyzing influence of the Communists and their apologists in America . . . No movement that maintains a double standard on the issue of human liberty can lay claim to the American liberal tradition."

But the ADA's militancy could not disguise the fact that only a month after its founding it was operating under severe handicaps in its struggle with the Progressive Citizens of America. The PCA had started with a nucleus of two large and—for liberal groups at least—affluent organizations. The ADA was attempting to expand a relatively small New York movement into a national force. A memorandum issued in February from PCA headquarters was not far from the truth when it said: "We *have* an organization; the ADA has only plans for one."

What plans the ADA had, moreover, were given a sharp setback on March 15, 1947, when the Executive Board of the CIO, acting upon president Philip Murray's urging, recommended that "all officers of the CIO, of affiliated unions, and of industrial union councils quit the ADA and the PCA."

The CIO Straddles the Fence. From the beginning of the split in the liberal movement over the Communist issue, the CIO—especially Philip Murray—had exhibited an ambivalent attitude toward this issue. Murray had first encouraged Loeb in his efforts to expand the Union for Democratic Action, then had personally participated on the committee which led to the formation of the Progressive Citizens of

America. Although he had not attended the founding conference of the PCA, he had not protested when that conference elected him vice-president of the organization. Despite this, he had sent CIO vice-president Allan Haywood to the ADA conference as his personal representative.

The reason for Murray's vacillation in his dealings with the liberal movement may be found in the hard realities of the distribution of power within the CIO during the immediate postwar years. If the estimate of commentators not unsympathetic to the labor movement is accurate, during these years "approximately one-fourth of the total CIO membership were enrolled in unions controlled by the Communists." The CIO was badly split, with such pro-Communist unions as the United Electrical Workers, the National Maritime Union, the Fur Workers and the Mine, Mill and Smelter Workers opposing the strongly anti-Communist Steelworkers, Textile Workers, United Automobile Workers, Retail and Wholesale Clerks, and others. Moreover, Lee Pressman—who in later years was to admit that he had been a Communist party member in the 1930's and had not broken ideologically with the party until 1950—was general counsel of the CIO and a close adviser to Murray. This division was not to be resolved until 1948 and 1949 when Pressman resigned to join the Wallace movement, and the CIO started its purge of pro-Communist unions by expelling the United Electrical Workers.

But in 1947 Pressman and the Communist-dominated unions were still entrenched, and, after the formation of the PCA, had begun to affiliate with that group. Some of the leaders of the anti-Communist unions had joined the ADA, thus creating a kind of ADA versus PCA atmosphere within the CIO Executive Board. Murray felt that the CIO would appear to be divided if its officers chose definite sides in the liberal struggle, and he wished to discourage the increasingly bitter split in the progressive movement. In February Murray announced that he was resigning as PCA vice-chairman, and in March he pushed through the resolution calling upon all union officers to pull out of both the PCA and ADA.

Of the two groups, the ADA was much harder hit by Murray's action than was the PCA. Mrs. Roosevelt, writing Murray to ask that he rescind his directives, felt that his neutrality "actually operated in favor of the Communists since most influential CIO members have shunned the PCA and given their backing to ADA." Walter Reuther, recently victorious over the Communists in a battle for control of the United Auto Workers, was an active member of the ADA organizing committee, as were John Green of the Shipbuilders, Willard Town-send of the Transport Service Employees, and Samuel Wolchok of the Retail Clerks. The loss of these and other CIO leaders, upon whom the ADA had been counting for financial as well as organizational support, was a severe blow. It destroyed perhaps the only advantage ADA held over the PCA.

While admitting the damage, ADA refused to back down from its anti-Communist position. In its first issue, the *ADA World,* the group's new house organ, said editorially: "We would be less than honest if we denied that Mr. Murray's decision will handicap the ADA. While we disagree with the CIO's action, we dissent even more from the publicly stated purpose of the action: to achieve unification of the two proscribed organizations."

Added the ADA organizing committee: "The CIO appeal to the liberal movement to drop its differences and unite can only be based on the theory that unity with Communists is possible. ADA flatly rejects this theory."

But in addition to the antagonism it had met with in some liberal circles because of its militant anti-Communist stand and to the blow dealt it by Murray's directive, in early 1947 ADA was facing another heavy obstacle in its attempt to became a national political force. This was the presence of Henry Wallace in the PCA camp.

Henry Wallace and the PCA. Since 1933 Henry Wallace had been an important figure in the New Deal. During World War II he held a special place in the affections of liberals; his wartime speeches, in which he had related the Allied war aims to the liberal goals of peace, prosperity, and one world, had established him as "the country's outstanding moral apologist for the conflict." Many liberals considered him the rightful heir to Roosevelt. In 1944 the UDA had hoped to enlist his aid in its first expansion attempt; in the following year UDA leaders had sponsored a testimonial dinner for Wallace to dramatize his fight for confirmation as Secretary of Commerce.

During 1945 and 1946, however, Wallace's criticisms of American policy toward Russia led to a strained relationship between him and the non-Communist UDA while drawing him closer to such popular front groups as the NCPAC and ICCASP.

Upon leaving Truman's cabinet and becoming editor of the *New Republic,* Wallace announced in the messianic overtones of a liberal prophet: "My field is the world. My strength is my conviction that a progressive America can unify the world and a reactionary America must divide it . . . If I have importance, it is because of the ideas that I have come to represent. They are major ideas, indestructible and on the march."

From his editorial chair Wallace began to voice the frustrations and fears of many liberals concerning the ominous developments of the postwar years. Peace must be kept at all costs, he held, and peace could not be kept unless the wartime alliance was preserved and America's great economic resources employed to bring about a rising standard of living throughout the world.

In the spring of 1947 Wallace, just returned from a well publicized European trip, began to tour the United States under PCA auspices. On March 31st a crowd of 19,000 turned out in Madison Square Garden to hear him denounce the newly formulated Truman Doctrine. On May 14th in the Chicago Stadium 20,000 heard Wallace call for a $150 billion foreign aid program as part of "a major effort to restore the world economy by the use of American resources." On May 17th in Los Angeles 20,000 paid as much as $2.40 each to hear Wallace speak. It was later estimated that his "brilliantly-staged speaking tour" had inspired a $300,000 flow of contributions into the PCA treasury.

The spring of 1947 was a particularly auspicious time for the type of appeal Wallace was making. The peaceful and plentiful postwar years Americans had fought for and looked forward to were proving to be a mirage.

Even before the war's end, it was apparent that the policy of Russia toward her Western allies was changing from an uneasy alliance to hostility. In 1945 the famous Duclos letter, in which a top French Communist attacked the American Communists' policy of wartime cooperation with capitalism, and which led to the abrupt deposal of Communist chieftan Earl Browder, indicated that an ill wind was beginning to blow from the East. In 1946 the continued presence of Russian troops in Iran had created a major crisis, and in early 1947 Communist pressure on Greece and Turkey evoked war alarms in all the Western capitals.

The domestic scene was equally dismal. In 1946, following wartime wage and price controls, the greatest strike wave in history swept the country. The Truman administration, faced with economic near-anarchy and unable to obtain concessions from industry, antagonized both labor and management by interfering with injunctions, industry seizure, and other government action. With the complete abandonment of price controls, consumer prices shot up 15% between June and December, 1946, with food prices rising almost 28%.

In view of these conditions the things Wallace was saying made sense to many liberals. Here was a man talking peace while others talked of war as if Hiroshima had never existed. While others pronounced the New Deal dead, Wallace called for its resurrection in America and its expansion throughout the world. Harold Ickes summed up the reaction to Wallace when he said: "The American people are looking for leadership. More than this, they are looking for leadership that has at least the appearance of idealism. Whether the qualities that the mine run of American citizens want do exist in Mr. Wallace or whether they exist at all, is beside the point. Thousands of people believe that Mr. Wallace possesses the qualities."

If many on the left were enthusiastic about Wallace, there were some—particularly in the ADA—who had doubts. They had no quarrel with most of the fine liberal sentiments voiced by the man and they did not question his credentials as a progressive, but they were becoming alarmed about Wallace's continued close association with some whose enlistment in a purportedly democratic liberal movement was of very recent origin and whose membership papers were not above suspicion. Watching the increasingly prominent role played in the PCA by such extreme left wingers as Lee Pressman, John Abt, Hannah Dorner, and Lew Frank, Jr., they were beginning to wonder whether Wallace was lending his great prestige to another Communist front.

Wallace himself appeared naive, even unconcerned, about Communist participation in the PCA. When asked how he stood on Communist activity in the group with which he was becoming identified in the public mind, he replied: "If they want to help us out on some of these problems, why God bless them, let them come along."

As the impact of Wallace's tour was being demonstrated by crowded halls and cheering throngs, and as his presence in a popular front group was luring many liberals into the PCA fold, the ADA announced—with more hope than conviction—that it "would continue to strive to correct the illusion that Wallace's opinions are the sole voice of American liberalism."

In April, 1947, it appeared that the battle for liberal supremacy might be a short war. The PCA, riding on the Wallace coat tails, seemed to be making good its boast that it was "the one organization which has the facilities, the experience—and above all the will—to fight your fight for a better America and a better world."

The ADA, considered by many liberals to be obsessed with the Communist issue, its one major advantage over the PCA destroyed by the CIO's neutrality policy, and without big-name leadership which could command headlines every day, appeared to be anchored in the backwater which had been predicted for its rival.

During the early months of 1947 ADA leaders had been attempting to add flesh to the skeleton of their national organization by holding local chapter meetings in Chicago, Los Angeles, Philadelphia, Pittsburgh, and other major cities. They had found much of their energies diverted into a defense of their non-Communist position in the court of liberal opinion. And as they were preparing for a second national conference scheduled for the end of March, events were already in motion which were to cause the ADA-PCA conflict over domestic communism to spill over into the broader battleground of American foreign policy.

The Clash Over Foreign Policy. The founding conferences of both the ADA and PCA had indicated that the two groups, despite their initial accord in domestic affairs, would represent opposing viewpoints in the foreign policy field and particularly in the area of American-Russian relations. During the first few weeks of 1947 this potential area of conflict was overshadowed by the differences over exclusion of Communists from the liberal movement.

On March 12, 1947, however, President Truman made a speech which placed U.S.-Russian relations in the very forefront of American politics. In a tense message to Congress he called for American economic and military aid to Greece and Turkey, giving as his reason the fact that both nations were in danger of an economic collapse which would make them easy bridges for Russian expansion into the Mediterranean. Here was an issue which, while giving pause to many non-Communist liberals who saw in it dangers of American imperialism, would also draw another battle line between the pro-Communists and anti-Communists on the left.

The PCA promptly denounced the Truman Doctrine as "an invitation to war" signifying the replacement "of an American policy based on one world" by "a policy in which he [Truman] divides the world into two camps." On April 7th the PCA ran a full-page advertisement in the *New Republic* which pictured the Truman Doctrine as a death blow to the United Nations.

For two weeks the ADA took no stand on the Truman Doctrine, leading Freda Kirchwey to charge that "the Americans for Democratic Action has uttered not one word on the greatest issue before the country."

Aware that there was division over the Truman Doctrine, ADA leaders withheld comment until the March conference could crystallize the organization's position. More than half of the two hundred delegates to the conference appeared before the commission charged with drafting a foreign policy statement. Although there was general recognition that channeling aid through the United Nations was impossible because of the Russian veto, there were long discussions about the possible effects unilateral American action would have upon the U.N. Despite strong opposition, the conference finally voted to back the Truman Doctrine.

The decision had not been an easy one. Debate over this one issue diverted the conference from major problems facing the ADA in other areas, and it divided key leaders who were united on all other issues. Charles Bolte, chairman of the American Veterans Committee and a member of the ADA organizing committee, voiced his dissent from the conference stand and revealed internal opposition to it.

Again, as in the battle over the Communist question, the ADA found itself at odds with the journals of liberal opinion. The *Nation* assailed the Truman Doctrine as "a plain declaration of political war against Russia" while the *New Republic* exclaimed that "the U.S. is now ready to excuse unholy alliances of its own by adopting the apology that the end might justify the means."

For the second time within three months the ADA had taken a position which alienated many of the liberals it had to attract if it was to survive and prosper. Again, the explanation lies in the now strange political atmosphere of 1947. Only two years earlier the United States had been allied with Russia in another war to end all wars. The hopes for world peace which hung upon the continuation of that alliance did not die easily. Many liberals believed with the PCA that Truman's action was an unnecessary provocation, especially when it appeared that he was willing to risk war to aid "the reactionary Greek and Turkish governments simply because they were anti-Communist."

Again ADA reaction to the criticism directed at its stand was voiced with the verbal militancy which was fast becoming characteristic of the organization. On April 8th Wilson Wyatt, newly elected ADA national chairman, spoke over the American Broadcasting Company network in ADA's first major effort to counter PCA influence. Holding that "the liberals who believe in the middle way have been too long inert, bewildered and homeless," Wyatt announced ADA's support for the Truman Doctrine and hit indirectly, but with force, at the PCA: "ADA rejects the theory that war with Russia is inevitable. It rejects with equal conviction the theory that we must purchase peace through continuous surrender to Soviet pressure . . . American liberals have a special responsibility today. The alarmist outcries of a hysterical minority have created the impression that all liberals believe that our government is embarked on a hopeless course and that the only salvation lies in Moscow."

Despite ADA efforts, the "hysterical minority" continued to cry out, and it was by no means clear that they were not a majority.

The ADA-PCA battle over the Truman Doctrine was still splitting the left in June, when the Administration put forth a sweeping proposal for large-scale aid to war-ravaged Europe. In a Harvard commencement address, Secretary of State George Marshall announced that the United States stood ready to aid any and all European nations to regain economic stability and to fight against "hunger, poverty, desperation, and chaos."

If the Truman Doctrine had been a bitter pill even for anti-Communist liberals, the Marshall Plan appeared certain to appeal to all liberals. It omitted the military aid features which had turned so many of them against the Doctrine, it pledged U.S. aid not to two small and reactionary regimes but to all of Europe, including Russia, and it was devoid of the bristling note of belligerence which had characterized Truman's March speech. Henry Wallace had been calling for a worldwide New Deal. Here *was* a worldwide New Deal, and one fathered by the despised Truman Administration.

The ADA, this time with no division within the ranks, backed the Marshall Plan without reservation. Chairman Wyatt, writing in the *New York Times Magazine,* declared: "The chance of ultimate world stabilization hinges primarily on the achievement of a new deal for the desperate, disillusioned, and embittered peoples of Europe. The Marshall Plan offers the essential base for world reconstruction. We are for it."

Henry Wallace, who had toured the country denouncing the Truman Doctrine before PCA crowds, announced that he was for the Marshall Plan as "a great advance over the Truman Doctrine," adding that "it embodies many of the things I have been saying in recent months." The remark was no vain boast. Marshall's original speech on the Plan had sounded as if it could have come from Wallace's crusading pen. The *New Republic,* also backing it, quoted a high

State Department official as saying: "Just how we'll distinguish it from Wallace's program we don't yet know." Wallace himself admitted to only one minor doubt when he emphasized that "we must reassure Russia that the Plan is not directed against her." Within six months, this doubt was to grow to such proportions that Wallace would reverse himself completely.

The PCA, although it had applauded the Wallace views which were now becoming official U.S. policy, was silent on the Marshall Plan. During the late summer and fall of 1947, while the ADA was concentrating its efforts behind the Plan, the Progressive Citizens ignored it. In October, however, the PCA national board issued a terse policy statement condemning both the Truman Doctrine and the Marshall Plan for "all but destroying the unity which existed among the nations that fought the Axis in World War II." The liberal battle over foreign policy, calmed for a moment by general acclaim for the Marshall Plan, was on again.

This time, however, it was the PCA which was defending a position at variance with the weight of liberal opinion. The ADA saw a chance to recoup some lost ground and exploited it with a full-page advertisement in the *New Republic* headlined: "We believe the Marshall Plan is the key to the fate of Europe." Calling attention to the PCA statement against the Plan, ADA noted that it was made at the same time officials of nine Communist parties of European countries were meeting to denounce the Plan in similar language. Liberal readers were invited to draw their own conclusions and were reminded that "this divergence between the ADA and PCA on the Marshall Plan should serve to clarify a difference which may have seemed obscure to some progressives."

From October on the liberal battle over foreign policy continued to center on the Marshall Plan. In December an ADA policy statement called upon Congress to give speedy approval to the Plan and described it as "the highest point United States foreign policy has achieved since the death of Roosevelt." In January the PCA national convention countered with a demand that both the Marshall Plan and the Truman Doctrine be abandoned and a U.N. program of rehabilitation be substituted for them.

While the respective positions of the two liberal antagonists remained unchanged, Henry Wallace's did not. Following his initial approval of the Marshall Plan, Wallace made another swing around the country turning his attention to domestic politics. By October he had returned to foreign policy, and his one minor doubt about the

Marshall Plan had begun to loom larger in his mind. Wallace felt that the aid contemplated in the Plan would be "too little and too late" because of Administration failure to implement it quickly. Adding that it had risen out of fear and distrust of Russia, Wallace disclosed that he was "not in sympathy with the present political objectives of the Marshall Plan." By January Wallace had swung fully around to the PCA position by presenting an alternative to the Administration program which called for a U.N. aid program.

James Wechsler later noted that Wallace's switch had come after Russia and her satellites had refused to participate in the Marshall Plan and had called upon Communists everywhere to oppose it. He attributed Wallace's reversal to the influence of the Communists and fellow travelers in the PCA and claimed that Wallace's speeches against the Plan "were prepared for him by a bright young man well versed in Communist doctrine."

By the end of 1947 it was evident that PCA opposition to the Marshall Plan had allowed the ADA to recoup some of the ground it had lost early in the year in the skirmishes over the Truman Doctrine and the Communist issue. However, PCA remained a very formidable opponent; it could claim 50,000 dues-paying members in 25 states, a well-filled treasury, and the far from negligible support of Henry Wallace. ADA had only 25,000 members and a relatively impecunious budget of less that $200,000 for the year. And while it had an impressive array of leaders, it had no one with the drawing power of a Wallace.

As 1947 drew to a close the fight for liberal supremacy was still very much in doubt. The first break in the year-long stalemate came on December 29th when Henry Wallace announced that he would run for President on a third party ticket in 1948.

Chapter VI

1948: YEAR OF DECISION

During 1947 it frequently seemed that the battle for supremacy on the left actually was a phony war. When the Americans for Democratic Action issued a call to arms under the banner of militant anti-Communism, the Progressive Citizens of America ignored the challenge and appealed to liberals to close ranks in a united front against the postwar reaction. When ADA continued to insist that Communist participation in the liberal movement would be a political kiss of death, PCA maintained an air of injured innocence, and the press of the left implied that it was bad form for a group of liberals to conduct themselves like reactionary Red-baiters. The labor movement, absorbed with its own problems, adopted a "plague-on-both-your-houses" attitude and refused to join either faction.

During 1947 ADA vigorously pushed an issue which many liberals considered minor beside the problem of rebuilding organized liberalism into a potent political force. Thus the battle for liberal supremacy remained in doubt because the antagonists never really came to grips over an issue which fully enlisted the attention and concern of the entire left.

Ironically, it was Henry Wallace, who had begun his crusade with an appeal for liberal unity, who supplied the issue which quickly transformed the phony war into a hot war and forced liberals to choose sides and render a final decision between ADA and PCA. Wallace's appeal to liberals to follow him into a third party was recognized immediately as a major issue, one which could not be ignored or straddled.

The third party move confronted those on the left with a basic decision: whether to renounce their longtime support of the Democratic party—thus almost certainly assuring a Republican victory in 1948—and join Wallace in a gesture of protest against what he denounced as reaction at home and warmongering aboard; or whether to reject Wallace and support a man and a party many could no longer consider liberal. The choice was a difficult one, and it would be made reluctantly, but by November, 1948, liberals had made it and delivered their verdict at the ballot box. And since PCA formed the base and shaped the policies of Wallace's third party, their verdict also involved an explicit or implicit choice between the opposing philosophies of ADA and PCA. Subsequent events have demonstrated that this choice was one of the most fateful decisions in the history of American liberalism.

The Third Party Background. Henry Wallace's announcement came as no surprise to liberals. Third party talk had been rampant on the left since the 1946 Republican Congressional victory and the liberal disillusionment with Truman; most of it had centered around Wallace and the PCA. In May, 1947, the *New York Times* reported that "tentative plans for a third party were being formed by certain sectors of the left," although it was not certain that Wallace would run. On June 28th the PCA national board issued a suggestive statement contending that "voters should be guaranteed the opportunity, by a new party if necessary, to have a choice between progressive and reactionary candidates for President." Wallace, who had been silent on the third party issue for several months, gave his approval in July to a Wallace-for-President meeting sponsored by the left wing of the California Democratic party.

In early 1947 support for a third party was reportedly widespread throughout the labor movement. In June the national convention of the International Ladies Garment Workers Union called for "action leading to the ultimate organization of a third party on a national scale." The railway unions, still seething over Truman's 1946 threat to draft striking railroad workers, were vocal in support of a third party. A. Philip Randolph, president of the Brotherhood of Sleeping Car Porters and chairman of a National Education Committee for a New Party, urged ADA to "get behind a liberal progressive political party similar to the British Labor Party."

Rejecting Randolph's advice, ADA attempted to block the tentative third party feelers put out to the liberal movement. Wilson Wyatt declared in a Chicago speech that "a third party in 1948 would be a catastrophe for American democratic liberalism." A third party on the left would cut into the Democratic vote and help elect a reactionary Republican, said Wyatt, "and only the Communists and the NAM would gain." The ADA chairman added: "As for Henry Wallace, when he fronts for a third party with the private cheering of the reactionaries and the beaverish industry of the Communists, he is fronting for a movement which can injure—perhaps irretrievably—the very liberalism for which Franklin D. Roosevelt fought."

But Henry Wallace was no longer listening to his old friends and new enemies. "If," he warned in September, "the Democratic party continues to stand for war and violation of civil liberties and both major parties to stand for high prices and depression, then the people must have a new party of liberty and peace." On December 16th the PCA executive committee urged Wallace to run on a third party ticket. By late in the month Wallace's "if" had become more definitive. In his Chicago speech announcing his candidacy, he denounced the Democratic party as "a party of war and depression" and urged liberals to join him in an attempt "to show the world that the United States is not behind the bipartisan reactionary war policy which is dividing the world into two armed camps and making inevitable the day when American soldiers will be dying in their Arctic suits in the Russian snow."

Henry Wallace obviously did not intend his third party venture as a serious attempt at the Presidency, but he obviously did intend it to be a spectacular demonstration of protest which would force the Democratic party to reverse or modify its policies, particularly its foreign policy. If this strategy were to succeed, Wallace would have to attract substantial support from liberal and labor ranks, and there was much in his experience during 1947 to cause him to believe that this support would be forthcoming. His numerous speeches had met with an enthusiastic response. Moreover, PCA had functioned as an efficient propaganda agency and was anxious to serve as the organizational base for a new party. Although the major unions had not backed him, neither had they come out against him. ADA, his most vocal opposition, had not proved too formidable. Despite some stir over the Communist issue, no one could say that Wallace himself was a Communist, and liberals had not appeared to take the matter too seriously.

Since Wallace has published no memoirs, we do not yet know what led him to cast his lot with a third party in late 1947 and go fishing for votes in the troubled waters of the left. Whatever the reasoning involved, and however promising the prospects may have looked at the time, 1948 was to demonstrate that Wallace and PCA had committed a major political blunder. The new year was only a few weeks old before it was evident that Wallace was using the wrong bait on his third party line, that the fish would not bite, and that a dramatic reversal of fortunes would occur in the battle for liberal supremacy.

The Left Backs Away. In 1945, speaking at a dinner sponsored in his honor by the Union for Democratic Action, Henry Wallace had warned of the futility of a third party. "There will be far less trouble in this country," he had said, "if the progressives can find full and free expression in the Democratic party." Three years later Wallace was leading a third party and many progressives were wondering why.

One plausible explanation might be found in the treatment Wallace had received at the hands of the Democratic party. In 1944 that party's national convention denied him a second nomination as Vice-President, and the man who got it became President. In 1946 he essayed some bold criticism of that party's foreign policy and it cost him his job as Secretary of Commerce.

In 1948 few liberals were willing to believe that Wallace was capable of using a third party as a purely personal weapon of revenge against the Democrats. It is an indication of his stature—and of the charismatic appeal to liberals which had almost killed off ADA—that not even his bitterest enemies ever accused him of this. Wallace's own explanation for the course he followed, as we have seen, was simply that the Democratic party no longer offered a means for the realization of liberal objectives and that it was time to start building a party which would.

While this explanation might have carried weight on the left in 1946 and early 1947, by December of 1947 it had lost much of its punch. President Truman's stubborn fight against the Republican-controlled 80th Congress had begun to revive waning liberal faith in the Democratic party. His Taft-Hartley veto had soothed the ruffled feelings of labor, and his veto of a regressive GOP tax bill had won general acclaim on the left. The bold, imaginative sweep of the Marshall Plan had helped to quiet liberal fears about an imperialistic American foreign policy. An indication of the turn in liberal opinion came when the *Nation*, reversing its earlier position, denounced PCA's demand for a third party. Citing polls showing a recent trend away from the Republicans, the *Nation* charged that a third party would wipe out Democratic gains and admonished: "Before concluding that the two major parties were identical and that only Wallace could give the voters a genuine choice next fall, the PCA's strategists might have asked themselves why political sentiment seems to have shifted so markedly in the past six months."

If neither of these explanations seemed adequate to account for the appearance of a third party, liberals were soon offered another one from a most surprising source. In the two weeks which had elapsed between the PCA call for a third party and Wallace's affirmative answer, several top PCA officers had resigned in protest. Following Wallace's announcement, Dr. Frank Kingdon, a PCA co-chairman, dropped a verbal bombshell into the battle for liberal supremacy by charging that the Wallace candidacy was engineered by Communists. "Who asked Henry Wallace to run?" queried Kingdon. "The answer is in the record. The Communist party, through William Z. Foster and Eugene Dennis, were the first . . . The call to Wallace came from the Communist party and the only progressive organization admitting Communists to its membership."

The ADA, happy to have confirmation of its long-standing charges from such an authoritative source, explained that Wallace's move was part of a Communist stratagem to force liberals to come to terms over the Marshall Plan or enter third party candidates against them in Congressional races. Communist control over the Wallace movement was further demonstrated, claimed ADA, by the fact that a delegation of Communists had visited Democratic party headquarters in Illinois and threatened to run a Wallace-backed candidate for Senator if the Democratic nomination went to the anti-Communist liberal, Paul Douglas.

Additional evidence that the Communists were calling the tune for Wallace came from Philip Murray, who disclosed that the third party "was inaugurated at a Communist party meeting in the city of New York in October of 1947." Murray claimed to have received his information from Mike Quill, a left-wing union leader who had defected from the Communists. Quill, who was present at the meeting, quoted Eugene Dennis, general secretary of the Communist party, as saying that "the national leaders of the Communist party had decided to form a third party led by Henry Wallace and that Wallace would come out in a few weeks and announce his candidacy."

Under the impact of these disclosures, the ADA charges of Communist domination of the PCA were beginning to receive a careful second look in liberal and labor circles. The *Nation,* weighing the evidence, urged liberals to reject the third party. "Our reason," explained the magazine, "for believing in the tentative nature of the Wallace movement is that, through no wish of its leader, it derives its only important organizational support from the Communists and their sympathizers." Contemporaneously Max Lerner predicted that Wallace's campaign would be a "futile insurgent gesture, with the main organizational strength provided by the Communists, whose prize trophy Wallace has become."

If liberals were doubtful about all these new-found revelations of Communist control over the Wallace movement, Wallace's reaction to the Communist seizure of power in Czechoslovakia furnished strong circumstantial evidence which few could ignore. When confronted with the news that a Communist coup had destroyed overnight one of the model democracies of the world, Wallace explained that—while the death of Czech democracy was lamentable—"one must not discount the degree to which American deeds had provoked the Russians."

By February, only six weeks after Wallace had thrown his hat into the ring, it was evident that the year-long ADA campaign against him was taking effect. "The people around Wallace are not the ones who followed him ten years ago or a year ago," said Cabell Phillips. "He has been forced to retreat into the desolate company of the most radical fringe of the Far Left."

By February, also, it was becoming clear that labor would not swallow the third party bait. The most dramatic example of erosion of Wallace support among labor ranks—an erosion traceable mainly to Truman's Taft-Hartley veto—was provided by the railway unions. In 1946, when Truman had broken the railroad strike, A. F. Whitney's Brotherhood of Railway Trainmen had voted a special two-and-a-half million dollar fund to be used to defeat Truman in 1948. Whitney later joined the PCA and became one of the most vocal third party backers. Before the year was out, however, he had come out for Truman's re-election on the grounds that his Taft-Hartley veto had "vindicated him in the eyes of labor."

The third party issue, which was forcing a decision upon liberals who otherwise might never have declared their allegiance in the ADA-PCA battle, was having a similar effect upon the CIO and its neutrality policy. Several left-wing CIO leaders, ignoring Murray's directive to stay out of both the PCA and ADA, had continued to furnish financial and organizational backing to the Progressive Citizens. Murray retaliated by freeing such anti-Communists as Walter Reuther and Emil Rieve to work with the ADA. In late January, over the opposition of representatives of ten Communist-controlled unions, the fifty-one member CIO executive board passed a resolution denouncing the formation of a third party as "politically unwise." In February the year-long struggle within the CIO between the ADA and PCA ended when Murray authorized a CIO alliance with the ADA.   ,

The first annual convention of the Americans for Democratic Action, held February 21-24, 1948, in Philadelphia, demonstrated that Wallace and the PCA would hook few of the big fish of the labor movement. The ADA could claim that the convention signalized "the widest labor participation in the organized liberal movement that has ever been attained." Walter Reuther of the CIO and president William Green of the AFL shared the convention rostrum, and many other lesser officials of both federations were in attendance. "In an unprecedented demonstration of liberal-labor unity," said the *ADA World,* "spokesmen for the AFL, CIO, Railway Brotherhoods, and the Machinists accepted posts on the ADA board."

The key issues before the convention were the Wallace candidacy and the Marshall Plan. The six hundred delegates dealt with both in a resolution "unreservedly condemning the third party candidacy of Henry Wallace" on the grounds that:

"1. It is committed to defeat of the Marshall Plan.

"2. It is an established fact that it owes its origin and principal organizational support to the Communist Party of America.

"3. Third party candidates in Congressional races can serve only to elect a reactionary and isolationist Congress."

ADA Versus the Third Party. By the time of the ADA convention the Progressive Citizens of America had begun to transform themselves into a full-fledged third party. The January PCA convention, after endorsing the Wallace candidacy, had authorized the merger of the national and local PCA groups with whatever party developed around Wallace. The decision provoked further resignations from several prominent PCA members and revealed that the organization had all along been split between one faction which was determined to create a third party and another which had wanted to use Wallace and the PCA as a lever to force the Democrats to abandon Truman for a more liberal candidate. Because of this division and because the PCA, despite its successes, was still a narrow base from which to launch a nationwide third party, the victorious faction sought to maintain the PCA in the position of supporting rather than generating a third party. One observer noted, however, that "a third party, if finally hatched, will have had much of its incubation at the PCA convention."

Henry Wallace followed up the convention with another nationwide tour in an effort to aid the birth of the party he had already announced. And despite his recent rebuffs at the hands of prominent liberal and labor leaders, the journey showed that he had lost little of his appeal for the rank and file. That the third party was far from a dead issue was demonstrated by a special election held February 17th in New York's Twenty-Fourth Congressional District, in which a third party candidate backed by Wallace won a two-to-one victory over the regular Democratic nominee. Four months earlier the PCA had shown Midwestern strength in a Chicago judicial election in which its candidate had captured 40 per cent of the total vote against candidates of the two major parties.

Wallace's campaign manager, refuting arguments that labor would not support Wallace, contended that "nobody controls the labor vote" and reminded liberals of John L. Lewis' ill-fated attempt to swing the labor rank and file against Roosevelt in 1940. Delegates to a Chicago Wallace-for-President meeting in April talked of "ten million votes in 1948."

Stepping up his campaign, Wallace began to hit hard on such domestic issues as civil rights, Taft-Hartley, and injustices to minorities. Seeing that the big names of labor and liberalism were lost to him, he began to appeal over their heads to the privates in the ranks. In the late spring Wallace made a stormy trip through the South, where his meetings were heckled and broken up and Wallace himself pelted with eggs, and where he "said a good many things that needed to be said about the brotherhood of man." Wallace's Southern tour, "probably the only occasion in American Presidential history when a candidate traveled so many miles in the South in order to win votes in the North," was having an obvious impact upon the various minority blocs of the urban East. Wallace was demonstrating that, even without the backing of organized labor and despite the new evidence of Communist manipulation, he might yet split off a large enough segment of the left to defeat the Democratic party.

Having won the battle for the allegiance of the leaders of the liberal-labor coalition, ADA was forced to carry the battle straight to the ranks. In April the organization published a thirty-four page pamphlet entitled *Henry Wallace: The First Three Months.* A blistering attack on Wallace's record and statements in the areas of foreign affairs, civil liberties, and labor, this pamphlet was circulated throughout the liberal movement by local ADA chapters. In May Leon Henderson, new ADA national chairman, attempted somewhat desperately to undercut Wallace's appeal to Negroes by claiming that as Secretary of Commerce Wallace had tolerated "the grossest kind of racial segregation in the Census Bureau." In Minnesota Hubert Humphrey, then mayor of Minneapolis and an ADA vice-chairman, led a fight to prevent Wallace forces from taking over the state Democratic party.

Humphrey credited state ADA leaders with having organized the successful precinct caucuses which stopped the Wallace partisans.

The most damaging ADA blow to the third party came indirectly. At the Democratic national convention in July ADA leaders, beaten in the platform committee, led a successful revolt on the convention floor which culminated in the strongest civil rights plank ever included in a major party platform. Further implications of the ADA civil rights fight will be explored in a later chapter. Its importance in the battle for liberal supremacy lies in the fact that— perhaps more than any other single factor—it was to cut the ground from under Wallace's appeal to Northern minority voters.

By mid-1948 the ADA had clearly become the focus of liberal opposition to the far left wing. For eighteen months ADA had mounted an almost ceaseless attack on the PCA, on the idea of a third party, and on Wallace himself. Despite the very provocative nature of this continued barrage, however, it had been unable to draw the opposition into an open fight. The far left had met all attacks upon it with silence or with professions of innocence.

In late July, however, the third party was preparing to hold its national convention. ADA leaders, sensing an opportunity to engage the opposition at close quarters, dispatched executive secretary Jim Loeb to Philadelphia to present the ADA position before the convention platform committee.

The third party leaders, apparently caught by surprise at Loeb's appearance, showed no inclination for infighting. Lee Pressman, the platform committee secretary, suggested that Loeb go home. Loeb remained, but committee chairman Rexford Tugwell ignored him while listening to a day-long parade of witnesses. Finally, late in the evening and amid sporadic heckling, the committee agreed to hear Loeb. It was an indulgence they would come to regret bitterly.

Loeb began quietly enough by reminding the committee that at the Democratic convention ADA had "fought the battle for a strong and unequivocal declaration on civil rights in the United States." His next words hinted at what was coming: "Accordingly, we propose to concentrate here on making sure that solicitude for freedom and minority rights does not wither away beyond the three-mile limit." The vast amount of territory existing beyond the three-mile limit was quickly narrowed: "We challenge the new party to renounce its double standard of political morality; to make clear that it opposes the police state and totalitarian dictatorship everywhere in the world—whether in Mississippi or in the Soviet Union."

Loeb warned his listeners that the third party "has an unprecedented opportunity—possibly its last—to show its independence of communism and totalitarianism." It could do so, said the ADA leader, by backing the Marshall Plan, which was meeting serious opposition only from American isolationists and the Communist parties of Europe. It could do so by withdrawing third party candidates from Congressional and local races. These candidates, who had no chance of being elected themselves, would only defeat outstanding liberals like Douglas and Stevenson in Illinois, Humphrey in Minnesota, and put isolationist and reactionary Republicans in office.

Loeb expressed doubt that the third party would take advantage of its opportunity: "We anticipate, however, that the new party once again will demonstrate that as an instrument of Soviet policy, it has sacrificed any claim to the support of independent liberals, that it will continue to betray its stated objectives of raising mass living standards, expanding freedom, and promoting peace throughout the world."

Despite the incongruous fact that the third party was led by an Iowa-born farmer, it remained a pawn of Soviet policy; Wallace's presence did not obscure the fact that "the Communists and their collaborators guide the major policies and word the major pronouncements of this party." Loeb pushed his attack: "We know that we speak for the great non-Communist liberal and labor majority when we state our conviction that your movement is a dangerous adventure undertaken by cynical men in whose hands Henry A. Wallace has placed his political fortunes. It is our conviction that, were the Communists to withdraw from your party today, your organization would soon join that long list of discarded groups which testify eloquently to the inevitable failure of the so-called 'united front'—which always becomes decreasingly united and increasingly 'front'."

Loeb's challenge, dismissed as "unscrupulous and demagogic denunciation" by Tugwell, hit the front pages all over the nation. Its impact cannot be precisely measured, but the publicity emanating from it constituted of itself something of a minor victory for ADA. Previously, liberal charges of Communist domination of the third party had seldom reverberated beyond the confines of a few liberal publications, and in many of these they had been given short shrift. In terms of national attention, these charges had been largely a monopoly of the right-wing press. This situation, while fortifying the preconceived beliefs of conservative readers, meant that such charges received a heavy discount among liberals. If the *Chicago Tri-*

bune said that the third party was a Communist front, liberal readers could reflect upon the source and react accordingly. But when the same charge was made by the **ADA**, whose liberal credentials were in good order, liberal readers were inclined to reflect a little longer. Thus the significance of Loeb's foray lay in the fact that liberal charges of Communist domination of the third party reached a much wider audience than before, and it was on this ground that the battle for liberal supremacy would be decided.

While the **ADA** charges were circulating throughout the country, the new party proceeded to substantiate them. Under the guidance of Pressman, the third party convention adopted a foreign policy plank condemning the Marshall Plan and the U.S. proposals for international control of atomic energy, proposals which had been accepted by all nations outside the Soviet bloc. In domestic affairs, also, the convention swung sharply to the far left, calling for "nationalization of the largest banks, the railroads, the Merchant Marine, the electric power and gas industry, and industries primarily dependent upon government purchases."

Communist control of the proceedings manifested itself crudely at times. One delegate, concerned about the wholesale condemnation of American foreign policy and the scarcely disguised support of Soviet policy, offered a modest floor amendment to the effect that "it is not our intention to give blanket endorsement to the foreign policy of any nation." The convention roared him down, with one speaker crying that "such words would be interpreted as an insinuation against a foreign ally."

The interests of a foreign ally were evident also on such minor points as the platform plank on Macedonia. The first draft, written several weeks before the convention, included a declaration of support for the Macedonian efforts to obtain national autonomy and independence from Greece. By July, however, the Macedonians had begun to turn for help to Marshal Tito of Yugoslavia, who was in open revolt against Moscow. In the platform draft circulated on the convention floor, the Macedonian plank had been dropped, and the efforts of a few delegates to find out what had happened to the Macedonians were ignored.

ADA work against the third party, which had adopted the name of Progressive party, did not cease with Loeb's appearance before the platform committee. In Massachusetts the state ADA organization took the lead in setting up a statewide United Labor Committee, which was a formal operational alliance of the ADA, the AFL and CIO, and various independent unions. The committee coordinated campaign work for the Democratic ticket, while the state ADA directed most of its efforts toward cutting down the strong Wallace movement in the state. In October ADA workers sent out 80,000 postal cards to persons who had signed petitions to put Wallace's name on the ballot.

A persistent ADA theme since the formation of the third party had been the charge that third party candidates would only siphon off votes which would normally go to liberal Democrats, and thus lead to the election of reactionary Republicans. The most glaring example of this occurred in Illinois, where Paul Douglas, running against Senator Wayland Brooks—dubbed the *"Chicago Tribune* Senator"— was also being attacked from the left by a Progressive party candidate. Third party candidates were also in the field against Humphrey in Minnesota, Helen Douglas and Chet Holifield in California, Henry Jackson in Washington, plus several liberal candidates in other states. Due to intricate qualification laws, the Progressive party had found it difficult to get on the ballot in many states, but it had succeeded in numerous districts and states where liberal but anti-Communist Democrats were running.

ADA proceeded to spell out the implications of this situation in a campaign pamphlet entitled *Henry A. Wallace, Bat Boy for Reaction.* Contending that the Progressive party was guaranteeing the defeat of liberal candidates where reactionary Congressmen presently held office, ADA charged: "There is more than one way of electing a reactionary Congress. In 1946 we did it by default when only thirty-four per cent of the voters went to the polls. In 1948 we may elect one by cynical Communist design. The third party—which the Communists have publicly claimed as their offspring—plans to pave the way for a reactionary isolationist Congress with the good intentions of honest supporters of Henry A. Wallace."

As election day drew near, ADA stepped up its attack. Another pamphlet, *Henry Wallace, the Last Seven Months of His Presidential Campaign,* highlighted the recent evidence of Communist influence in the Progressive party and predicted that ADA's civil rights plank would destroy Wallace's appeal to Negro voters. The Massachusetts ADA sponsored half-hour weekly radio broadcasts in the month immediately preceding the election. "An Appeal to the Liberals of America," circulated by the national ADA and signed by prominent figures of the Roosevelt Administration, refuted Wallace's claim to be the "heir to Roosevelt" and condemned the Progressive party as "the most serious attempt in the history of our nation by a totalitarian group to capture and destroy American liberalism."

Early in 1948 the PCA had predicted that Wallace would get ten million votes. In October the ADA had found "no evidence that he would get more than two million." When the ballots were counted in November, it was found that Wallace had received a total vote of only 1,157,326. The Progressive party's Congressional candidates had fared no better. Many had withdrawn prior to the election, and only one of those who remained in contention had been elected. The party's strength was concentrated primarily in New York, where it had been potent enough to cost the Democrats the state's forty-five electoral votes, but even this had not prevented Truman from scoring the most amazing upset in U.S. political history.

In a moment of exuberant rhetoric, Henry Wallace once told his followers that they were members of "Gideon's army" and were fighting for the right. An unsympathetic observer had claimed that they were a division of "Stalin's foreign legion." The election of 1948 demonstrated that they were only a small and impotent band of far left-wingers whose promised roar of protest was barely audible.

Following the decisive defeat of 1948, the Progressive party died a slow but certain death. In 1950, the party mustered only fifty Congressional candidates, none of whom made a serious bid for election. Wallace himself repudiated it after America's entry into the Korean conflict, which the party opposed. Although a token Presidential ticket was put forth in 1952, the Progressive party had become merely one more of those minute left-wing sects which eke out a precarious existence on the fringes of American politics.

*   *   *

American political history is largely a history of success; few words are wasted on the "also rans." Perhaps for this reason the movement represented first by the Progressive Citizens of America and then by the Progressive party has received little consideration. But this movement, although it left no permanent imprint on American political life, was of great significance in the history and development of American liberalism. It was significant for two reasons: first, because it was the most successful of a long series of attempts by American Communists to infiltrate and dominate the American liberal movement and, second, because it failed.

From the period of the Russian Revolution onward, domestic

Communists had been an important factor on the American left. With varying degrees of success, they had exerted a sometimes open and sometimes subterranean influence on the liberal-labor movement. This influence, probably at its peak during the depression years, declined sharply as a result of the Moscow purges of 1936 and the Hitler-Stalin pact of 1939. It rose to new heights during the wartime alliance with Russia and, as we have seen, reached the point where it covered one-fourth of the labor movement and, through the PCA, a large sector of the non-labor left. At this point, just when Russian actions again threatened to destroy what had been built up, the domestic Communists were presented with a power factor they had long desired—the use of a prominent American politician as a front.

The reasons for Henry Wallace's continued involvement with the PCA and the Progressive party, despite the very full evidence that these groups were run by Communists, are still obscure. Wallace himself has said little about it, and the whole episode remains one of the minor—and tragic—mysteries of American politics.

If Wallace's intentions are unclear, however, the intentions of the Communists and fellow-travelers in these two groups are obvious: the PCA and the Progressive party were to be used immediately as a lever to force a reversal of American foreign policy, specifically to kill the Marshall Plan, and ultimately as a nucleus of a revived and stronger Popular Front.

This attempt was a complete failure. The reasons for this failure are many, but not the least of them was the existence of the Americans for Democratic Action. For over two years, and at first with indifferent success, the ADA opposed and exposed every move made by the far left in its efforts to redirect American liberalism along the road toward Moscow. It precipitated the battle for liberal supremacy by insisting that liberals could not work in harmony with Communists. When many of them insisted upon doing so, it maintained a stubborn and vocal independence. When Henry Wallace threw his great influence to the opposition and called for a united liberal third party, the ADA began a war of attrition against him which was finally decided at the ballot box and out of which it emerged a clear winner.

The significance of these two developments—the defeat of the third party and the victory of the ADA—were summed up by James Wechsler in these words: "The crushing setback suffered by the Progressive party marked the turning point in American Communist fortunes in the decade of the forties . . . The newly born Americans for Democratic Action emerged from the campaign as a far more significant political force than the still-born Progressive party."

At the beginning of 1947, when it appeared that American liberalism had had its turn at bat and struck out, the founders of Americans for Democratic Action proclaimed as their goal "the reconstruction of the American liberal movement." They added, as if in recognition of the magnitude of the task they had set for themselves: "Our objective is to show that American progressivism is not dead."

In the battle for liberal supremacy, the ADA had played a large role in preventing the burial of liberalism in the wake of the Progressive party. But this had been essentially a negative victory. It had checked a detour to the left, but it had not moved liberalism very far along the road to reconstruction.

In the past the chief means of liberal transportation had been the coattails of Franklin Roosevelt. Under Roosevelt liberals had enjoyed a short cut to the realization of their goals because they had access to the power of the Presidency. They had not found it necessary—or possible—to build a center of liberal power independent of Roosevelt. But this relatively painless means of realizing liberal objectives had obscured the question of what was to be done when the Roosevelt free ride ended. As one liberal, Wilson Wyatt, put the matter: "When Franklin D. Roosevelt died it was tragically clear that liberalism—in an organized sense—was a fiction rallied around his name . . . The real question, after his death, was whether liberals would quietly fold their tents and steal silently into the night, perhaps to await the coming of a new leader, or whether they would recognize that this was the time for them to set out on their own."

The founders of ADA obviously considered their organization the answer to the question Wyatt posed. Their announced intention of forming a "country-wide liberal, labor, farmer progressive movement" indicated that they hoped to regroup and revitalize the coalition which had previously clustered around Roosevelt. Humorously referred to by Elmer Davis as "the New Deal government-in-exile," they gladly accepted the designation, resolving only that the exile would not last.

The question remained, however, as to what road the new group should follow as it set out to find its way out of the post-Rooseveltian wilderness. At the beginning it was faced with a basic decision on strategy which would shape the development of ADA in the years ahead. In 1947, three alternatives appeared open to it:

1. To attempt to form a third party based on those elements— labor, the more progressive farm elements, minorities, and non-labor

liberals—which had always backed Roosevelt and were looking for new leadership.

2. To become a quasi-political ideological group, in the tradition of the British Fabian Society, and try to effect liberal reforms by promulgating comprehensive and logically coherent policy positions which would be taken over and translated into action by more narrowly political groups or parties.

3. To work within the Democratic party and attempt to shape its policies and personnel along more liberal lines.

There is some evidence to indicate that, had Wallace not pre-empted the field, ADA might have chosen the first of these alternatives. In 1948 an *ADA World* editorial, while deploring the Wallace version of a third party, predicted that American liberals would nevertheless eventually be forced to form a party of their own. Perhaps because of the unhappy example of the Progressive party, that step has never been taken.

The Fabian concept, although it has never prevailed, has caused intermittent friction in ADA from the beginning. Various ADA leaders have advocated such a policy, and much of the organization's educational and propaganda activity can be viewed in this light. The ADA has never committed itself to a clear-cut Fabian concept, however, perhaps because the primary vehicle of Fabian success in Britain —a centralized and disciplined political party—has never existed in the United States.

As a result of a decision made very early in its history, the bulk of ADA's efforts—national and local, educational and electoral— has been directed toward working for liberal objectives within the framework of the Democratic party. Chester Bowles, at the ADA founding conference, declared that—despite its shortcomings from the liberal point of view—ADA had no choice but to "struggle to establish liberal control of the Democratic Party." ADA leaders have voiced intense dissatisfaction at times over the necessity for this choice, and the organization has often cast about desperately for practicable alternatives, but the ADA has continued to function primarily as a liberal wing of the Democratic party.

The struggle for liberal control of that party has assumed various forms, ranging from gentle persuasion to intraparty warfare. By late 1948, two years after its founding, it appeared that ADA had succeeded in establishing, if not liberal control over the Democratic party, at least a semblance of such control.

Part Three

THE LIBERAL ROAD BACK

Chapter VII

EISENHOWER, TRUMAN, AND CIVIL RIGHTS

When Harry Truman replaced Franklin D. Roosevelt as President, liberals felt that their short cut to power had been short-circuited. As previously noted, the early liberal disillusionment with Truman, although a result of many factors, was due largely to his failure to retain the New Deal officialdom left by Roosevelt. ADA inherited this disillusionment, which was in fact one of the reasons for its formation. But the Democratic party had inherited Mr. Truman; if ADA was to exert any influence within the party it would have to deal with him whether it liked him or not.

During 1947, while struggling to establish itself and warring against the PCA, ADA had failed to define clearly its position toward the Democratic party and its leader. The bitter battle against Wallace, which might have drawn the group closer to Truman, evoked no such response. "The ADA's disavowal of a third party movement," the *New York Times* noted in mid-1947, "is not necessarily a commitment to President Truman's candidacy . . . Without threatening to support the Republican ticket or a third party, ADA leaders hope to summon sufficient strength to influence the course of the Democratic party."

With an election year coming up, ADA's position toward the President would have to be made clear. The first annual ADA convention, meeting in Philadelphia toward the end of February, 1948, proved to be a straw in the wind. The 600-odd delegates were reported "restless over being bound to Truman." During the convention sessions several speakers "angrily declared that Mr. Truman's actions belied his New Deal words." The platform resolution on domestic policy, without mentioning Truman by name, denounced "the dismissal of outstanding liberal officials."

Other resolutions indicated that antipathy to Truman was rubbing off on the party as a whole. Modifying the policy of the previous year, the delegates adopted resolutions emphasizing ADA's "independence of any political party" and announced that ADA would support liberal Congressional candidates "regardless of party label."

Toward the close of the convention several delegates carried their opposition to Truman to the point of proposing that ADA ask him to withdraw as a candidate for re-election. This proposal was overwhelmingly defeated, but the convention did vote to withhold endorsement of any candidate until after the major party nominating conventions.

Despite all the furor against Truman, the ADA convention revealed a curious paradox. It's platform—which backed the Marshall Plan, called for a national health insurance program, demanded a strong civil rights policy, and proposed extensive federal aid to education—sounded as if it might have been lifted wholesale from Truman's recent messages to Congress. ADA's position, frequently manifested by the convention, was that Truman's words were not backed up by deeds, but the similarities pointed up the group's dilemma.

Naturally inclined by present policy and past ties to the Democratic party, and yet in revolt against that party's leader, ADA was like a sailor aboard a ship whose captain—while plotting the correct course—was unable to get the ship underway. Perhaps more to the point of ADA's discontent, he had fired most of the old crew before sailing. The problem was further compounded by the fact that ADA had no other choice of berths. The major competing vessel was slated to sail under Senator Robert A. Taft or Governor Thomas E. Dewey, and the rowboat being floated by Henry Wallace was obviously unseaworthy. The ADA, as one observer noted, was "pretty uncertain about its own course of action."

Mutiny Against Truman. Within two weeks after the convention, ADA leaders were embarked on a decisive course of action which involved the organization in one of the most fantastic episodes in American political history. On March 10th executive secretary James Loeb sent a memorandum to ADA officers noting that the national office had received numerous communications voicing concern over "the catastrophic possibility of a Truman nomination." Loeb added: "One of the staff members of the CIO Political Action Committee approached me unofficially with the suggestion that the liberal and labor people start campaigning for someone else, because a Truman nomination would be disastrous to the whole liberal-labor coalition, to say nothing of success in the campaign. This wave of seemingly justified defeatism should be given serious attention by the ADA Executive Committee and the National Board."

On March 26th Franklin D. Roosevelt, Jr., an ADA vice-chairman, revealed who the "someone else" would be. Calling for a candidate

A Herblock cartoon about Senator McCarthy's reaction to ADA reprints of copies of a critical Senate report which the Subcommittee refused to disseminate.

Title page of a pamphlet printed when Nixon was nominated Vice President.

Cover of a 1958 leaflet.

who could "unify the country," the younger Roosevelt came straight to the point: "In times of crisis the Democratic party has provided such great leaders as Jefferson, Jackson, Wilson, and Franklin D. Roosevelt. In keeping with this tradition, I am convinced that the Democratic party will again mirror the overwhelming will of the American people, when its leaders meet at the Democratic national convention in Philadelphia, and will draft General Dwight D. Eisenhower for President."

Within hours after this announcement, ADA chairman Leon Henderson called on ADA state chapters to send delegates to a meeting in Pittsburgh on April 10th with authority to endorse a candidate for the Presidency. Clearly reluctant to abandon ship, ADA was preparing to stage a mutiny and throw the captain overboard.

As new developments unfolded it became obvious that the mutiny had been carefully planned. On March 27th the national chairman of Students for Democratic Action, ADA's campus affiliate, announced adoption of a resolution backing Eisenhower. He explained that this SDA action had been taken at Henderson's request. On April 3rd the New York state ADA convention urged the nomination of Eisenhower and Supreme Court Justice William O. Douglas. The state organization said it was acting "in the firm conviction that the present state of the Union and the world at large constitutes an obvious and overriding reason for the nomination of such standard bearers of progressivism."

By early April President Truman, as expected, had announced that he would run for re-election. General Eisenhower had politely but firmly discouraged a movement to draft him as the Republican nominee. Despite these developments, the ADA national board, meeting in Pittsburgh on April 12th, challenged the Democratic party to an open convention and backed Eisenhower and Douglas as "men this nation has a right to call on." While commending President Truman for his stands on foreign policy, civil rights, and other liberal programs, the board explained that it "could not overlook the fact that poor appointments and faltering support of his aides have resulted in a failure to rally the people behind policies which in large measure we whole-heartedly support."

Moving from words to action, the national office instructed local ADA groups to work for Democratic convention delegates who would be for Eisenhower and Douglas, uninstructed, or for favorite sons— anyone but Truman.

The ADA-inspired revolt began to gather momentum. The leaders

of New York's Liberal party, which frequently held a balance of power
in that state, were supporting the draft-Eisenhower movement. Political polls, showing that Truman would be overwhelmed by any likely
Republican candidate, evoked a "what-the-hell-Harry's-licked-any-
way" attitude among Democratic party leaders. The President's
stock had fallen so low that Washington wits were saying that Truman's best chance was to talk Wallace into giving him second place on
the third party ticket. Democratic national chairman J. Howard Mc-
Grath admitted that Truman did not have the votes to win on the first
ballot.

The ship appeared to be sinking, and the mutiny—which had
originated in liberal-labor circles on the Democratic left—began to
pick up some strange allies. Jake Arvey, boss of the Chicago Democratic machine and a frequent target of the Chicago ADA, revealed the
motivating force behind the revolt when he said that "Eisenhower is
the kind of liberal with whom we could win, both nationally and
locally." The Southern Democrats, agitated about the militant
program recommended by President Truman's Commission on Civil
Rights, also were making rebellious noises. Senator Byrd of Virginia
openly confided: "I hope that Virginia Democrats will cast their
votes for Eisenhower and lead the Democratic Party to victory." The
Georgia Democratic convention resolved that "Eisenhower is the one
man, the only proper man to lead the people in their fight against Communism, tyranny, and slavery." In late March Senator Stennis of
Mississippi also came out for Eisenhower.

Despite these signs of possible success, some members of the
liberal-labor coalition were becoming restive. President William
Green of the American Federation of Labor denounced the draft-Ike
movement, pointing out that "labor doesn't know the social, economic
and industrial views of General Eisenhower."

ADA members also were raising questions. Within six weeks after
the ADA convention had rejected demands that Truman be asked to
withdraw, ADA leadership had completely reversed this position.
Liberals had always prided themselves on a high moral approach to
politics, and now they were gathering in one smoke-filled room after
another. Robert Bendiner, an ADA member, wrote that ADA was
rationalizing its mutiny on the grounds that a Democratic defeat
would result in a Congress whose isolationist views would heighten the
danger of war. "At the same time", Bendiner added, "an organization
based on program and principle cannot, without a certain loss of
character, go panting after a candidate about whom it knows no

more than that he has a marked humanitarianism, a warm smile, and an excellent chance of winning an election."

But the mutineers, having gone so far, had no intention of striking their colors. While conceding that Truman, "if he insists," could probably take the nomination, ADA leaders nevertheless stepped up their campaign against him. The Chicago ADA, in an open letter to the President, informed him that "only four per cent of our members want to see you as a candidate for re-election." An ADA member from Missouri wrote Truman, urging him to withdraw despite the personal sacrifice involved. "You will recall when the Savior of mankind was upon a mountain top he was confronted with this identical problem. His road to glory was the road of personal sacrifice." Truman answered: "I read your letter of . . . with a lot of interest and for your information I was not brought up to run from a fight." As the Democratic convention drew near, Henderson called attention to the fact that only 310 of a total 1,234 delegates were pledged to Truman. Moreover, 110 ADA members had been elected as delegates, and one week before the convention opened the ADA national office began mailing a series of daily leaflets to all delegates urging the nomination of Eisenhower.

While failing to intimidate Truman into withdrawing, ADA had obviously succeeded in creating a situation unique in U.S. political history. For the first time it seemed possible that an incumbent President might be denied a renomination he wanted. The large bloc of uncommitted delegates indicated that a lot of political professionals were sitting on the fence and waiting to see the outcome. The prospect for a successful revolt looked so promising, in fact, that some of the professionals began to climb off the fence and join the mutiny. On July 4th Boss Frank Hague of New Jersey, a vice-chairman of the Democratic National Committee, switched the New Jersey delegation from Truman to Eisenhower.

All that was needed to start a stampede, apparently, was a word from Eisenhower himself. But for three months, as one Democratic faction after another rallied behind his name, Eisenhower had either remained silent or issued mild statements that he was not a candidate. During this time it was frequently recalled that talk of Eisenhower for President had first been heard in labor circles in 1946, when he had addressed the CIO convention and received a tumultuous welcome. Aside from this, there was little evidence to indicate whether he was a Democrat or Republican. But the mutineers had carefully nursed their revolt for weeks and were preparing to carry it into the Democratic convention.

On July 5th, however, Eisenhower announced that he "could not accept nomination for any public office." The Democratic national chairman, notified in advance of the announcement, seized the occasion to appeal to all factions to unite behind the President. Southern delegations immediately pulled out of the revolt and began preparing for a fight over their pet issue, the controversial platform plank on civil rights. The mutiny, gathering steam one day, seemed on the verge of collapse the next.

ADA leaders, watching the work of months deteriorate overnight, reacted hastily—and in retrospect—ludicrously. Joined by various big-city Democratic leaders who had seized a premature hold on the Eisenhower coattails and were reluctant to let go, they began a series of moves which haunt the organization even today. Chairman Henderson, rejecting McGrath's unity appeal with the declaration that "party unity would best be achieved by the President withdrawing his candidacy," expressed hope that the convention would nominate Eisenhower anyway. Arvey of Illinois felt that Ike would not decline if the convention insisted upon having him. Hague predicted that New Jersey would go Republican by 300,000 votes if Truman ran and suggested that the President save the party by withdrawing and nominating Eisenhower himself. In a last-minute effort, several New York ADA chapters organized a motorcade to Eisenhower's residence and picketed him with signs reading "Ike, Don't Be a Draft Dodger," and "Ike, You're A-1 With Us, Be 1-A in the Draft." These frantic efforts succeeded only in provoking a Sherman-like statement from Eisenhower that he would not take the nomination under any "terms, conditions, or premises." By July 10th, two days before the convention opened, the Eisenhower boom was dead. The *New York Star* noted that "if General Eisenhower had waited only a few more days Leon Henderson and his ADA might have brought it off."

ADA leaders, still refusing to accept defeat, attempted to transfer the momentum of the Eisenhower drive behind Justice Douglas. "In our judgment the Democratic Party must choose Douglas or invite a disaster that will imperil the future of progressivism in America," said Henderson. Acting on the theory that the convention might turn to Douglas or some other candidate if an early Truman nomination could be stopped, the ADA chairman went so far as to join in a movement for restoration of the two-thirds rule which until 1936 had given Southern conservatives a veto over Democratic candidates.

But this time Southern leaders, well aware of Douglas' liberal views, refused to go along. The brief Douglas boom expired when Arvey, O'Dwyer of New York, and other leaders of big-state delegations announced that, since Eisenhower was unavailable, "it is in the best interest of our country and party that our democracy unite behind President Truman." The mutiny dragged to an end when the convention unenthusiastically nominated Truman on the first ballot.

In its anti-Truman revolt, the ADA had attempted to take the most direct route available to implement its policy of liberalizing the Democratic party. It had tried to play the role of king-maker, hoping to recapture some of the power behind the throne which liberals had been accustomed to wielding under a former monarch. The adventure led the group down some strange paths, the memory of which causes acute embarrassment today, and it failed dismally. In succeeding years ADA has suffered numerous defeats, but none so complete, or with which it was so completely identified, as the Eisenhower fiasco of 1948.

Civil War Over Civil Rights. Much of ADA's resources, as well as its reputation, had been put on the line in the effort to unseat President Truman. If its activity in the 1948 Democratic convention had ended with Truman's nomination, ADA might well have joined the PCA in political oblivion.

For several months prior to the convention, however, ADA had been preparing for a battle over the Democratic platform. Concurrent with their anti-Truman drive, but with much less fanfare, ADA leaders were laying the groundwork for a floor flight designed to alter radically the party's position on civil rights. The ultimate success of that strategy, coming as it did in the midst of the Eisenhower debacle, enabled the ADA to turn what would have been a disastrous defeat into a surprising political victory.

ADA's concern with the Democratic party's position on civil rights had not sprung up overnight. At its founding conference the group had served notice that it considered the New Deal unfinished business, and one of the major gaps in the New Deal was its failure to cope with the problem of discrimination against Negroes and other minorities. In the late 1930's it had appeared that the Roosevelt Administration might be moving in on this area. But the failure of Roosevelt's attempt to purge prominent Southern conservatives in the election of 1938 and his subsequent need for Southern support for his preparedness policies put an end to such efforts. During the war years Roosevelt had some success in curbing discrimination against Negroes in defense industries, but the larger problems of discrimination in housing, in the armed services, and in education and voting rights in the South remained largely untouched. Southern leaders, entrenched in positions of Congressional seniority and wielding a powerful veto in national party affairs, had blocked all liberal moves to commit the Democratic party to a vigorous stand on these issues.

In the immediate postwar years the prospects for reversing this trend did not appear bright. The 1947 ADA convention contented itself with a general statement calling for an expanded civil rights program. In late 1947, however, a Presidential Commission on Civil Rights issued a report which stirred new hope among liberals and made civil rights a national issue. While conceding that the nation had made great strides toward ending discrimination, the Commission pointed to glaring inconsistencies between professed belief and actual practice. Its specific recommendations included demands for federal antilynching and antipoll tax legislation, an immediate end to segregation in the armed services, enactment of a compulsory Fair Employment Practices Act, and establishment of a permanent Commission on Civil Rights.

The report set off alarms throughout the South. When President Truman endorsed certain of its recommendations in a special message to Congress, the first threats of a Southern bolt of the party were heard. The 1948 ADA convention, finding little room for improvement, incorporated the Commission's report as part of its platform. The national office made civil rights a focus of ADA activity in preparation for the Democratic convention. As early as March, Democratic leaders throughout the country were sent a letter signed by Hubert Humphrey and James Roosevelt asking their pledge for an uncompromising civil rights plank in the Democratic platform.

By July, Democratic strategists were playing down the civil rights issue. The party was given little chance of winning in 1948 as it was; it would be political suicide to write off safe Southern electoral votes by adopting a civil rights plank which the South could not swallow. Democratic strategy called for offering the Southerners a mild civil rights plank and balancing it with a states rights plank. Senator Francis Myers of Pennsylvania was named chairman of the convention platform committee with instructions to push through this compromise. Truman himself advised party leaders to keep the specific points of his civil rights program out of the platform.

Thus the ADA, fighting Truman's renomination, also found itself lined up against the party leadership on the platform. The lineup, moreover, seemed heavily weighted against it. ADA's demand for an uncompromising civil rights plank would have to run the gauntlet of an eighteen-member platform drafting subcommittee and the full 108-member convention platform committee, both dominated by Administration supporters. The compromise position of the leadership was further bolstered when Southern delegations appeared at the convention opposing even the mild civil rights plank of 1944 and insisting upon an off-setting states rights plank.

Despite the odds, ADA leaders decided to press the civil rights fight. Hubert Humphrey, one of four ADA members on the platform committee, was given the task of directing ADA strategy. On July 12th the subcommittee released its draft of the 1948 platform. As expected, the civil rights plank, full of generalities, was a "virtual rewriting of the 1944 compromise." The next day Humphrey presented ADA's version to the full committee in the form of four amendments which called for "federal action" to guarantee to all Americans: (1) personal safety from the crime of lynching and mob violence; (2) equal opportunity in employment; (3) full and free political participation; (4) equal treatment in the armed forces.

After a tumultuous and acrimonious session, the committee rejected the ADA amendments by a "substantial voice vote." Humphrey announced that ADA would take its case to the convention by way of a minority report and fight it out on the floor. Senator Scott Lucas of Illinois stormed out of the committee meeting and accused the ADA of "attempting to wreck the Democratic party by insisting on its civil rights plank."

Lucas' attack revealed that Administration leaders were unsure of their ability to control the convention. The delegates, unhappily certain they were picking a loser in Truman, were restless. An indication of their mood broke through the surface of an otherwise dispirited gathering on the convention's second day. The spark was provided by a dispute over the seating of the Mississippi delegation, whose members had pledged themselves not to support Truman and to walk out if the convention adopted a platform incorporating his civil rights program. When George L. Vaughn, a Negro delegate from Missouri, brought in a minority report from the credentials committee recommending that the Mississippians not be seated, the convention erupted. Southern delegates arose, booing and shaking their fists, while Northern delegates cheered Vaughn on. Temporary chairman Alben Barkley, aware that Administration leaders wished to placate the South, ordered a voice vote, ruled the minority report defeated, and turned a deaf ear to Illinois and California delegates who charged the rostrum demanding a roll call.

For months the North-South split had been a time bomb ticking away in the middle of the Democratic party. Barkley's maneuver merely postponed the explosion one day longer. Liberal delegates, meeting at an all-night caucus presided over by Leon Henderson, prepared to set it off by getting behind ADA's drive for a strong civil rights plank. Acting through their 100-plus members sprinkled throughout all the large Northern delegations, ADA leaders began rounding up support for their minority report. At the same time, three Southern minority reports demanding a states rights plank were in preparation.

The following day, after presentation of the majority report of the platform committee, Governor Dan Moody of Texas led off the Southern demands for a states rights plank. Delegates from Tennessee and Mississippi demanded even more unequivocal guarantees to the states. Former Congressman Andrew Biemiller of Wisconsin followed with ADA's four-point civil rights program.

The drift of the convention became clear when Hubert Humphrey arose to plead for adoption of the ADA resolution. In a speech punctuated by frequent and prolonged applause, he referred to the Truman civil rights program as a new emancipation proclamation. "This convention," declared Humphrey, "must set out more specifically the direction in which our party efforts are to go . . . To those who say that we are rushing this issue of civil rights, I say to them, we are 172 years too late. To those who say that this civil rights program is an infringement of states rights, I say this, that the time has arrived in America for the Democratic party to get out of the shadow of states rights and walk forthrightly into the sunshine of human rights."

Humphrey's speech brought Northern delegates to their feet in a long and loud demonstration; it also brought down upon his head Southern epithets which may still be heard today. In the voting following it, however, the Moody resolution was buried by a vote of 925 to 309. The Tennessee and Mississippi resolutions were shouted down. The chairman of the California delegation, carrying out the strategy decided upon the night before, demanded and got a roll call on the ADA report. Faced with the threat of a public poll of their members, doubtful Northern and Western delegations swung behind the ADA resolution, which carried by a count of 651½ to 581½.

For the Democratic party, which on the question of civil rights had long walked a tightrope along the Mason and Dixon Line, the vote was unprecedented. "Never since 1932," said the *New York Times*, "had there been such a material change in a party platform after it had reached the convention floor."

For the ADA and its liberal allies the civil rights victory was doubly welcome. The humiliation of the Eisenhower debacle was partially erased, and Southern conservatives, an increasingly powerful counterweight to any attempts to liberalize the Democratic party, had met a severe setback. With its civil rights plank, ADA had scored its first success in a drive to "restore some of the Rooseveltian vigor to the Democratic party."

Chapter VIII

ADA AND THE 1948 ELECTION

Following the 1948 national convention ADA found itself in an uneasy position vis-à-vis the Democratic party. ADA's official policy was to work to liberalize the party, but from the point of view of Democratic leaders, especially President Truman, ADA seemed bent upon liquidating the party. Prior to and during the convention, ADA had worked diligently to plant a knife in Truman's back. While this had failed, it had nevertheless left wounds which could be easily exploited by Republican campaigners.

It appeared, moreover, that ADA's civil rights plank might be the final straw which would break the donkey's back in November. The Solid South had always provided Democratic Presidential candidates with a sure cushion of electoral votes, but this year the South was loud with revolt. Two Southern delegations stalked out of the Democratic convention in protest against the civil rights plank. On July 17th delegates from several Southern states met in Birmingham to form the States Rights party and nominate Governors Strom Thurmond of South Carolina and Fielding Wright of Mississippi for President and Vice-President. The rebels made it known that their action stemmed primarily from the Democratic convention position on civil rights.

Thus ADA, fighting vigorously against the Progressive party to the left of Truman, was also attempting to depose the President while playing midwife to the formation of the Dixiecrat party on his right. The harassed Truman, assured by every poll that he had enough enemies, gave no public indication of his position toward ADA, but it is doubtful that he viewed its contributions with equanimity.

ADA's own position toward Truman, however, underwent a quick reversal. ADA in any case had no place else to go, but the President's postconvention actions provided a ready rationalization for turnabout. To a special session of the 80th Congress, Truman presented a militant eleven-point program calling for an increase in the minimum wage, added social security benefits, federal aid to education, an excess profits tax, and other liberal measures. The *World* noted that eight of the eleven measures had been urged by ADA earlier in the year.

On August 29th the ADA national board, declaring that "the Democratic party carries forward the principles for which the American liberal-labor coalition stands," endorsed Truman and Barkley. The board added that ADA's civil rights victory and the Democratic platform as a whole "justify our hope that the Democratic party can be made the most effective national instrument for the achievement of ADA's objectives." Yet even at this late date the old complaint of liberal unemployment could not be kept down: "ADA has frequently criticized President Truman, especially in the matter of appointments. We shall continue to do so when we believe he is not acting in the public interest. It is our hope that the Chief Executive, in exercising his appointive rights, will in the future choose men who conform to his aggressive campaign statements and stated liberal views."

Finally, ADA had made its choice and in the weeks preceding the election the organization threw its resources behind the Democratic ticket on national and local levels. Chairman Henderson explained that while ADA would not enter into any formal alliance with the Democratic National Committee, it would "work in harmony with it." The *World* disclosed that ADA chapters had endorsed and were campaigning for Congressional candidates, almost all of them Democrats, in twelve states.

Like everyone but Truman himself, ADA leaders were convinced they were backing a loser. Three weeks before the election, Henderson sent the President a telegram urging him to appoint a bipartisan commission of prominent citizens to investigate the government's controversial loyalty program. The telegram "urged action before November 2nd."

After November 2nd ADA was paying tribute "to the personal fortitude of a President who clung to faith in himself when we and many others were convinced he could not win." Attributing Truman's stunning victory to his stand on "clear-cut, fighting liberal principles," the ADA happily ate its words: "We were wrong when we argued before the Democratic convention that President Truman could not rally the people under progressive banners. We were wrong because we misjudged his readiness to carry the fight for a liberal progam to the people who once gave their allegiance to Franklin D. Roosevelt. We were right only in believing that the New Deal still lived."

ADA's interpretation of the election as a liberal victory was one of the many postmortems which sprang up to explain how the impossible had happened. In many situations ADA itself appeared to be a factor for success. "When the election returns were in," according to one account, "ADA's significance as a national force was established." Westbrook Pegler assured the President that he owed nothing to the ADA for his victory, which suggested that those on the right were afraid that he might.

Unlike its earlier opposition to Truman, highly visible and always vocal, ADA's contributions to his election are difficult to assess with any precision, but in at least four areas ADA appears to have exerted an active influence on the 1948 election, an influence it has been unable to duplicate since but which for a while promised to make it a force of some consequence in Democratic politics.

The first of these areas, that of an auxiliary arm of the Democratic party on a national basis, was probably the least important. In a number of communities ADA members worked as ward and precinct workers, performing the many tasks involved in the mechanics of every election campaign. In areas of ADA strength—Illinois, New York, Michigan, and Massachusetts—this activity may have been of some moment. In 1948, be it noted, ADA could claim a national membership of only 28,000, and its campaign efforts were often merged with and overshadowed by the huge political army of the CIO-PAC.

If ADA's influence on the Presidential campaign was obscure and perhaps negligible, its impact on the Congressional and local level was obvious and in some areas startling. Two newly-elected U.S. Senators, Humphrey of Minnesota and Douglas of Illinois, were ADA leaders. Nine members of the new House of Representatives would be ADA members. All told, 79 Congressmen, 5 Senators, and 4 governors who had been endorsed and backed by ADA were elected. In Indiana's Third Congressional District ADA member Thomas Crook ousted a five-term GOP Congressman. Richard Bolling, former ADA Midwest Field Director, was elected to Congress from Missouri.

On local levels the results were even clearer. In Detroit ADA could count 30 winners on an endorsed slate of 35 candidates. Ten of the winners were members of the local ADA chapter. In Chicago 12 of 14 ADA-endorsed candidates won easily. If in the past liberal groups had too often confined their political activities to sharing platforms with prominent personages, the 1948 election demonstrated that a new kind of liberal organization had entered the field.

But ADA's greatest impact in 1948 was in the positions it staked out, not in the numbers it helped elect. This is most evident in the relationship between Wallace on one hand and the ADA and Truman on the other. With Wallace operating well to the left of the President and enjoying—or suffering—open Communist support, Republican charges of Democratic radicalism, which had such effect in 1946, were blunted. The corollary of these gains, of course, was the danger of losses on the left. But the pull of Wallace's appeal to liberal Democratic elements, obviously potent in early 1948, was largely erased by ADA's ceaseless exposures of Communist manipulation of the Progressive party. ADA seriously damaged Wallace's pose as the heir of Roosevelt. Without its hard-hitting intervention between Wallace and those dissatisfied progressives who were longing for the second coming of Roosevelt, the Progressive party's claim of ten million votes would not have been so ludicrous.

Paradoxically, ADA's position on civil rights—forced upon an unwilling President as the official policy of his party and interpreted at the time as the death blow to his chances—may have been a decisive factor in his victory. Accepting the verdict of the convention, Truman wrote off the South in advance, waged a hard-hitting campaign on the civil rights issue and became the first President to stump Harlem in search of votes. Samuel Lubell details some of the effects of this campaign on Negro voters in the North; he quotes a Harlem editor as saying that "After the Dixiecrats walked out of the Democratic convention there was no question how Negroes would vote." Despite Wallace's repeated appeals to minority voters, the Democratic platform and Truman's vigorous campaign prevented serious inroads into this crucial sector. One national survey showed that Negroes voted almost two-to-one for Truman over Dewey, with Wallace getting less than one-half of one per cent of the Negro vote cast.

However one evaluates ADA's impact upon the 1948 election, the impact of that election upon ADA and other liberal groups is unmistakable. Truman's triumph was interpreted by them as a liberal victory with a surprising mandate for an extension of the New Deal into what had seemed an inevitable period of postwar reaction. "So now," exulted T.R.B. in the *New Republic,* "we have in the White House a man with the most radical platform in Presidential history. On the basis of two months of campaign speechmaking, Truman is well to the left of the Roosevelt New Deal." This was no liberal victory in a depression period, Eric Goldman pointed out, "this was a reform triumph in a boom."

Referring to Truman's championship of sweeping social reforms, his attacks on big business lobbies, and his espousal of a program "which at least contains the first elements of a new New Deal in American life," ADA could claim that "Without undue pride of authorship, it is not unfair to say that he campaigned on a domestic platform that ADA urged many months before the campaign began."

For an organization whose reason for being was to regain the liberal momentum lost after Roosevelt's death and to revive the New Deal reform spirit, the election of 1948 promised to usher in a new era of liberal power and influence.

After November, 1948, American liberals felt they could permit themselves a certain degree of satisfaction. In just two years the liberal movement had come a long way back from the dark days of November, 1946. The reactionary resurgence which had followed World War I and which loomed so ominously on the horizon after World War II apparently had been averted. Labor and its liberal allies had proved valuable assets to the Democrats in the election and could look forward to political dividends in the form of more liberal policies and appointments. Southern Bourbons, who had long assumed that they held a blank check against the Democratic party, had attempted to cash that check and had seen it bounce. And the liberals who had suffered from charges of Communism or pro-Communism had good reason to believe that this issue, which had been used so indiscriminately and so effectively against them, had been laid at rest.

ADA, emerging from the election as the most effective national liberal organization in the field, could regard itself as the spearhead of the liberal movement. The *New Republic,* originally opposed to the ADA, recognized that it could "now speak with . . . authority for the country's liberals and independents." In late 1948 liberals felt that the future held great promise for them.

The future actually was to be a cruel joke for the liberals and ADA. By 1954 the great hopes of 1948 were gone and liberals were forced to abandon the offensive and fall back on a weak holding action. Access to the power of the Presidency, always their most effective political leverage, was denied them. In Congress most of the liberals of 1948 either were gone or had made their peace with a new era of moderation. The liberal-labor alliance, so close in 1948, showed signs of fatigue and strain. The Democratic party, which had once welcomed ADA support, came to consider it a liability, and prominent Democratic leaders repudiated the organization.

But the most serious reversal of all for liberals in general and ADA in particular was the revival of the old conservative charges that liberals were tainted with Communism. ADA thought it had buried this issue in 1948 when it helped destroy the Progressive party. Within three years it was to learn that this particular ghost would walk again and, in company with demagogues ranging all the way from local American Legion officials to the Vice-President of the United States, would almost destroy the ADA.

Part Four

YEARS OF FRUSTRATION

Chapter IX

THE LIBERAL FAILURE IN CONGRESS

Speaking at the national Jefferson-Jackson Day dinner in February, 1949, President Truman told his audience that "Campaigns and elections are just preliminary exhibition matches—the fight in Congress is the main bout." New Deal liberals, long accustomed to proposing and drafting legislation and passing it up to F.D.R. to push through the Congressional obstacle course, tended to overlook this fact of political life. In the years following the 1948 election liberals were to be reminded of it many times.

As measured by the success or failure of legislation which ADA has favored or opposed, much of the postwar liberal legislative record has been a dismal one. That record in the 81st Congress will be examined in some detail in an attempt to discover the factors leading to liberal frustration in the Congressional arena. Following this will come a summary overview of the ADA record in subsequent Congresses, supplementing and building upon the factors uncovered in the analysis of the 81st.

In the liberal book the 81st was supposed to be a very liberal Congress. Many of the leading lights of reaction in the "no-good, do-nothing Eightieth Congress" had been retired to private life in the election of 1948. And in a surprising number of cases their seats had been taken over by certified liberals. One reason for this was the apparent certainty of Democratic defeat in November. *The New Republic* noted that "many young crusaders were nominated in 1948 because party bosses, certain of Democratic defeat, had put forward liberals." Whatever the reason, the 81st Congress contained more young crusaders than any since the early 1930's, and they supposedly were bent upon a legislative revolution.

President Truman's State of the Union message seemed to indicate that he was also a revolutionist. Among the progressive proposals he recommended were measures calling for government construction of a million low-cost housing units in the next seven years, repeal of the Taft-Hartley Act, increased taxes on corporations and higher incomes, an increase in the minimum wage, a national health insurance program, federal aid to education, and implementation of his earlier civil rights recommendations. His most radical proposal called for federal loans for construction of new steel plants and federal operation if the steel industry failed to cooperate in increasing output. Much impressed, ADA commended the President for calling upon Congress to "act on every critical issue supported by ADA."

Three days after Truman's message liberals scored a significant victory in the organizational maneuvering which developed as the 81st Congress got underway. Shortly after the election, ADA political secretary Vi Gunther prepared a memorandum outlining plans for cutting down the dictatorial power of the House Rules Committee. In previous Congresses this committee, through its authority to grant or withold a rule for any bill reported out by other House committees, had held the power of life or death over legislation. On January 3rd the newly-elected House, much as ADA had outlined, adopted the so-called "twenty-one day rule," by which any bill held up by the Rules Committee longer than twenty-one days could be brought to the floor by a simple majority of the House members present and voting. The *Nation* hailed the change as one of "more far-reaching importance than any bill or group of bills that may be affected in the current session." ADA rejoiced that one of its "major legislative goals" had been achieved.

After the Rules Committee victory and the President's message, ADA concluded that "on the evidence of its first fifteen days, the 81st Congress is taking the November election returns as its marching orders." The Fair Deal revolution seemed well underway.

But, as one writer observed, "Revolutions need lieutenants," and it soon became apparent that the lieutenants in this revolution would not be liberals. Over the opposition of ADA and other liberal groups, Senator Scott Lucas of Illinois was named Senate majority leader. Among other actions considered treasonous by liberals, Lucas had voted for the Taft-Hartley Act, and he had led the fight for a mild civil rights plank in the Democratic convention. The Speaker of the House would be Sam Rayburn of Texas, once a New Deal stalwart but now—like so many other Southerners—becoming increasingly conservative. Whatever else Rayburn might do, he could be counted upon to oppose liberal proposals on civil rights.

Moreover, it also quickly became apparent that those Southerners who had bolted the party and backed the Dixiecrat ticket in 1948 would retain their positions of power in the new Congress. Senator James Eastland of Mississippi, along with twelve House members, campaigned for Thurmond, and most other Southern Congressmen had done nothing to help the national Democratic ticket in their

THE HOUSE
The Issues

1. ADMIT HAWAII TO THE UNION
--Passed 323-89, March 12
The House voted by a commanding margin to grant statehood to Hawaii. (A vote for passage is marked plus; a vote against, minus.)

2. RESTRICT AUTHORITY OF TVA TO ISSUE BONDS
--Defeated 182-231, May 7
The House rejected the move by Rep. Scherer (R., Ohio) to recommit (turn down) a bill authorizing the Tennessee Valley Authority to sell revenue bonds to finance expansion and improvement of facilities. The Scherer motion would have added language providing for Budget Bureau control over TVA projects. (A vote for recommittal is marked minus; a vote against, plus.)

3. BAR DIRECT TREASURY FINANCING FOR PUBLIC HOUSING, URBAN RENEWAL
--Passed 222-201, May 21
The House accepted this amendment to the first housing bill offered by Rep. Thomas (D., Tex.). Amendment made funds available for urban renewal and public housing programs only after approval by Appropriations Committee instead of through authorization bill and public debt transaction with Treasury. The amendment was dropped in conference. (A vote for the amendment is marked minus; a vote against, plus.)

4. STRIKE PUBLIC HOUSING AUTHORIZATION, CUT URBAN RENEWAL
--Defeated 189-234, May 21
The House rejected this move to reject the first housing bill in favor of a substitute offered by Rep. Herlong (D., Fla.). The Herlong bill would have eliminated authority to build new public housing units and cut the urban renewal authorization drastically. (A vote for recommittal is marked minus; a vote against, plus.)

5. FOREIGN AID PROGRAM
--Passed 271-142, June 18
The House approved this $3.5 billion mutual security bill, including a $700 million authorization for the Development Loan Fund.

But substantial cuts in funds were made later in the appropriation bill. (A vote for the bill is marked plus; a vote against, minus.)

6. REJECT "STATES RIGHTS" ANTI-PREEMPTION BILL
--Defeated 191-227, June 24
The House rejected this motion by Rep. Lindsay (R., N. Y.) to recommit (turn down) a bill permitting states to legislate in any area of concurrent jurisdiction not specifically preempted by Congress, and to resurrect state anti-subversive laws. (A vote for recommittal is marked plus; a vote against, minus.)

7. REJECT MOVE TO UPSET SUPREME COURT MALLORY DECISION
--Defeated 138-261, July 7
The House turned down this Lindsay motion to recommit (turn down) a bill making a confession admissible in the Federal Courts even though it was obtained from a defendant while he was being detained for an unreasonable time before arraignment. (A vote for recommittal is marked plus; a vote against, minus.)

8. SUBSTITUTE TOUGH LABOR BILL FOR REFORM MEASURE
--Passed 229-201, August 13
The House accepted this bill sponsored by Reps. Landrum (D., Ga.) and Griffin (R., Mich.) which, by curbing picketing and boycotts, impairs union bargaining powers in dealing with management. The Landrum-Griffin bill was voted in preference to a measure limited to internal union reform. (A vote for the substitute is marked minus; a vote against, plus.)

9. ESTABLISH FOOD STAMP PROGRAM
--Passed 232-127, August 21
The House adopted the Sullivan amendment to an overseas food surplus disposal program, permitting the Secretary of Agriculture to distribute surplus food to needy persons in the U. S. through a food stamp system. (A vote for the amendment is marked plus; a vote against, minus.)

Extracts from a voting record issued in October 1959

House Voting Record

	1	2	3	4	5	6	7	8	9
Alabama									
1 BOYKIN	+	+	+	+	A	-	-	-	A
2 GRANT	-	+	+	+	+	-	-	-	-
3 ANDREWS	-	+	-	+	+	-	-	-	+
4 ROBERTS	-	+	+p	+p	+	-	-	-	+
5 RAINS	-	+	+	+	-	-	-	+	+
6 SELDEN	-	+	+	+	+	-	-	-	+
7 ELLIOTT	-	+	+	+	+	-	-	A	A
8 JONES	-	+	+	+	+	-	-	+	+
9 HUDDLESTON	-	+	+	+	+	-	-	-	+
Alaska									
AL RIVERS	+	+	+	+	+	+	-	+	+
Arizona									
1 Rhodes	+	-	-	-	-	-	+	-	-
2 UDALL	+	+	+	+	+	+	+	+	A
Arkansas									
1 GATHINGS	-	+	-	-	-	-	-	-	+
2 MILLS	-	+	-	+	-	-	-	+	+
3 TRIMBLE	-	+	+	+	-	-	-	+	+
4 HARRIS	-	+	-	+	-	-	-	+	+
5 ALFORD	-	+	-	-	-	-	-	+	A
6 NORRELL	-	+	-	-	-	-	-	-	+
California									
1 MILLER, C.W.	+	+	+	+	+	+	+	+	+
2 JOHNSON	+	+	+	+	+	+	+	+	+
3 MOSS	+	+	+	+	+	+	+	+	+
4 Mailliard	+	-	+	+	+	+	+	+	-
5 SHELLEY	+	+	+	+	+	+	+	+	+
6 Baldwin	+	+	+	+	+	+	+	+	+
7 COHELAN	+	+	+	+	+p	+	+	+	+
8 MILLER, G.P.	+	+	+	+	+	+	+	+	+
9 Younger	+	-	-	-	+	-	-	-	-
10 Gubser	+	-	-	-	+	-	-	-	-
11 McFALL	+	+	+	+	+	+	+	+	+
12 SISK	+	+	+	+	+	+	+	+	+
13 Teague	+	-	-	-	-	-	-	-	-p
14 HAGEN	+	+	+	+	A	-	+	-	-
15 McDonough	+	-	-	-	-	-	-	-	-
16 Jackson	+	-	-	-	+	-	-	-	A
17 KING	+	+	-	+	+	+	+	+	+
18 Hosmer	+	-p	-	-	+	-	-	-	-
19 HOLIFIELD	+	+	-	+	+	+	+	+	+
20 Smith	+	-	-	-	-	-	-	-	-p
21 Hiestand	+	-	-	-	-	-	-	-	-
22 Holt	+	-	-	-	-	-	-	-	-
23 DOYLE	+	+	+	+	+	+	+	+	+
24 Lipscomb	+	-	-	-	-	-	-	-	-p
25 KASEM	+	+	-	+	A	+	A	+	+
26 ROOSEVELT	+	+	+	+	+	+	+	+	+
27 SHEPPARD	+	+	+p	+	+	-	-	+	+
28 Utt	+	-	-	-	-	-	-	-	-
29 SAUND	+	+	+	+	+.	+	+	+	+
30 Wilson	+	-	-	-	+p	-	-	-	-
Colorado									
1 ROGERS	+	+	+	+	+	-	-	+	+
2 JOHNSON	+	+	+	+	+	+	+	+	A
3 Chenoweth	+	-	-	+	-	-	-	-	-
4 ASPINALL	+	+	+	+	+	-	-	+	+
Connecticut									
AL KOWALSKI	+	+	+	+	+	+	+	+	+
1 DADDARIO	+	-	+	+	+	+	+	+	+
2 BOWLES	+	+	+	+	+	+	+	+	A
3 GIAIMO	+	+	+	+	+	+	+	+	+
4 IRWIN	+	+	+	+	+	+	+	+	-
5 MONAGAN	+	-	+	+	+	+	+	+	A
Delaware									
1 McDOWELL	+	+	+	+	+	+	A	+	+

	1	2	3	4	5	6	7	8	9
Illinois									
1 DAWSON	+	+	+	+	+	+	+	+	A
2 O'HARA	+	+	+	+	+	+	+	+	+
3 MURPHY	+	+	+	+	+	+	+	+	+
4 Derwinski	+	-	-	-	-	-	-	-	-
5 KLUCZYNSKI	+	+	+	+	+	+	+	+	+
6 O'BRIEN	+	+	+	+	+	+	+	+	+
7 LIBONATI	+	+	+	+	+	+	+	+	+
8 ROSTENKOWSKI	+	+	+	+	A	+	+	+	A
9 YATES	+	+	+	+	+	+	+	+	+
10 Collier	+	-	-	-	-	-	-	-	+p
11 PUCINSKI	+	+	+	+	+	+	+	+	+
12 BOYLE	+	+	+	+	+	+	+	+	+
13 Church	+	-	-	-	-	-	-	-	+
14 Hoffman	-	-	-	-	-	-	-	-	-
15 Mason	-	-	-	-	-	-	-	-	A
16 Allen	-	-	-	-	-	-	-	-	-
17 Arends	-	-	-	-	-	-	-	-	-
18 Michel	+	-	-	-	-p	-	-	-	-
19 Chiperfield	+	-	-	-	-p	-	-	-	-
20 Simpson	+	-	-	-	-	-	-	-	-
21 MACK	+	+	+	+	+p	+	+	+	+
22 Springer	+	-	-	+	-	-	-	-	-
23 SHIPLEY	+	+	+	+	+	+	+	+	A
24 PRICE	+	+	+	+	+	+	+	+	+
25 GRAY	+	-	+	+	+	+	+	+	+
Indiana									
1 MADDEN	+	+	+	+	+	+	+	+	+
2 Halleck	+	-	-	-	-	-	-	-	A
3 BRADEMAS	+	+	+	+	+	+	+	+	+
4 Adair	+	-	-	+	-	-	+	-	+
5 ROUSH	+	+	+	+	+	-	+	-	+
6 WAMPLER	+	+	-	+	-	+	+	+	+p
7 Bray	+	-	-	-	-	-	-	-	-
8 DENTON	A	+	-	+	-	+	+	+	+
9 HOGAN	+	-	+	-	+	-	+	+	+
10 HARMON	+	+	-	+	+	+	+	+	+
11 BARR	+	+	+	+	-	-	-	+	+
Iowa									
1 Schwengel	+	-	-	+	+	-	+	-	
2 WOLF	+	-	+	+	+	+	+	-	
3 Gross	+	-	-	-	-	-	-	-	
4 CARTER	+	-	+	+	+	+	+	+	
5 SMITH	+	+	+	+	+	+	+	+	
6 COAD	+	+	+	+	+	+	+	+	
7 Jensen	+	-	-	-	-	-	A	-	
8 Hoeven	+	-	.-	-	-	-	-	-	
Kansas									
1 Avery	+	-	-	-	+	-	-	-	
2 GEORGE	A	+	+	+	+	+	+	+	
3 HARGIS	A	+	+	+	+	+	+	+	
4 Rees	+	-	-	-	-	-	-	-	
5 BREEDING	+	+	+	+	-	+	-	+	
6 Smith	-	-	-	-	-	-	A	-	
Kentucky									
1 STUBBLEFIELD	+	+	+	+	+	-	-	+	+
2 NATCHER	+	+	+	+	+	+	-	+	+
3 BURKE	+	+	+	+	+	-	-	+	+p
4 CHELF	+	+	+	+	+	-	A	+	+
5 SPENCE	+	+	+	+	+	-p	-	+	+
6 WATTS	+	+	+	+	+	-	+	+	+
7 PERKINS	+	+	+	+	+	-	+	+	+
8 Siler	-	-	-	-	-	-	-	-	+
Louisiana									
1 HEBERT	+	+	-	-	+p	-	-	+	
2 BOGGS	+	+	+	+	+p	-	-	+	
3 WILLIS	-p	+p	-	-	A	-	-	+	
4 BROOKS	+	-	-	-	-	-p	-	+	
5 PASSMAN	+	-	-	-	-	-	-	+p	
6 MORRISON	+p	A	A	A	-	-p	+	+p	
7 THOMPSON	-p	+	-	-	-	-p	+p		
8 McSWEEN	+	-	-	-	-	-	-	-p	

Extract from voting record of 86th Congress, First Session states. In December the ADA national board had called for the "expulsion of all members of Congress who had supported Thurmond from both Senate and House caucuses and their removal from all important posts on Congressional committees." After the election, informed sources reported that President Truman intended to cut the Dixiecrats down to size by depriving them of their patronage and seniority rights on committees. These intentions, if they existed, were never carried out. When the new Congress was finally organized, the rebellious Southerners assumed their usual high-ranking committee posts, the strategic points from which they had been striking down liberal legislation since the late 1930's.

And in the first big test of the Fair Deal revolution, Southern Senators demonstrated that—whatever mandate liberals might read into the election returns—it did not apply South of the Mason and Dixon Line. This test came over the Administration attempt of liberalize the Senate's cloture rule so as to curb the effectiveness of Southern filibusters, and upon its outcome rested the fate of civil rights legislation in the 81st Congress.

ADA felt a proprietary interest in such legislation. In December it had announced that, "As the organization which initiated the successful battle for a strong civil rights plank in the Democratic convention, ADA will insist on legislation implementing every point in that plank." At a January conference ADA leaders decided to try to muster two-thirds of the Senate votes in one major drive to cut off debate and enact a resolution for cloture by a simple majority, rather than to rely on getting two-thirds on each of several controversial civil rights measures which were due to come up.

Debate on modification of the cloture rule opened on February 28th. President Truman ordered Administration forces to make an all-out fight on the filibuster and personally came out for cloture by a simple majority, exactly what ADA was demanding. But on March 11th, after two weeks of complicated maneuvering and intense debate, the Senate voted 46 to 41 against the Administration position. Civil rights became a dead letter in the 81st Congress. While a few measures passed the House, no civil rights bills even came to a vote in the Senate. The ADA, for the first of many times, found that the conversion of party platform planks into legislative enactments could be a difficult process.

Four days after the Senate defeat a coalition of House Republicans and Southern Democrats joined forces to beat down an Administration effort to maintain federal jurisdiction over rent decontrols. One week later the Senate followed suit.

The second annual ADA convention, meeting April 7th-10th in Chicago, found liberals in a chastened mood. Vi Gunther warned that the filibuster defeat not only doomed civil rights legislation but also boded ill for other liberal measures: "Any illusion that the liberal Democrats dominate either the House or the Senate has been completely blasted." The convention delegates issued a call for an "emergency legislative conference" to bring together liberal, labor and farm groups in an effort to halt "the reactionary coalition in Congress." Hubert Humphrey concluded that the 1948 election was "not so much a victory as a reprieve" and upbraided liberals for their "post-election complacency."

In its Political Policy Statement, the convention attempted to assess the weaknesses which had developed in liberal ranks since November. One major weakness was the fact that "separate elements of the liberal coalition tended in the post-election months to pursue their special aims to the detriment of their collective strength." This was a euphemistic way of saying that ADA was concerned because the labor movement, determined to repeal the Taft-Hartley Act, was neglecting other liberal aims. Another major weakness had arisen because "there has been an ineffective—if not nonexistent—liasion between the Administration and the liberal forces which played so large a part in continuing it in power." This was the old, pre-election liberal complaint that Truman was not taking liberals into his confidence. Together, they indicated that the liberal-labor-Democratic party alliance of the previous fall was showing signs of strain.

Subsequent developments indicated that this alliance, even when acting in concert, was far less powerful in Congress than it thought itself to be in the country at large. In January an ADA-sponsored conference of national liberal and labor leaders issued a manifesto declaring: "The liberal-labor coalition expects results in this session on labor legislation, which includes repeal of Taft-Hartley and restoration of the Wagner Act; a substantial civil rights program; aid to education; a health program which includes an insurance scheme; and aid to the family-sized farm."

These demands, along with demands for reimposition of the excess profits tax and development of additional valley authorities like TVA, constituted "must" legislation for the liberal-labor coalition. We have seen the results on civil rights. An examination of the fate of the other measures listed illustrates why some liberals dubbed the 81st Congress the "Eighty-worst" Congress.

When the Senate, on May 5th, passed a federal aid to education measure by a 58-15 vote, liberals thought they could foresee realization of a long-standing goal. While the Senate bill contained several states rights guarantees which liberals thought unnecessary, it did authorize an annual appropriation of $300 million in direct federal aid to education in the states. Despite the overwhelming vote in the Senate, however, a companion measure in the House died in the Education and Labor Committee. This was due primarily to an acrimonious debate over the question of restricting aid to tax-supported schools, a debate which quickly spread beyond the halls of Congress and ended in a personal feud between Mrs. Roosevelt and Cardinal Spellman. One Congressman figured that the federal aid bill would have passed the House by a three-to-one margin if this controversy had not arisen.

The liberal demand for a comprehensive national health insurance program, included in President Truman's State of the Union message and backed by ADA, the CIO, and the AFL, proved to be one of the most controversial issues considered by the 81st Congress. The American Medical Association, which spent more than any other registered lobby group in 1949, led the opposition against it. The AMA's high-pressure campaign against "socialized medicine" proved so effective that the Administration's health insurance bill did not get beyond the hearing stage in either House or Senate.

ADA's demand for reimposition of the excess profits tax did not get that far. Also included in Truman's January message, it was heard respectfully by Congress and quietly ignored. Hearings were held on the Administration proposal for a Columbia Valley Authority, but this measure, like the health insurance program, died in committee. A long-range farm program did pass both houses, but it contained none of the features of the Brannan Plan, which was backed enthusiastically by the liberal-labor coalition.

By late May these and other liberal proposals were being strangled in various Congressional committees, and many of those which had been reported to the floor of the Senate and House faced crippling amendments. Five months deep into the session, when it had become obvious that the Fair Deal revolution was an abortive putsch, the Administration prepared to pull in its lines and concentrate on limited objectives. On May 4th, Senate Majority Leader Lucas, after conferring with Truman, announced that only three items of the President's original program would remain on the Administration's "must" list. Those were repeal of Taft-Hartley, ratification of the North Atlantic Treaty, and extension of the reciprocal trade program.

The announcement stunned liberals in and out of Congress. ADA reacted quickly, blasting the action as "more than a flag of surrender; it is a flat betrayal of the Democratic platform." Editorialized the *ADA World*: "We believed that the leaders of this Administration were ready to fight . . . We suffered a profound shock this week when the Democratic Congressional leaders, with a silent nod from the Chief Executive, meekly declared that the Fair Deal could wait."

The *New Republic* noted that "the ADA phrasing was rough, and there are Fair Dealers in Congress who think the charge excessive." Nevertheless, many liberals were remarking cynically that "the difference between the ADA and the Democrats is that ADA believes in the Democratic platform."

Along with civil rights, the most important plank in the 1948 Democratic platform was the demand for outright repeal of the Taft-Hartley Act. Taft-Hartley had been dubbed a "slave labor" law by both the AFL and CIO. Its passage by the 80th Congress had spurred the labor movement to intensive action in 1948, and many Democratic congressmen owed their seats to labor support. Truman himself, upon learning of his victory, had said that "Labor did it." The liberal-labor coalition was determined to repeal Taft-Hartley in the 81st Congress, and the Administration was equally determined to pay off a huge political debt. Within a month after Lucas' announcement, all this determination had come to naught, and liberals had suffered what was probably their greatest Congressional defeat of the postwar years.

The fight for Taft-Hartley repeal began in February when Administration forces brought forward the Thomas-Lesinski bill, which proposed complete repeal of Taft-Hartley and return to the Wagner Act. Senate and House Republicans were said to be preparing for a "rearguard action" against it.

After weeks of intensive committee maneuvering, House debate on repeal began on April 28th. The Administration bill, reported unchanged from the Education and Labor Committee, was immediately attacked by a Republican-Southern Democratic coalition. Representative John Wood of Georgia offered an amendment which was in reality a substitute bill which would have left Taft-Hartley essentially unchanged. On May 3rd the Wood Amendment passed the House by a 217-203 vote. There followed a day and night of intensive pressure on the part of liberal, labor, and Administration forces. On May 4th, the House approved a surprise motion to return the Wood Bill to committee for further study by a 212-209 margin. Thus by only a three-vote margin was the liberal-labor coalition able to prevent virtual re-enactment of Taft-Hartley in the House. The Wood Amendment was heard from no more, but neither was the Thomas-Lesinski measure.

The Senate did not begin debate on repeal until June 6th, after the House had already acted. Administration leaders hoped to force a bill through the Senate and gain reconsideration in the House. But, as in the House, the Administration bill was subjected to a Republican-Southern Democratic counter-attack led by Senators Taft and Holland. The liberal-labor coalition was divided, with some factions calling for complete repeal of Taft-Hartley and restoration of the original Wagner Act and others being willing to settle, even if somewhat reluctantly, for substitution of a new law containing some features of Taft-Hartley.

After three weeks of debate, the question was no longer repeal but whether the Senate would reaffirm its previous approval of Taft-Hartley. The key vote came on June 28th on an Administration amendment offered by Senator Lucas which would eliminate the injunction provisions against labor included in Senator Taft's substitute.

Thus, of the seven measures listed as "must" liberal legislation by ADA, not one was passed in the first session of the 81st Congress. While noting some successes, primarily in the area of foreign affairs, the *ADA World* termed the session one of "disheartening rebuffs." Few of these "must issues" came to a vote in the second session, and again not one passed. Glumly surveying the performance of the Congress which was supposed to have resurrected the New Deal, the *World* concluded that "the 81st Congress is not a liberal Congress."

ADA's evaluation of subsequent Congresses is equally negative. The 82nd, "while not matching the mediocrity of the Republican dominated 80th, came very near to it." The 83rd Congress wrote "a record of expediency, timidity and inconsistency." The 84th "dealt the people out." The 85th was not quite a "do-nothing Congress," but its record was "meager." The 86th Congress was one of "minuscule achievement."

The first session of the 87th Congress produced at best a record of "callous expediency" and at worse, "one of astonishing indifference to real national needs."

Running through all these criticisms of postwar Congresses is the consistent theme that a "Republican-Dixiecrat" coalition has stifled liberal legislation and kept Congress several years behind sentiment in the country. Lack of vigorous Presidential leadership of Congress has formed a subsidiary theme, particularly during the Truman and Eisenhower years. Neither strand of criticism, it may be noted, has disappeared with the election of a Democratic President with nominally overwhelming majorities in both Houses of Congress. Although ADA concluded that the dismal record of the 86th Congress made the election of John F. Kennedy "imperative," one year later the *World* said of the first session of a Kennedy Congress: "The door to the New Frontier remains closed. The key—a combined program of bold Presidential initiative and determined Congressional execution—has not been found."

The ADA Record in Congress. Obviously, in ADA's opinion, liberals have not fared well in the Congressional arena since World War II. A study of the ADA record in the 81st through the 86th Congresses bears out this opinion.

Each year the *ADA World* publishes a special "Congressional Supplement" evaluating the work of each session of Congress. For both House and Senate, a number of roll-call votes—usually ten to thirteen from each chamber—is selected, and the votes of each Senator and Representative are rated "plus" or "minus" according to ADA's judgment of whether he voted for or against the liberal position. An analysis of the outcome of these votes should give one measure of the success or failure of liberalism in Congress. Table 1, with breakdowns by Senate and House and by votes on domestic and foreign policy issues, gives the results of this analysis. The figures show the percentage of victories for the ADA position on roll calls during each Congress from 1949 through 1960. The figures in brackets show the number of roll-call votes in each category.

Several things should be noted about the data in Table 1. The votes analyzed are not a random sample of all roll-calls in Congress during these years; they were selected by ADA primarily because they tend to show a liberal-conservative split in the voting. A vote was counted as a liberal victory if the liberal position, as defined by ADA, achieved a majority. But the percentages are not particularly meaningful as measures of the overall success of liberal policy, primarily because we are dealing with a bicameral legislature and largely with votes on different issues in the House and Senate. In many cases, an issue voted on in one House might not come to a vote in the other House, or might be compromised within conference between the two Houses. In other cases, the liberal position might achieve a majority on one roll-call only to be amended by a later vote. This situation is explored in more detail below in the section on liberal fortunes back of the voting stage. For the moment, it should be emphasized that the percentages in Table 1 represent primarily a measure of liberal success or lack of success when these selected issues reached the voting stage in either the Senate or the House of Representatives.

Given these qualifications, several interesting factors emerge. Although the votes on foreign policy issues are few, they show a much greater degree of liberal success than do the domestic policy votes. This may be due to several factors but presumably is a reflection of the general consensus between the two parties and within the nation as a whole on questions of foreign policy. Despite occasional sharp differences, since the rise of the Soviet threat after World War II Congress has been dominated in foreign affairs by a bipartisan internationalist bloc. The liberal position, as interpreted by ADA, has been whole-heartedly internationalist. ADA has consistently favored foreign aid, reciprocal trade, regional alliances, etc. Its differences with the bipartisan coalition on specific issues have been more differences of degree than of kind, with ADA favoring *more* foreign aid, *more* reciprocal trade, etc., than Congress has often been willing to grant. In foreign policy, therefore, liberals met with much greater success than in domestic policy. This is reflected in the comments on Congress in each ADA Congressional Supplement, in Table 1 and various measures mentioned below.

The picture in domestic policy is quite different. Table 1 shows that, despite great fluctuations over the twelve-year period covered, the liberal position on these selected domestic issues has been successful only 30 per cent of the time in the Senate and 29 per cent of the time in the House.

At first glance, it might seem tenuous to interpret positions taken by one interest group as the "liberal" position and infer from this a general liberal futility in Congress. But in the case of ADA this does not seem unwarranted. ADA, unlike many or perhaps most pressure groups, is not based on narrow economic, regional, occupational, or other interests. It is almost an ideological group, taking a position on virtually all political, economic, and other issues which form the stuff of national debate and find their resolution in Congress. Indeed, as noted below, this "cover the waterfront" approach is the source of one of ADA's greatest weaknesses as a pressure group.

A check of the positions taken by ADA with those taken by the AFL-CIO, the National Farmer's Union, the NAACP, and other liberal

TABLE 1

LIBERAL SUCCESS ON SELECTED ROLL CALL VOTES,
81st THROUGH 86th CONGRESSES

Congress	SENATE			HOUSE		
	% All votes	Votes on % domestic issues	Votes on % Foreign issues	% All votes	Votes on % domestic issues	Votes on foreign issues %
81st 1949-50	27(30)	17(22)	57(8)	39(28)	32(22)	66(6)
82nd 1951-52	31(26)	29(17)	33(9)	8(26)	10(21)	0(5)
83rd 1953-54	32(28)	26(19)	44(9)	30(20)	19(16)	75(4)
84th 1955-56	47(24)	47(17)	43(7)	64(17)	40(11)	100(6)
85th 1957-58	42(24)	32(19)	80(5)	43(21)	27(15)	83(6)
86th 1959-60	36(25)	33(21)	50(4)	61(18)	56(16)	100(2)
Avg.	34	30	49	38	29	70
No. of roll-call votes	157	115	42	130	101	29

groups bears out the impression that ADA is the most representative liberal group operating on the national scene. The positions taken by ADA seldom differ from those taken by these groups, while ADA assumes positions on many issues which one or another of these groups will ignore because of their narrower base. Thus, it does not seem unwarranted to assume that the views on issues expressed by ADA represent a general liberal viewpoint, perhaps slightly to the left of the consensus of other liberal groups, but nevertheless representative of the liberal position in the nation as a whole.

If this is the case, on the basis of these ADA-selected votes, liberals have taken a beating in Congress during the postwar years, being victorious on just over one-third of the occasions when issues important to them have come to a vote in either House of Congress.

In recent years the Senate generally has been considered a more liberal body than the House. Such an evaluation is not reflected in Table 1, but the nonrandom nature of the sample of votes may have skewed the results. The high tide of liberal success came in the 84th Congress, after the Democrats had taken control of Congress following the Eisenhower sweep of 1952. But the abnormally high percentage in the House for the 84th Congress seems due to the heavier weighting of foreign policy issues than to a resurgent liberalism.

Sources of Support for and Opposition to Liberalism. There seems to be general agreement that, on the whole, the Republicans are the most conservative force and the Northern and Western Democrats the most liberal force in Congress. Controversy in this area has usually focused on the Southern Democrats. Senator Barry Goldwater, on a 1960 campaign swing through the South, concluded that "there's hardly enough difference between Republican conservatives and the Southern Democrats to put a piece of paper between." The AFL-CIO, which usually does not see eye-to-eye with Senator Goldwater, agrees that "a coalition of conservative forces from both the Democratic and Republican parties . . . has shaped the nation's political direction for the past twenty-three years." One academic writer, however, contends that the idea of a conservative South is a "myth" and says that no GOP-Dixiecrat alliance exists. "The Southern Democrats differ from both Northern Democrats and Republicans," says Norman R. Phillips, "but have much more in common with their fellow Democrats than with the GOP."

Most Congressional voting analyses have focused on party cohesion or on party solidarity or lack of solidarity with the President. ADA's voting records, however, furnish the basis for an analysis along a liberal-conservative dichotomy, thus allowing a more direct approach to the question of sources of liberal support and opposition in Congress. In an attempt to isolate and measure these sources, the votes of each Senator and Representative on the roll-call votes in Table 1 were tabulated. The results are presented in Tables 2 and 3. Each member of Congress was classified as a Republican, Southern Democrat, or Northern Democrat. The Republican category requires no explanation. In these tables Southern Democrats are those Senators or Repre-

TABLE 2
SENATE SOURCES OF SUPPORT FOR LIBERAL POSITION ON SELECTED ROLL CALL VOTES, 81ST THROUGH 86TH CONGRESSES

Congress	All votes					Votes on domestic issues					Votes on foreign issues				
	S	D	R %	SD	ND	S	D	R %	SD	ND	S	D	R %	SD	ND
81st	46	62	25	42	74	44	59	24	38	75	53	69	27	53	73
82nd	45	65	23	45	79	45	61	27	39	77	46	73	16	57	85
83rd	43	61	26	43	76	42	67	17	47	84	47	48	46	36	59
84th	46	67	24	49	81	47	73	21	55	88	42	53	30	37	65
85th	51	66	38	38	83	47	63	32	36	86	61	61	62	47	72
86th	49	62	26	25	81	49	63	22	24	83	56	59	52	30	74
Avg.	47	64	27	40	79	46	64	24	40	82	51	61	39	43	71

S — All Senate votes
D — All Democrats
R — Republicans

SD — Southern Democrats
ND — Northern Democrats

TABLE 3
HOUSE SOURCES OF SUPPORT FOR LIBERAL POSITION ON SELECTED ROLL CALL VOTES, 81ST THROUGH 86TH CONGRESSES

Congress	All votes					Votes on domestic issues					Votes on foreign issues				
	H	D	R %	SD	ND	H	D	R %	SD	ND	H	D	R %	SD	ND
81st	48	69	16	40	87	46	65	16	32	86	58	82	15	68	92
82nd	42	63	20	29	89	43	61	23	25	89	41	70	9	45	88
83rd	45	68	25	44	89	42	66	20	41	86	58	74	43	55	90
84th	54	69	37	42	88	50	66	31	36	95	61	74	46	55	88
85th	49	62	35	29	85	47	64	27	29	89	55	56	53	30	75
86th	55	72	24	33	92	54	72	20	33	93	64	67	58	34	85
Avg.	49	67	26	36	88	47	66	23	34	90	56	71	37	48	88

H — All House votes
D — All Democrats·
R — Republicans

SD — Southern Democrats
ND — Northern Democrats

sentatives from the eleven former Confederate states. Northern Democrats are those members from any of the other states.

During these years there were two mavericks in Congress, Wayne Morse in the Senate and Frazier Reames in the House. Morse's votes were carried in the Republican column during the years he called himself a Republican and in the Democratic column after he officially became a Democrat; his votes as an independent were not counted. The votes by Reames, who remained an independent throughout his service, were not counted. It should be noted that in each of its Congressional Supplements ADA lists paired votes and announced vote intentions as well as actual votes. All of these were included in the tabulation.

The data in Tables 2 and 3 bear out the general impression that the Democrats are the more liberal party. In both House and Senate, the Democrats overall support liberal measures more than twice as often as their GOP colleagues. The data also show that by far the greatest support for the liberal position comes from the Northern Democrats. In the House Northern Democrats support the liberal position over three times as often as Republicans, and the difference in the Senate is just under three-to-one.

Both ADA pronouncements and the policy it has followed indicate that it considers the Republicans in Congress to be its worst enemy. This voting analysis shows that it does not err in this respect. But Southern Democrats occupy an equally high place in the ADA's roster of political devils. In the *World*, reference is seldom made to the iniquities of Congressional conservatives without a bow in the direction of the Southern Democrats. Liberal failures in Congress usually are attributed to the machinations of a "Republican-Dixiecrat" coalition. Such a coalition has been operative in Congress in recent years, and its force is reflected in these two tables.

It would appear, however, that ADA overstates the case slightly when it implies that Southern Democrats are just disguised Republicans. In both Houses of Congress, in overall voting and on both domestic and foreign issues, Southern Democrats have been more liberal than Republicans.

In every Congress Southern Senators were more liberal than Republican Senators on domestic policy issues. On foreign policy, however, they fell below their GOP colleagues in three of the six Congresses. But the decline of liberal support among the Southerners in the 85th and 86th Congresses is noticeable.

In the House, on domestic issues, the Southern Democrats had a higher liberal support record than the Republicans in each Congress. Overall, they dropped below the Republicans only in the 85th Congress. As in the Senate, the decline of liberalism among the Southerners in the last two Congresses is evident.

Nevertheless, on an average over the twelve-year period, the data show that Southern Democrats were much closer in their voting patterns to the Republicans than to their own Northern colleagues. Table 4, showing the percentage-point differences between Southern Democrats and Republicans and between Southern Democrats and Northern Democrats, illustrates this point.

TABLE 4

DIFFERENCE IN LIBERAL-SUPPORT PERCENTAGES BETWEEN REPUBLICANS AND SOUTHERN DEMOCRATS AND BETWEEN SOUTHERN DEMOCRATS AND NORTHERN DEMOCRATS

	Percent of Difference between R and SD	Percent of Difference between SD and ND
Senate—All votes	13	39
—Domestic votes	16	42
—Foreign votes	4	28
House—All votes	10	52
—Domestic votes	11	56
—Foreign votes	11	40

Thus, on all issues except domestic policy in the Senate, Southern Democrats in House and Senate had a "liberalism" score at least three times as close to the Republicans as to the Northern Democrats.

Liberal Fortunes Back of the Voting Stage. The liberal victory percentages in Table 1 are based on roll-call votes, and therefore may be suspect as a measure of liberals' effectiveness in getting their views enacted into law. At best, the figures in the table merely represent liberal power or lack of power when issues actually come to a vote in one or the other House of Congress.

The most obvious difficulty with this attempt to employ voting data as a general measure of liberal effectiveness is that no allowance is made for the existence of a bicameral legislature or for possible inter-vention by Presidential veto. The passage of a liberal measure in one house of Congress does not mean that that particular liberal policy becomes the law of the land; it is necessary to pass it through both houses and get Presidential approval. Defeat in either house of a measure which liberals oppose does represent an effectuation of liberal policy, since in such a case the liberal policy is effectuated simply by maintaining the status quo. But we cannot assume that these two factors balance each other out. As will be seen below, the balance is heavily weighted against liberals.

David Truman, who makes very successful use of highly sophisticated voting analysis techniques in his book on *The Congressional Party,* has warned of the chief difficulty of a purely voting analysis approach: "Reservations properly can and should be registered against an uncritical reliance upon roll calls as indicators of the full range of legislative behavior. They are unmistakably a record of decisions taken, of choices made, but they are evidence of only the most public choices. Ordinarily they indicate nothing about measures that never reach the floor of the House or Senate, and they directly reveal nothing of what has occurred behind the scenes. In the Congress, as in most American legislatures, the choices made in committees . . . are of great consequence."

Only a very few of the proposals submitted to Congress ever reach the voting stage; most die along the way in one of numerous labryinthine Congressional byways. After referral to the appropriate standing committee, they may simply gather dust there and be heard of no more. A few may reach the hearing stage but not be reported out of committee. If reported out, they may never come to a vote. Thus, before reaching the voting stage in either house, legislative proposals must clear a number of hurdles. The whole structure of Congress operates as a brake upon any proposals to disturb the status quo. Primarily because of these structual factors, voting records alone do not present a realistic picture of liberal fortunes in Congress.

What is needed, of course, is some method of measuring the power of an interest or the groups which support it. This is a problem which has fascinated interest group students since Bentley published his seminal work down to today. No one has yet come up with a methodological solution to this problem, and no claims are made along those lines here. All that has been attempted in this study is to obtain a simple—and somewhat superficial—measure of liberal power which goes a few steps back of the voting stage analysis covered above.

This was done by studying the positions taken by ADA—as reported in the *Congressional Quarterly Almanac*—on legislative proposals in the hearing stage. The period covered is from 1947 through 1960. During these years the *Almanac* recorded ninety usable ADA positions, either in the form of testimony by various ADA officials before Congressional committees or in the form of statements submitted in writing to these committees.

The details of this measure, including the scoring procedures, are summarized below.[1] The main point of interest here is that this procedure enables us to go back of the Congressional committee stage, where so many legislative proposals come to an end, and forward through both houses of Congress and Presidential scrutiny, and thus obtain what should be a more valid estimate of liberal effectiveness in Congress. We can assume that the issues included in this measure were important to liberals, since they stimulated ADA and other liberal groups to make appearances or draft statements in behalf of the liberal position on these issues. As a counterpoint to the measure of liberal effectiveness, the same procedure was followed with a recognized conservative group, the National Association of Manufacturers. The results of these two measures are as follows:

TABLE 5

ADA VERSUS NAM SUCCESS IN CONGRESS, 1947-1960

	ADA	NAM
All issues—	32% (90)	67% (90)
Domestic policy issues—	24% (70)	65% (86)
Foreign policy issues—	65% (20)	50% (4)

(Numbers in brackets are the number of issues in each category.)

According to this analysis, during the fourteen postwar years from 1947 through 1960, liberals were able to make their policies effective on just one-third of occasions. As in other measures applied, again liberals appear to be much more effective in foreign policy then in domestic policy. On the whole, however, the picture is one of liberal futility and conservative success.

The measure used in connection with Table 5 is subject to many qualifications. It was based on *Congressional Quarterly's* selection of positions assumed by the two groups, and this selection presumably was not random. Also, the measure was not purely quantitative, but involved a large degree of qualitative judgment.

At first glance the closeness of ADA success percentages in Tables 1 and 5 seems unusual. The logical assumption might be that since the measure in Table 5 made allowances for a bicameral legislature, the obstructive effect of the committee system, and intervention by veto, liberal success as measured by this technique would be lower than simple roll-call measures in both Houses of Congress.

The explanation seems to lie in the different criteria for selection of data in the two samples. The roll-call votes analyzed in Table 1 and again in Tables 2 and 3 were selected by ADA after the voting occurred and were selected primarily because they showed a liberal-conservative split. Presumably this tended to overemphasize votes on which the Republican-Southern Democratic coalition was operating and to depress the ADA success percentage. It can be assumed that a universe or a purely random selection of all votes on which liberal-conservative positions possibly might be differentiated would produce different results. One would expect such a procedure to show a higher liberal success percentage and to narrow somewhat the striking differences between Southern and Northern Democrats which Tables 2 and 3 exhibit.

On the other hand, the positions which furnished the sample for Table 5 were taken by ADA prior to Congressional action. The issues involved drew testimony by ADA and other groups in favor of the liberal position. They were "gut" issues for liberals, issues on which liberal forces presumably were exerting maximum pressure. The same can be said, of course, for NAM on the conservative side. It is believed that the procedure used in Table 5, despite its imperfections, is a reasonably valid measure of the relative power of the liberal and conservative forces operating on Congress. If this is the case, then liberals have some reason to feel "unbelieving, incredulous, bitter frustration" when they watch the American Congress at work.

Why Liberal Failure in Congress? If the relative impotence of Congressional liberals vis-à-vis Congressional conservatives is accepted as evident, the question remains as to why this should be the case. The major studies of Congress, such as those by Gross, Griffith, Bailey and Samuel, Young, Burns, and others do not go specifically or in depth into this question. The tentative explanations advanced below are, however, largely an extension or elaboration of ideas developed in several of the above-mentioned works. No attempt is made at a unified, exhaustive analysis.

One obvious explanation of liberal futility in Congress might be simply that not enough liberals are elected to Congress. Since its disappointment with the 81st Congress, this has been a constant theme of ADA internal and external propaganda. This factor has ramifications far beyond the scope of this study, ranging from the political attitudes of the electorate as a whole through the structure of the entire electoral process. Some students contend that the ground rules for election of members of Congress are so drawn as to distort and minimize the essential liberalism of the electorate. Rural over-representation, for instance, prevents Congress from being a true reflection of the electorate and operates to the advantage of conservatism.

There is some question, however, whether the simple fact of election of more liberals to Congress, by itself, would be such a boon to liberal policy as ADA seems to believe. Liberal experience with the 86th Congress effectively destroys any notion that an increase in the number of liberals in Congress will be reflected by direct ratio in the success of liberal policy. ADA, along with other liberal groups and the liberal weeklies, was ecstatic over the election of 1958. The percentage of Northern liberal Democrats in the 86th Congress was greater than in any postwar Congress. By all odds, this was supposed to be the most liberal Congress since the New Deal. Yet ADA disillusionment with the record of the 86th Congress was, if anything, greater than with that of the 81st.

Another relevant factor, and one constantly emphasized by ADA, is the programmatical schizophrenia of the Democratic party. The Northern Democrats, in ADA's estimation and from the data of this study as well as others, are the most liberal force in Congress. If the Southern Democrats were equally liberal, or even as close in their voting patterns to their Northern colleagues as they are to the Republicans, liberal fortunes in Congress would certainly improve. They are not, however, and ADA realizes that nothing is likely to change this situation in the near future.

All this suggests that factors other than greater or less liberal representation in Congress are operating to reduce liberal effectiveness in that body. These factors appear to be rooted in the structure of Congress, in the ideological nature of liberal interests, and in the nature of liberal demands made upon Congress.

All students of Congress have emphasized the importance and power of its standing committees. It is in committee that the real work of Congress is done, or —as the case may be—is not done. In 1885 Woodrow Wilson labelled the committees of Congress "little legislatures" and referred to American government as "government by the standing committees of Congress." "Legislation," said Wilson in another place, "is not conducted in the open. It is not threshed out in open debate upon the floors of our assemblies. It is, on the contrary, framed, digested and concluded in committee rooms."

Contemporary students of Congress have seen little reason to revise Wilson's estimate of the power of Congressional committees. The members of these committees occupy the most strategic point in Congress with relation to proposed legislation. To emphasize what this can mean for the success or failure of liberal legislation, the membership of each Senate and House standing committee in the 81st through the 86th Congress was tabulated. Members were classified as Republicans, Southern Democrats, and Northern Democrats. During these six Congresses, in the Senate, Republicans and Southern Democrats held a two-to-one or greater majority on 60 per cent of the standing committees. In the House they held a two-to-one or greater majority on 58 per cent of the committees. In the Senate, Northern Democrats held a simple majority on only 6 per cent of committees, and they held a simple majority on only 3 per cent of the House committees.

These proportions, of course, are in line with the weight of each of these three groups in the House and Senate as a whole. But there is evidence that the anonymity of committee operations permits conservative Southern Democrats and Republicans to stifle measures which they might be reluctant to oppose in an open vote.

If the power of Congressional committees is great, a large part of that power is in the hands of committee chairmen. Burns refers to the members of committees as "court-barons" and to the chairmen as "lords-proprietors." The Committee on Political Parties of the American Political Science Association concluded that, "In effect, the committee chairmen are able in large measure to dictate what proposals may be considered by Congress. The ordinary member proposes, but the chairman disposes."

Committee chairmen are selected, or emerge out of, the seniority system. Regardless of which party controls Congress, this system operates so as to place committee chairmanships in the hands of Senators and Representatives who are likely to be insulated from the prevailing political winds by virtue of safe constituencies. Bertram Gross has summed up what this means for liberal fortunes in Congress: "The significant effect of the seniority system is that it tends to concentrate political power in the hands of members from 'safe and solid' areas of the country, areas where there is very little real competition between the two major parties. This tends to insulate committee chairmanships from the real meanings and mandates of

national electoral conflicts. It tends to undermine the ability of party
leaders to carry out campaign pledges. Above all, it tends to bring
a greater number of conservatives than of liberals into committee chairmanships."

The effects of the seniority system when the Democratic party
controls Congress are evident in this table:

TABLE 6

RELATIVE WEIGHT OF SOUTHERN DEMOCRATS IN CONGRESS
AS A WHOLE AND IN COMMITTEE CHAIRMANSHIPS,
81st THROUGH 86th CONGRESSES

Congress	% of SD in Senate to % of SD committee chairmen	% of SD in House to % of SD committee chairmen
81st	23 - 40	24 - 47
82nd	23 - 53	24 - 47
84th	23 - 53	23 - 63
85th	23 - 53	23 - 58
86th	22 - 62	23 - 60
Avg.	23 - 52	23 - 55

Thus Southern Democrats, comprising less than one-fourth of the
membership of each House, held more than one-half of the standing
committee chairmanships when the Democrats controlled Congress.
While a liberal Northern Democrat may propose progressive measures, more often than not it is a conservative Southern Democrat who
has wide latitude to dispose of them as he sees fit. This has been a
major, if not precisely calculable, reason for liberal futility in Congress.

The ideological nature of liberal interest groups, as contrasted with
conservative groups, is another imprecise but evident factor tending
to frustrate liberal efforts in Congress. Whatever may be the case
with other liberal groups, this is certainly true of ADA, which has
no institutionalized or even homogeneous membership base. ADA's
membership is not tied to any specific economic or other tangible
interest. ADA has no "natural" constituency. Its members appear
to be primarily academic intellectuals, the more socially conscious labor
leaders and union members, municipal reformers, and other assorted
groups and individuals of liberal political and economic inclination.
They range from a union leader like Walter Reuther, who would like to
see the labor movement direct its efforts toward broader social goals
than the usual "bread and butter" union issues, through liberal politi-

cians like Hubert Humphrey, to academics like Reinhold Neibuhr and James MacGregor Burns. These people are attracted to ADA for various reasons, but primarily because they share a relatively cohesive and integrated liberal viewpoint on current political, economic, and social questions.

One result of this heterogeneity of membership and homogeneity of viewpoint is a very wide-ranging policy program. ADA takes a position on virtually every issue of national import, whether it be Taft-Hartley, TVA appropriations, social security, civil rights, recognition of Franco Spain, or federal aid to education. While to a less extent than ADA, other liberal groups also appear to encompass very broad objectives. In any session of Congress, the legislative goals of the AFL-CIO cover a much wider field than do those of the NAM.

This attempt to realize a wide range of firmly-held, ideologically-based policy goals prevents ADA from engaging in "logrolling," one of the most effective tactics available to interest groups in the Congressional arena. Logrolling, according to David Truman, "involves a group's giving support to a proposal that may bear no relation or only the most tenuous relation to its own objectives, in return receiving similar support from the group it has assisted."

Few issues arise on the national scene which bear no relation to ADA's objectives. It cannot trade its own efforts in behalf of federal FEPC legislation for NAACP assistance in behalf of high price supports for agricultural commodities, nor can it trade its own support for federal aid to education for assistance from the National Education Association in opposing the Bricker Amendment. While happy to gain possible benefit from ADA support for their own objectives, the NAACP and the NEA, because of their specialized interests, are not likely to agitate themselves unduly for high price supports or against the Bricker Amendment. Since they know that ADA is going to support their position on these issues anyway, they are under no compulsion to engage in any *quid pro quo*. And because of its consistently liberal stance on all issues, ADA cannot engage in bargaining with business or other conservative interest groups. Thus ADA's wide policy goals, based on its liberal ideology, prevent it from making effective use of logrolling tactics.

Another result of ADA's encompassing of numerous policy goals is a diffusion of effort which hampers its chances of success on any one issue. The more goals a group tries to achieve, the weaker it becomes in pursuit of any of them. When, in the same Congressional session, ADA exerts itself in an attempt to repeal Taft-Hartley, enact a national health insurance program, effect an increase in the federal minimum wage, pass an FEPC law, and shepherd through Congress a baker's dozen other legislative proposals, it cannot expect to emerge with a very high batting average. In summing up ADA's experience in trying to exert pressure on such a broad front, one can do no better than to paraphrase Churchill and say that never have so few tried to do so much for so many.

A final factor contributing to liberal futility in Congress is the nature of liberal policy goals. Congress, as noted above, is so structured as to place a great handicap in the way of positive legislative proposals. David Truman, who has spelled out in detail the specific Congressional practices leading to this situation, concludes that "the complicated procedures of a body like Congress and the strength of established relationships in society as a whole tend to give an advantage to the group that is on the defensive in the legislative struggle." In other words, the Congressional terrain, with its built-in obstacle courses, operates against groups which are "for" and in favor of groups which are "against" new legislation.

Within this categorization of interest groups as offensive or defensive, ADA is overwhelmingly an offensive group, while the NAM is primarily defensive. The ADA and NAM testimony before Congressional committees, which formed the basis for Table 5, was reclassified according to an offensive-defensive dichotomy, *i.e.*, according to whether each group, on a given issue, was attempting to pass new legislation or attempting to prevent the passage of legislation. The results are presented in Table 7. The figures show the percentage of successes in each category. Figures in brackets show number of cases in each category.

TABLE 7

RELATIONSHIP BETWEEN OFFENSIVE-DEFENSIVE POSITION
AND INTEREST GROUP SUCCESS

	ADA	*NAM*
Offensive position—	23% (69)	49% (37)
Defensive position—	67% (21)	75% (53)
Overall success—	32% (90)	67% (90)

Thus, while liberals are only half as potent offensively as conservatives, they do almost as well defensively. Their much greater failure in Congress may be due more to their offensive stance than to any intrinsic power disadvantage.

These factors—the structure and composition of Congress, the ideological nature of liberal interests, and the offensive nature of liberal demands—suggest that American liberals operate in the Congressional arena with the dice loaded against them.

[1] Issues in this measure were traced to their final disposition, which might range all the way from death in the committee stage to re-passage over a veto. ADA was assigned a "victory" or "defeat" on each issue, depending upon its final resolution. In cases where no legislation was passed, scoring was automatic. In cases where legislation was enacted, however, scoring was more difficult. In such instances, victory or defeat in the legislative struggle is seldom clear-cut. A group may get part of what it asks for, or succeed in watering down proposals it opposes, but still not get exactly what it called for in testimony. In such cases, scoring required a further step. ADA publications, primarily the *World*, were checked to see what ADA had to say about the legislation finally passed. If ADA said something to the effect that it was "totally inadequate," ADA was assessed a defeat on that issue. If it said something to the effect that the legislation was "better than nothing," it was credited with a victory. This introduces a qualitative factor into an otherwise quantitative measure, but it seems unavoidable. Groups know that legislation is a matter of compromise, and they do not expect to get everything they ask for on every issue. To assume that they do, and score accordingly, would be unrealistic. No attempt was made to weigh issues according to their importance to ADA. This is one of the rocks upon which any attempt at constructing an interest group "power index" would certainly founder. It is undoubtedly the weakest point in this less rigorous scoring procedure. The same procedure was followed with NAM, with doubtful issues being scored according to the evaluation of final legislation in NAM publications, primarily the *NAM News*.

Chapter X

THE UTILITY OF ENEMIES ON THE LEFT

While the failure of organized liberalism in Congress may have its own rationale, this failure also is intimately bound up with the general decline in status or respectability of liberalism in the postwar years. This decline, most marked during the years of the "McCarthy era," came about largely because conservative elements were somehow able to implant in the public mind doubts about the loyalty of liberalism in general and of some liberals in particular. In this battle for public opinion, right-wing tactics—some subtle and some not so subtle—were dictated by the overall strategy of attempting to associate and equate American liberalism first with socialism and then with communism. From 1949 through 1954 ADA was a prime conservative target in this propaganda battle. Probably more than to any other single factor, the precipitate decline in ADA influence after 1948 can be traced to its defeat on this issue.

In Part II we found that one major reason for the founding of ADA was the concern of several liberal groups and leading individuals that Communists might succeed in infiltrating and assuming direction of the liberal movement. We saw that the conservative press at that time considered ADA a welcome antidote to the fellow-traveling Progressive Citizens of America, and we traced the bitter ADA struggle against Henry Wallace and the Communist-dominated Progressive party.

One would have thought, after 1948, that ADA's credentials as a staunchly anti-Communist group were not in doubt. Few dreamed that in six years ADA and the things it stood for would be virtually synonymous—in the conservative press, in speeches of right-wing politicians, and to a large extent in the public mind—with socialism, communism, and un-Americanism in general. This virtual rewriting of the plain historical record in the case of ADA is one of the lesser-known but more disturbing ironies of the postwar period.

The first move toward historical revisionism came in 1949 with an attack on ADA on the floor of the Senate. On April 7th, during a debate on renewal of the European Recovery Program, Senator

132

Congressional Record

PROCEEDINGS AND DEBATES OF THE 85th CONGRESS, SECOND SESSION

Statement of Legislative Program of Americans for Democratic Action

❖ ❖

Extension of Remarks of

Hon. Joseph S. Clark

of Pennsylvania

in the

Senate of the United States

Monday, January 27, 1958

*Not printed
at Government
expense*

United States Government Printing Office, Washington : 1958

454618—64906

Title page of a leaflet widely circulated in 1958

The ADA: Its Impact on the New Frontier

Once Aloof From Kennedy, It Staffs His Administration

ADA Impatient With Congress

Irked by 'Apathy,' They Would 'Light Fire' Under Lawmakers

ADA Lists State as 1961 Target

Bay Area First, Los Angeles Will Follow Under Program

Views Far Apart on Aims of ADA

Called Leftists by GOP Unit, 'Imperialists' by Daily Worker

ADA Has Its Own Loyalty Oath

Group Excludes All Totalitarians in Drive for Expanding Democracy

What and Why Is ADA?

Headlines of Los Angeles Times articles in September 1961

William Jenner of Indiana arose to denounce an ADA booklet advertising the summer study tours to Britain which the group had organized. The particular statement which drew Jenner's ire was one declaring that "ADA has a deep and sympathetic interest in the program of Britain's Labor Government." Jenner complained that the booklet was being circulated among government employees. "Worse than that," said the Senator, as if describing a piece of pornographic literature, "it has been circulated to young boys, 15, 16, and 17 years old, here within the very shadows of the Senate chamber." Thus the initial tactic in the campaign to destroy ADA's reputation was to associate it with the British Labor government.

This campaign received a significant boost in late 1949 with the publication of John T. Flynn's *The Road Ahead,* a bitter little book predicting a dire future for America if it did not mend its ways and return to laissez faire capitalism. Flynn's thesis was that the United States was in danger of taking the road followed by Britain, where the socialists had assumed power in the election of 1945. Liberals, in alliance with the labor movement, were acting as the U.S. equivalent of the British Fabian Society and were plotting a socialist future for America. Labor would provide the numbers and money for this socialist takeover. ADA, which would furnish the political and economic brains, was already acting as "the spearhead and central planning and propaganda machine of the National Socialist Economic Planners in this country." The publication of Flynn's book was subsidized by the Committee for Constitutional Government, a right-wing propaganda group whose chairman, Edwin A. Rumely, was cited for contempt of Congress. Rumely testified before a Congressional investigating committee that 700,000 copies of *The Road Ahead* were distributed to schools, libraries, churches and other educational institutions across the country.

In October Westbrook Pegler had his say and carried the attack one step further. ADA "is not yet frankly a Communist force," said Pegler. "You could put it this way, however: the ADA advocates nothing which a Communist would oppose except the North Atlantic Pact and a strong American war machine." Just how an "almost Communist" force could be for the Atlantic Pact, currently the primary target of Soviet propaganda, Pegler did not bother to explain. ADA's national board considered bringing a libel suit against Pegler but decided in favor of a policy of "silence and contempt."

Silence and contempt were to prove most ineffective weapons, however, and were shortly abandoned. In the heat of a municipal election campaign in Philadelphia, Republican City Chairman William F. Meade, in several radio broadcasts, charged that ADA was "Communist infiltrated." The Philadelphia ADA chapter promptly served a $100,000 libel suit against Meade. Two chapter members also brought suits as individuals against the GOP leader.

These libel suits stopped—for a time at least—the attempt to smear ADA with a Red brush by progressing rapidly, through the guilt by association technique, from liberalism to socialism to communism, and right-wing extremists were forced to stop at socialism.

In November, 1949, the *ADA World* had noted that, while "welfare state" had been the scare slogan of previous campaigns, "socialism" was likely to be used in 1950. On February 6, 1950, the Republican National Committee and the GOP Senate and House conferences issued a joint statement declaring that the major domestic issue in the 1950 Congressional elections would be "liberty versus socialism." On the following day, Senator Homer Capehart of Indiana arose in the Senate and announced that he wished to "talk on the subject of socialism." Launching immediately into a blast at ADA, Capehart charged that "In their [ADA's] official organ, their official newspaper, they are advocating the election of a socialistic government in England. Birds of a feather flock together." Capehart added, "There is under way an international conspiracy to socialize America," and ADA was participating in this conspiracy. "Every night, Mr. President, when we go to bed, we are one day nearer to state socialism in the United States."

At the conclusion of his speech, Capehart asked permission to introduce into the record a collection of articles, evidently compiled by the GOP Senate Policy Committee staff, entitled *The PCA, the ADA, and Henry Wallace*. The Senator explained that this document showed that the ADA was an outgrowth of the NCPAC and the ICCASP, "which became PCA, then ADA."

Capehart's genealogy was, of course, directly contrary to the facts. The Progressive Citizens of America was formed out of the National Citizens Political Action Committee and the Independent Citizens Committee of the Arts, Sciences, and Professions, but ADA evolved not out of—but as a counter to—the PCA. Capehart did not read his document on the floor, but it was printed in the *Record*. On reading it, one can reach only one of two conclusions: either Capehart himself had not read it or he was incapable of understanding what he read.

Among the statements in Capehart's material was one paragraph which clearly showed the anti-Communist origins of ADA. Headed

"Rival Group of Non-Communist Liberals Form ADA," it read: "Probably the most conclusive evidence of the Communist tinge within the PCA is the fact that a rival set of liberals felt it imperative within a week's time of the formation of the PCA, to form a separate organization as a non-Communist haven for the more respectable liberals who could find no stomach for the Red-tainted PCA."

In what turned out to be a gross understatement, the *ADA World* observed that "It seems probable that ADA will be somewhat of a whipping boy in the conservative attack." The whipping began immediately, and with a much more potent lash than ADA anticipated. In its February, 1950, issue, the *Reader's Digest* printed a condensed version of *The Road Ahead*. ADA, with no means of publicity remotely comparable to the *Digest's* circulation of nine million, tried to get editor DeWitt Wallace to print ADA's reply. National chairman Francis Biddle complained that "Flynn and the *Reader's Digest* don't mention the fact that ADA excludes Communists" and that it "was organized to rid the liberal movement of Communists and has been highly successful in doing so." Senator Hubert Humphrey engaged in a lengthly correspondence with editor Wallace, in which Humphrey contended that the *Digest's* condensation of Flynn's book contained serious misrepresentations about ADA. After Wallace asked for and got a statement of what Humphrey considered to be misrepresentations, Wallace finally refused to publish ADA's rebuttal. "Any article," he explained, "which would have to deal so largely with interpretations and implications could hardly have that simple, down-to-the-ground reader interest which a mass-circulation magazine must continually strive for."

Evidence that these mass-circulation attacks were having an effect cropped up all over the country. The *ADA World* began publishing a column called "What They're Saying," which soon became a recitation of the more extreme slurs on ADA. The pastor of the First Presbyterian Church in Nashville, Tennessee, for instance, informed his congregation that the Americans for Democratic Action were "about as Democratic as Stalin." Fulton Lewis, Jr., in a broadcast attacking ADA's support for the Brannan Plan, referred to the "OPA long-haired, left-wing, star-gazing, mouth-hanging-open, fair-haired boys, who, when they were bounced out of the government, formed the Americans for Democratic Action."

In Los Angeles a "Wage Earners Committee of the U.S.A." popped up to oppose Helen Douglas, James Roosevelt, and other liberals in the Democratic primary campaigns. These "wage earners" somehow found enough money to buy full-page advertisements linking liberal candidates to ADA and saying: "Many of the leaders of this Socialist front organization imitate Stalin and Hitler even to the extent of riding around in $35,000 bullet-proof cars and spending thousands of dollars daily of their members money for personal bodyguards."

No one in ADA, which usually had difficulty paying its printing bills, was able to identify such well-heeled adherents.

In a rhythm which was to become routine in future years, the number and intensity of right-wing attacks on ADA increased as election day approached. The violence of the distortions, and the extent to which they had penetrated down to the grass roots, was evident from a letter written by a resident of Elmira, New York, to his newspaper stating that ADA had been cited as a Communist front organization by the Department of Justice. This particular statement, incidentally, was made to the author on a number of occasions—by students and faculty members at two different universities—during the course of research and writing for this book. Attempts to refute it were met with skepticism—sometimes accompanied by embarrassed glances and an immediate change of subject—and on one occasion necessitated a joint check of the "subversive list," where no mention of ADA could be found.

Twelve days prior to the election, Republican Congressional Campaign Committee Chairman Leonard Hall complained to the press that the "Democratic-CIO-ADA" had "five times as much money as the Republicans." ADA's Jim Loeb retorted: "This is the unkindest cut of all. Never before have American liberals been accused of ability to meet a payroll . . . Obviously, Hall has got us mixed up with the American Dental Association."

Thrown on the defensive and with inadequate means of retaliation, ADA could not keep up with the attacks upon it. Hubert Humphrey and other ADA members in Congress attempted to take up the slack. Calling the Senate's attention to ADA's record of opposition to communism, Humphrey emphasized: "In policy, platform, and performance ADA has opposed the Communists on all the important issues of our time: aid to Greece and Turkey, the Marshall Plan, Henry Wallace and the Progressive party, Point Four, the military aid program, atomic energy controls, and Korea." But the readership of the *Congressional Record* was considerably less than that of the *Reader's Digest*, and ADA was losing the propaganda battle by default.

In a pre-election column in the *New York Times*, James Reston called attention to this situation, pointing out that the "intellectual left" had remained silent in the campaign because it was "fearful of the Red tarnish." The furor over Communist oath provisions for teachers, the damaging revelations of the Hiss trial, McCarthy's wild charges of Communist infiltration of the State Department, and the Korean War had silenced the left.

"The experience of Americans for Democratic Action in this campaign," Reston reported, "illustrates the caution on the left. The support of this organization of young intellectuals was welcomed by many candidates in the 1948 election . . . Though this organization was formed to dramatize the non-Communist left, it has been widely attacked since 1948 as a left-wing organization, with the result that in this election, candidates are showing a distinct lack of enthusiasm for its support . . . "

In 1946, there had been at least some justification for right-wing charges of communism on the liberal left. In 1948, ADA had been the primary factor in erasing such Communist influence. With the PCA and the Progressive party eliminated, however, ADA itself became the only force of any consequence on the left. While far more moderate than the PCA, and unimpeachably anti-Communist to any objective observer, it found itself in a very exposed position. In 1950, ADA began to realize the utility of having enemies on the left to serve as lightning rods for conservative propaganda.

The 1952 Election. Sporadic attacks on ADA continued to appear in 1951. Westbrook Pegler returned to the fray in November with a column assailing David Williams, ADA director of Research and Education. Williams, a former Rhodes Scholar, had returned to England for a visit and while there had written an article called "The Intelligent Socialist's Guide to America." Pegler offered this as evidence that Williams was a socialist. Williams retorted that he was merely "interpreting America to socialists, of whom there were a great many in England. The government was socialist, as a matter of fact."

It was in 1952 that ADA first became a significant secondary, if not a major, issue in a nationwide campaign. From the beginning in 1949, the conservative attacks had been motivated by a desire to embarrass the Democratic party. For ADA, while never formally aligning itself with the Democratic party as such, had continued to campaign for liberal Democrats and support Democratic policies. In some states, particularly in Massachusetts, ADA had been instrumental in uniting the political arms of the AFL and CIO behind

Democratic candidates. This support was of some importance in 1948 and 1950 and had been welcomed by the Democrats.

By 1952, in part because of the sustained fire it had been subjected to, ADA was a far less potent political force. A situation had developed in which the ADA, while it had little of tangible value to offer the Democrats, was still closely identified with that party. In political terms, ADA in effect occupied a position in relation to the Democratic party similar to that which had been filled in 1946 by the ICCASP. It was a small, vociferous, and suspect group sitting out in the open on the party's left flank. Fanatical right-wing publicists had succeeded in identifying the ADA with socialism, if not communism. More respectable Republicans now took over the job of identifying it with the Democratic party and thus equating the Democrats with socialism.

This process was facilitated when Adlai Stevenson, after his nomination in 1952, appointed Wilson Wyatt and Arthur M. Schlesinger, Jr., to his staff as campaign manager and speechwriter, respectively. Wyatt and Schlesinger, both ADA founders, had been prominent leaders of the organization since 1949.

Republican National Chairman Guy Gabrielson promptly shot straight from his hips: "The appointment of Wilson Wyatt by the Democratic nominee for President as his campaign manager clearly demonstrates that the ultra-left-wingers of the country, not the Democratic party, will have complete charge of his campaign. It is significant that Mr. Wyatt was formerly the head of Americans for Democratic Action, an organization dedicated to the promotion of Socialistic schemes in America."

Linking of Stevenson to ADA through Wyatt and Schlesinger contained a double irony. In the first place, there had been some opposition—and a considerable lack of enthusiasm—within ADA to Stevenson's nomination. Several top leaders had backed Harriman or Kefauver, and the 1952 ADA annual meeting had voted not to make a preconvention endorsement of any candidate. Also, after the Wyatt and Schlesinger appointments, *ADA World* revealed: "ADA must, with some chagrin, confess to have had nothing to do with the selection of either Mr. Wyatt or Dr. Schlesinger by Governor Stevenson."

There appeared to be no valid grounds for the contention that Wyatt and Schlesinger had been appointed because they were members of the ADA. Wyatt had been a high-level political figure for years and was active in Kentucky politics. Schlesinger was a noted Harvard historian with a facility for pungent phrase-making. Thus both men possessed individual talents of great value to any candidate, irrespective of their organizational ties. Republican campaigners were not to be deterred by such considerations, however.

The fact that Stevenson and Wyatt immediately reacted defensively, while perhaps politically necessary, provides a significant indication of the deterioration in ADA's public image in the four years since 1948. Two days after Gabrielson's statement, Stevenson termed as "nonsense" the charge that Wyatt's appointment meant he had been taken over by the Democratic left wing, adding that he "had known very little about Mr. Wyatt's connection with the Americans for Democratic Action."

Two days later Wyatt, when asked by reporters to explain the positions he had taken in ADA, replied that he had usually been "identified with the conservative wing of that organization and had not been among those ADA members who had sought to 'ditch' President Truman in 1948." This statement aroused the ire of many ADA members. "What," demanded one member, "is Wyatt doing apologizing for being a member of ADA? What is a 'conservative ADA member' anyway? Mr. Wyatt should have said he is a liberal and that he is proud of it."

The issue plagued Stevenson all through the 1952 campaign. Three weeks prior to election day, Senator Jenner brought it to a delicate conclusion: "Stevenson's campaign manager is Wilson Wyatt, former chairman of the ruthless and reckless gang of Marxist lobbyists who call themselves 'ADA.' Stevenson's speeches are largely written by Professor Arthur Schlesinger, Jr., one of the top ADA commissars . . ."

It was inevitable that Senator Joseph McCarthy of Wisconsin would join the pack. He did so in late October on a nationwide radio and television broadcast, charging ADA with a number of heinous crimes and attempting to tie it firmly to Stevenson's coattails. Among other things, McCarthy "charged" ADA with favoring repeal of the Smith Act, opposing government security procedures, "condemning the FBI for exposing traitors," opposing the House Committee on Un-American Activities, and favoring the recognition of Red China. Stevenson, McCarthy concluded, had given "sympathy and aid to the Communist cause" and was "unfit to be President" because of his association with a group like ADA. McCarthy noted that Stevenson had been listed by the *ADA World* as a "charter member" of ADA and showed his audience what he described as a "photostat" of a letter from Stevenson to Senator Pat McCarran denying membership in ADA.

McCarthy's attack on ADA is a perfect illustration of the famous "method" which made his career, and is worth a brief digression. In the first place, his speech contained so many detailed "charges" that several days were consumed before the opposition could refute it. Five days later, for instance, the Democratic National Committee issued a five thousand word analysis of McCarthy's speech showing that he had "used at least eighteen false statements, distortions, or quotations out of context . . . " By then, of course, McCarthy had made other speeches and held several press conferences, which gave his opponents another month's work to do. And the refutation, while it made headlines, could not reach the millions who had seen and heard McCarthy.

Perhaps more to the point, every one of McCarthy's "charges" had just enough basis in historical fact to provide a platform for his takeoff. Taking them one by one, the Senator had first accused ADA of wanting to repeal the Smith Act—period. ADA pointed out that it had "opposed certain provisions of the Smith Act that would prosecute people for what they think rather than for what they do." It is worthy of note in passing that McCarthy's charge appeared on page one of the *Times,* while ADA's rebuttal was buried on page twenty-six.

The Senator also accused ADA of opposing government security regulations. This was a reference to ADA's criticism of certain aspects of the loyalty-security program initiated by President Truman in 1947. The "Civil Liberties" section of the 1951 ADA platform had expressed its policy on this issue:

"We recognize the right of the government to require loyalty to free institutions as a qualification of public employment. However, on the basis of the experience of past years, we are convinced that the crude and indiscriminate methods by which wholesale loyalty investigations of Americans have been conducted have done the country more harm than good. We continue to recognize the necessity for guarding truly vulnerable agencies from the activities of Communists and Fascists whose divided loyalties render them untrustworthy in security-sensitive positions.

"Accordingly we propose the following:

" (1) The loyalty check provided by presidential order should be eliminated in those agencies and positions which do not clearly affect national security . . .

" (2) Loyalty tests for security agencies or security-sensitive positions must guarantee every individual the full right and opportunity to defend himself. No organization or individual should be adjudged disloyal without a fair hearing, based on specific written charges and disclosed evidence, confrontation of accusers, a full opportunity to be represented by counsel and to examine and cross-examine witnesses . . . "

In 1959, after a firm push from the Supreme Court, the Eisenhower Administration did almost exactly what ADA had advocated eight years earlier.

Another of McCarthy's charges was that ADA had "condemned the FBI for exposing treason," with reference being made to specific successful FBI efforts in exposing espionage. This was McCarthy's way of saying that ADA opposed the use of evidence obtained by wiretapping in these cases. ADA's position on this issue had been spelled out in its 1950 platform: "We are opposed to current proposals that Congress legalize wiretapping and revise the espionage laws to cover unintentional acts. We regard wiretapping as a dangerous invasion of personal liberty and we do not believe that any disclosures of espionage activity warrant such drastic and dangerous measures."

McCarthy's charge that ADA was opposed to the House Un-American Activities Committee was fully warranted. The 1950 ADA convention had unequivocally stated: "While we recognize the right of Congress to conduct investigations, the House Committee on Un-American Activities has proved itself a threat to freedom of political opinion. We therefore call for its abolition."

Today reasonable men can oppose the House Un-American Activities Committee and not be accused of harboring dark designs on the Republic. But in 1952 in McCarthy's hands this opposition was "proof" of ADA's "sympathy and aid to communism." The great difference in atmosphere today from yesterday and the repressive effect of the earlier climate on ADA can be illustrated by its position on this issue. ADA first called for the abolition of the Un-American Activities Committee in 1950, before the "McCarthy era" had begun. This demand was not repeated in 1951 and did not reappear in an ADA platform until 1959, and then in a much more mildly-worded resolution.

Because of the bitterness of the Korean War issue in 1952, McCarthy's charge that ADA favored recognition of Red China was probably the most damaging made against it. Moreover, if certain important qualifications were ignored, and given the atmosphere of the time, it could be made to stick. Unlike many liberal groups of the immediate postwar years, ADA had not been taken in by the "agrarian reformer" image of the Chinese Communists which bemused many observers, including some Old China Hands. "This was one of those issues which separated the sheep from the goats," one ADA leader notes today. In 1950, however, the ADA convention had adopted a platform plank on China which read: "We believe that the principal objective of American policy in China must be the maintenance of communication and traditional friendly contact with the Chinese people. We believe that sooner or later we will be compelled to establish diplomatic relations with the Mao Tse-tung regime as the effective government of China, however much we detest its devotion to totalitarianism. Our continuing policy must be to counter any Kremlin policy of isolating China from the non-Commupnist world . . ."

This statement, innocent enough when it was made, had much to commend it as a possible alternative to U.S. policy toward China. The trouble was that it was made in April, 1950. Three months later North Korean troops crossed the thirty-eighth parallel, and five months after that Red China entered the Korean War. In McCarthy's 1952 speech, therefore, it became closely akin to treason.

After June, 1950, ADA, of course, revised its China policy. Prior to China's entrance into the war, it had urged that negotiations for the recognition of Red China be considered if the Communist regime would give positive assurances that they would not enter the Korean conflict and if it would also agree to a nonmilitary solution to the problem of Formosa. Today a strong case can be made that such a move would have been a very good bargain for the U.S. if it could have been effected in 1950. But in 1952 it served only as evidence that ADA was a suspect group.

Finally, there is McCarthy's linking of Stevenson with ADA. It is not clear even today whether or not Stevenson was ever an ADA member. As McCarthy claimed, the *ADA World,* in its February, 1952, issue had described Stevenson as a "charter member". Whether or not Stevenson did write Senator McCarran denying such membership has apparently never been verified beyond McCarthy's assertion. Stevenson himself merely denied that he was "a captive of a girl named Ada."

Whether or not Stevenson was an ADA member is hardly significant. What is significant is that the question could become significant in the 1952 campaign. Our involvement with it here illustrates the dilemma ADA faced then and the absurdly cumulative effect of the right-wing campaign against it. Taking off from an ADA expression of sympathy with the British Labor government, this campaign had proceeded mathematically to the conclusion that ADA=Communism, sometimes backtracked to an ADA=socialism equation, then went on to ADA=the Democratic party, and advanced finally and with great fanfare to ADA=socialism/communism/Marxism=Stevenson. By any standards of logic or reason, this exercise in political algebra was absurd. In 1952, however, as was intended, it received a passing mark at the polls.

It would be equally absurd, of course, to attribute Stevenson's defeat to his tenuous connection with ADA, which was only a minor refrain in the symphony of "Korea, Communism, and Corruption." But the "communist ADA" was an issue in several Congressional and local campaigns in 1952, and Democratic candidates suffered—or thought they suffered—from their association with it. In a few cities such as Chicago and Philadelphia ADA could claim with some justification that its own organizational strength more than offset any negative effects its support for a candidate might entail. But such strongholds were few and far between.

Out in the state of Washington, for instance, Democrat Hugh Mitchell was defeated in a gubernatorial race in which his ADA membership was made a prime issue.

ADA was the victim of a particularly bad stroke of luck—or timing—in Washington. In 1949 an investigating committee of the state legislature had accused ten University of Washington professors of being present or past members of the Communist party, and three years later the resulting furor was still a subject of political debate. During the campaign Mitchell's opponent made good use of an ADA booklet which, among other things, upheld the right of nonconformist organizations, including Communist groups, to organize on the campuses of colleges and universities. Mitchell's campaign manager, himself a former ADA staff member, said: "If I had to point to one single cause for losing the election this statement in the ADA booklet would be it."

ADA's reputation was beginning to run to areas where its organization did not.

1953: The Man Who Came to Dinner. After the 1952 election the campaign of the radical right continued unabated. In April of the following year, ADA again crossed verbal swords with McCarthy when Chairman Francis Biddle called upon Attorney-General Herbert Brownell to "institute a thorough investigation into the personal affairs" of the Senator. The basis for such an investigation lay in the report issued by a Senate Privileges and Election Sub-committee which had looked into charges made by Senator William Benton against McCarthy. Biddle contended that the report raised serious questions as to whether McCarthy had violated laws dealing with embezzlement, mail fraud, kickbacks, and income taxes. McCarthy's reaction is worthy of extended quotation:

"It should be recalled that the ADA, of which Biddle is national chairman, has viciously attacked the FBI, has attacked the Smith Act, has urged the recognition of Communist China, and in many other respects had followed the Communist party line.

"Normally, I would call Biddle's case to the attention of the United States Attorney or the Attorney-General for criminal libel. However, he and his crowd of Communist defenders may even be doing me a favor by this libelous attack.

"Besides, I am much too busy with work of much greater importance than to take time out to waste it on a man who has been so thoroughly discredited and who is as well known for what he is as Biddle."

ADA, in a deliberate attempt to draw McCarthy into a libel suit, reprinted the subcommittee's report and sold thousands of copies as did many other individuals and groups during the early 1950's. Since Senator Jenner effectively blocked official distribution of the report, it was ADA's reprint that Senator Flanders used to start censure proceedings against McCarthy.

ADA for a time suffered from a "McCarthy complex." By September, 1953, so much of the organization's effort had been diverted to the McCarthy front that the executive committee concluded that "activities in regard to McCarthy should not dominate ADA's interest."

Joseph Rauh, however, became involved in a curious episode which somewhat tarnished ADA's anti-McCarthy image. In 1954 a certain Paul Hughes approached Clayton Fritchey, editor of the *Democratic Digest,* and Rauh with a story that he was an undercover member of McCarthy's staff, had become disillusioned with McCarthy, and had inside information on certain shady or illegal activities of McCarthy and his committee. For nine months Hughes fed Rauh, Fritchey, and a *Washington Post* editor "information" for which he received $8,500 from Rauh and $2,300 from Fritchey and others for expense money before it was discovered that Hughes was an imposter. (William Buckley, editor of the *National Review,* tells the story in detail—and with great glee—in his book, *Up From Liberalism.*) Today Rauh admits simply that he was "taken," says he knew he was taking a chance, but insists that he was risking only his own reputation and money. Because of Rauh's close association, however, both he and ADA felt some of the repercussions.

In June, 1953, Dr. J. B. Mathews, a former clergyman who had participated in several Communist front groups in the 1930's and was now a favorite witness for Congressional investigating committees, assailed ADA in the pages of the *American Mercury*. Taking Reinhold Niebuhr to task for criticizing Chiang Kai-shek's regime, Mathews charged that this view of Chiang "is not only the official Kremlin falsification of history; it is also the mendacious interpretation in which Socialists and Americans for Democratic Action (ADA'ers) like Niebuhr join the gangsters in Moscow in their seduction of history for the purpose of hiding from posterity the New Deal's shameful betrayal of hundreds of millions of human beings."

In August ADA discovered that one of its members had been denied security clearance for work being done under a Defense Department contract "because of his membership in ADA and the American Civil Liberties Union." Secretary of Defense Charles Wilson replied to ADA's inquiry that the Department used only the Attorney-General's list as a basis for denying security clearance, and that ADA was not on that list. Another query as to whether membership in ADA or ACLU was considered cause for a full background check received no answer.

Through the 1950 and 1952 campaigns, the right-wing attacks on ADA had been largely ignored by the Democratic party. Prominent Democrats had defended themselves against the charges of "leftism," but only a few—primarily Hubert Humphrey—had attempted to defend ADA. Most said nothing, hoping the issue would die down. As the 1954 Congressional campaign approached, however, it became clear that this issue would not go away. Democrats had reason to be chary of riding in the same boat with ADA, and some of them began to bail out.

In December, Foster Furcolo, Massachusetts State Treasurer who was slated to be the Democratic Senate nominee, was invited to address a dinner meeting at the state ADA convention. Furcolo had been close to ADA for years and had welcomed its support in three previous campaigns. Leaders of the state group were on friendly terms with Furcolo and expected to back him again in 1954.

Realizing, however, that his identification with ADA might no longer be such an asset, Mrs. Arthur Rotch, vice chairman of the state ADA, approached Furcolo several days before the convention and asked if he would prefer to cancel his engagement. Assured that the State Treasurer wished to speak to the ADA, convention preparations proceeded as planned.

On December 12, 1953, Furcolo was guest of honor at the convention's opening dinner session. Rising from his place at the head table, he moved to the rostrum and proceeded to tell his hosts that they should abolish ADA: "ADA has never been able to attract ... the broad base that is vital to any political movement . . . Leadership that loses contact with its followers . . . is a pitiful and tragic waste. You are rendering a disservice to the people of America . . . You are hurting programs that are good for America. You are weakening the Democatic party, which is the only party that will carry out these programs. Rightly or wrongly, fairly or unfairly, the fact is that the public is apt to immediately oppose whatever you support . . . I do not think you should discuss anything at this convention except one question: Should ADA continue or not."

Most observers concluded that Furcolo's action had been tailored to the peculiar political conditions prevailing in Massachusetts, which was nominally Democratic but an area where McCarthy had made great inroads. An intensive study of one Boston ward showed that voters' attitudes were ambivalent. There was wide support for the Democratic party and its program but fear of international communism, and a belief that McCarthy was doing an excellent job in fighting it. Furcolo himself noted that McCarthy had "alerted the nation" to the danger of communism and said he did not wish to take a position on McCarthy without "close personal observation" of the man in action.

The "Furcolo affair" agitated Massachusetts politics for years. Needless to say, ADA did not support him again. Jim Loeb summed up the ADA attitude when he remarked, "It has been said that the trouble in Washington is not the heat, but the timidity. Why add to it?"

But the timidity soon spread to higher Democratic circles. Speaking on a television panel in Chicago, Democratic National Chairman Stephen Mitchell felt that the party "could get along without" ADA's endorsement. "ADA," said Mitchell, "has been developed very much in the press and by Republican speakers—out of proportion to what little I know of the organization's size and importance."

Long before the 1954 campaign started, the Democratic Party was attempting to shake the ADA albatross off its neck.

"Demon ADA". In previous years the conservative attack on ADA had been largely the property of the far out right wing, symbolized by Flynn, Jenner, Mathews, and McCarthy. These generals of the ultra-

right did not cease operations in 1954. Flynn, for instance, elaborated on his earlier allegations by dubbing ADA the "Socialist politburo" in America: "ADA's purpose is not merely political. It is revolutionary . . . Here is a group doing infinitely more to lay the foundations for a Communist America than the Communist leaders can do."

In 1954 a new general took over. In what was probably the roughest Congressional campaign in American political history, command of the offensive against ADA was assumed by the Vice-President of the United States, Richard Nixon.

Mr. Nixon began quietly enough, at first staying within the wide bounds of what a frontier tradition might define as good, clean political fun. On September 16th in a speech at Wichita, Kansas, ADA was no more than a "left-wing mouthpiece" for "Trumanism," calling for "deficit financing and inflation." In Albany, New York, on September 29th, ADA was the "left-wing element" which would "call the signals" if a Democratic Congress were elected.

By October 1st at Norwalk, Connecticut, the pace had stepped up a bit. Here Nixon regretted that, because of statements by Democratic leaders, "the issue of how to handle Communists in government will be an issue in this campaign." This was "unfortunate," said Nixon. But these statements—made, incidentally, by Stephen Mitchell and Senator Olin Johnston of South Carolina—indicated that "the Americans for Democratic Action wing of the Democratic party still underestimates the danger of communism." The ADA record on the internal Communist menace, said Nixon, "is not one which inspires confidence."

ADA, deciding to join in the spirit of the game, attempted to identify Nixon with itself. ADA's national board passed a resolution commending Nixon for his recent statement in Delaware against the perpetuation of segregation in public schools: "The Vice President in that speech expressed a position that has been a basic principle of the ADA for years. The national board of ADA hopes and believes that as Mr. Nixon goes around the country and learns the problems facing the American people he will become converted to the ADA point of view on many issues."

But on October 13th in California Nixon continued his assault. The Vice-President claimed that when the Republican Administration took over in 1952 it had "found in the files a blueprint for socializing America," and many ADA members had contributed to this blueprint.

As election day approached, Nixon's attack gained momentum. In a speech prepared for delivery in Wyoming, but cancelled because of bad weather, Nixon listed four major points on which he claimed that "Communist party members" and "the left-wing clique of Americans for Democratic Action" had joined forces.

"It is time to talk bluntly and frankly about the most sinister development of this campaign to date . . . The Communist party has agreed enthusiastically with Americans for Democratic Action in the latter's position on four major points. These are:

"1. Calling for recognition of Communist China just before the Korean War.

"2. Attacking the Eisenhower security program.

"3. Calling for the abolition of the committee which brought out the evidence which convicted Alger Hiss.

"4. Constant sniping at J. Edgar Hoover and the Federal Bureau of Investigation."

The issues contained in these points were not, of course, "new developments." All were at least three to four years old. All were precisely the same points Senator McCarthy had made in 1952.

Nixon brought his orchestration of slurs on ADA to a climax from Seattle in a direct telegram to Stevenson, in which he referred to "Americans for Democratic Action, the cell of left-wingers which has spawned your speechwriters." Thus, in speech after speech in city after city, and with the Vice-Presidency as his sounding board, Nixon had made of ADA "the whipping boy of the 1954 campaign."

Eric Sevareid, reviewing the campaign as it came to a close, devoted an entire broadcast to ADA's record and Nixon's distortion of it: "No political campaign seems to be complete without its conspiracies, myths, and invisible demons. This campaign too is laboring hard to give birth to a demon bearing the mystic, cabalistic title 'ADA'."

"To Mr. Nixon," Sevareid explained, "ADA is a 'wing' of the Democratic party whose anti-Communism is suspect." He added: "It is questionable whether ADA could be called a 'wing' of the Democratic party; one feather in a wing might be more accurate . . . ADA is not only anti-Communist, but so strongly anti-Communist that a new member not only has to be vouched for but is required to sign what amounts to a loyalty oath."

Reviewing ADA's record against the PCA and Henry Wallace, Sevareid pointed out: "The Communists were well aware of the threat such a new group meant to their tactics of confusion and infiltration. I covered one of the original ADA organization meetings, and I remember Communist hecklers trying to stop it before it could start . . . The political role and policies of the ADA are no doubt open to criticism on many grounds, but not on the grounds of loyalty."

* * *

ADA deserved a better press than the one it received in the early 1950's. Fortunately, some of the distorted accounts of that period are being rewritten.

Peter Viereck, customarily an acid-penned critic of liberalism, is one who has attempted to set the record straight on the Communist issue. Writing of the "fight for the souls of liberal intellectuals" which raged after 1945, Viereck recently credited ADA for exposing Communist control of the Progressive party: "By that act of 'premature' anti-communism, long before more headlined demagogues took any interest in the Soviet threat, ADA has earned a place of honor among defenders of liberty . . . That special honor of these effectively anti-Communist liberals can never be tarnished, even if ADA has subsequently declined into a increasingly deracinated organization."

In an earlier chapter we saw what happened to ADA's organizational apparatus during the decade of the 1950's. Despite the stiff-upper-lip front of its leaders, plus desperate membership and financial drives directed at those who might be expected to be sympathetic to any group attacked by McCarthy and Nixon, ADA after 1954 was not what it had been before 1950. While its objectives remained essentially unchanged, its resources were badly depleted. It needed members to function as a political action organization—"the heart and soul of ADA are in its chapters," said one national chairman—and members became increasingly hard to find and keep. Money was required to operate as a political education group, and for ADA money was scarce during this most prosperous decade. Perhaps most important of all for an organization which depended so heavily upon publicity, a good public image was required, and between 1950 and 1954 ADA's public image underwent a Jekyll and Hyde transformation.

Not all of ADA's difficulties can be ascribed to McCarthyism or Nixonism, of course; it has proved adept at making plenty of trouble for itself without assistance. But it is obvious that the attacks the group sustained in the early 1950's caused great damage. Some of the public evidence of that damage has been reviewed. The letters in ADA's files contain voluminous private evidence which reflects much more than the effect of McCarthyism on one particular liberal organization.

One uninhibited letter, postmarked March 4, 1954, from a small town in Illinois and addressed to "James RED Doyle, Communist Head of the ADA," can be quoted only in part: "You are 100 per cent a dirty Communist, just like all ADAers . . . God bless Joe McCarthy . . . Did you know that the true Americans are wising up to you traitors? I hope they put a rope around your Red neck, you traitor."

Another letter, dated August 4, 1953, from a young man in a California city, requires no comment:

"I am joining your organization over the objections of my parents. Despite the fact that they are militant liberals they did not want me to become an ADAer because that action might return to plague me as an older person. My mother's father was a Socialist and an all-out Debs man; my father is the chairman of the local county Democratic Central Committee. So you can imagine my surprise and consternation when they opposed my joining an organization that includes Mrs. Roosevelt, Michael Straight, and Paul Douglas, among others.

"I suppose my parents merely reflect the fear and hysteria that is so widespread today. But I want to do my part to help liberalism in my country, and I feel that by joining the ADA I would have taken the first step."

In his 1952 speech attacking Stevenson, Senator McCarthy had also taken a sideswipe at Arthur M. Schlesinger, Jr., accusing the latter of saying that Communists "should be allowed to teach your children" and of "being against God." Schlesinger fired right back, noting that he was "tired of these Joe-come-latelys" in the fight against communism: "At the time some of us were alerting the American people to the dangers of communism, McCarthy was accepting Communist support in his fight against Bob LaFollette."

But the artillery was not evenly matched. From 1952 onward, ADA members could reflect ruefully that they had been impaled on two of the three points in Mr. Dooley's famous trinity of American politics. They had been convicted of being against God and country. Luckily, ADA had never staked out a position on motherhood.

Chapter XI

ADA IN THE IKE AGE

"The defeat of Adlai Stevenson," announced the ADA national board in January, 1953, "provides no evidence of a repudiation of liberalism." "The condition of U.S. liberalism is sound and vigorous," insisted national director Ed Hollander. "ADA's strength, in numbers and influence, is greater than ever," claimed the board as it issued a call for the organization's sixth annual convention. It wasn't so —and ADA knew it.

In tracing the record of liberal frustration in Congress and the rise of the right-wing assault to its high point in 1954, we have slighted one event of major significance for ADA and the liberal movement. Perhaps ADA, which had once seen Dwight Eisenhower as the savior of American liberalism, had more reason than most liberal groups to whistle in the dark. Despite the hopeful assurances of its leaders, ADA was soon to realize that the election of 1952, far more so than the election of 1946, presented liberals with a fundamental change in the facts of political life.

Since the First Hundred Days of the New Deal, if not since the time of Woodrow Wilson's New Freedom, American liberals had looked to the executive branch to supply the political power for the great changes which slowly transformed the nation from a laissez faire to a welfare state. Except for a brief period in the late Twenties, when rising discontent and somnolent White House leadership made the Congress seem a hot-bed of progressivism by comparison, liberals had carried on a long love affair with the Presidency. Unable to fuze the many but divergent liberal impulses of labor, agriculture, and urban groups into a mass, united political base, and frustrated by the chaotic legislative obstacle course that was Congress, they had fallen back upon the Strong President to "short-cut the necessity for electoral organization."

Liberals had, of course, engaged in intermittent marital strife with particular Presidents, even Roosevelt. And ADA, as we have seen, brought suit for divorce against Truman on the grounds that he was unwilling or unable to act as a Strong President should. Despite the temporary coolness resulting from its efforts to block his renomination, ADA's relations with Truman between 1949 and 1952 were cordial if not close. Truman's occasional blasts at "hot-house" or "fake" liberals, generally interpreted as being aimed in the direction of ADA, did not prevent him from addressing its gatherings, and, more important, proposing policies which it could consider liberal. If these policies did not go far enough, if they too often ran out of gas between the White House and Capitol Hill or were lost in the confused maze of the bureaucracy, at least they went in the direction liberals wanted to move. In retrospect it is clear that the Presidency under Truman, if not the dynamic ally which liberals wanted and needed, was at least a positive liberal force. By the late 1950's ADA leaders were looking back with some nostalgia—and perhaps some forgetfulness of their own words and actions—to the Truman years.

There is not space here to review in detail ADA's intense and frequently-voiced frustration as it watched the great engine of the Presidency idle through what it now calls the "dismal Eisenhower years," nor much point in doing so. By May, 1953, ADA was admitting that its early hope that Eisenhower would translate that vague but reassuring term "Modern Republicanism" into at least a program of "responsible conservatism" was vain. A year later it found the President's program "neither positive nor dynamic and wholly inadequate to the issues this country faces." National chairman Joe Rauh, never a man to mince words, charged in 1955 that "Eisenhower has produced the saddest excuse for a legislative program since President McKinley. We have drift, confusion, bluff, blunder and a sunburnt Coolidge in the White House." ADA saw little reason to change its mind in subsequent years. This was a period when "complacency came in on little fat-cat feet and stayed to blanket the country," when "ADA could do little more than fight a holding action in its struggle for progress."

For liberals the central political fact of the Ike Age was the loss of access to and influence within the executive branch, which came largely under the direction of their old enemy, the businessman. The Presidency, no longer the spawning ground and impetus for liberal programs, became for six years the weakest link in the federal system and, after 1958, a surprisingly effective bulwark against the belated liberalism of a Democratic Congress. For ADA this loss meant falling back on other resources—Congress, the national Democratic party, the liberal-labor alliance, and its own organizational reserves— and these were to prove inadequate to produce the results which liberals demanded.

The Congress, as we saw in Chapter IX, was a slender reed for liberals to lean upon. Long before 1953, ADA was aware that no Congress was going to take the ADA platform as it marching orders. But with a Republican Administration in power, the Democrats in Congress—for the first time in twenty years—were to all intents and purposes the Democratic party itself, and ADA did expect them to present clear-cut liberal alternatives to the "moderation" of the President and the "obstructionism" of the Republican Congressional party.

These expectations were to survive only slightly longer than the vain hopes about Eisenhower. By April, 1955, Rauh was lamenting "the passage of three months of a Democratically controlled Congress with little progress made in enacting liberal legislation." The national board, in a statement more critical of the Democrats in Congress than of the Administration, accused the Democratic Congressional leadership of "using the pretext of 'party unity' to avoid action on liberal legislation." Listing seven areas of "legislative default" in the 84th Congress for which the Democrats must take responsibility, the board warned that "the Democratic leadership in Congress must understand that if the American people want a do-nothing, care-nothing government, they will choose the Republicans every time." By March, 1956, Rauh was charging the Congressional leadership with "bringing the Democratic party to its lowest point in twenty-five years."

Aside from frustration at the paucity of liberal legislation coming out of Congress, there was another—and related—reason for ADA's sustained criticism of the Congressional Democrats. It was convinced that the party in Congress was writing a record which would handicap the national party efforts to recapture the White House, and it rather suspected that this suicide by proxy might not be accidental. As the Presidential election of 1956 approached, however, some in ADA became concerned that such sharp censure might boomerang. ADA blasts at Democrats were making headlines, while its anti-GOP press releases were being ignored. A discussion broke out in the executive committee about whether "ADA had not unwittingly helped the Republican Administration and the Republican Congressional leadership to escape responsibility for their actions and failure to act." ADA's public criticism of Congressional Democrats became somewhat more muted after 1956, but the subsequent performance of Congress did little to change the belief of liberals that the whole legislative branch was, as William S. White said of the Senate, an essentially conservative, backward-looking place.

In assailing the "Congressional Democratic leadership," ADA was, of course, aiming squarely at Senate Majority Leader Lyndon Johnson, House Speaker Sam Rayburn, and the Southerners who dominated most of the committees of both Houses. But liberal frustration over Southern control of Congress was nothing new. Long before ADA was founded liberals viewed Congress as a place where militant Northern Democrats went to fight a valiant if somewhat ineffective guerrilla warfare against the entrenched Bourbons. From the beginning, one of the main reasons for ADA's emphasis on local political action was the conviction that without the election and re-election of more Northern liberals Congress would continue to be a conservative bastion against the Presidency. In 1948, following the lesson administered by the 80th Congress, ADA leaders had joined other liberals in forming a National Committee for an Effective Congress. The purpose of the Committee was to raise funds for and otherwise "contribute effective campaign assistance to qualified liberal candidates." For a time during the 1950's, however, ADA began to have doubts about the militancy and the liberalism of some of the candidates it had helped to put in Congress.

The trouble began during the closing days of the 83rd Congress when Democratic liberals, weary of McCarthy's attacks and fearful of his effect in the forthcoming elections, tried to be more royalist than the king. Senator Hubert Humphrey, an ADA vice-chairman, introduced a surprise proposal to outlaw the Communist party. Wayne Morse, also a vice-chairman, hailed the measure as proof that liberals were not soft on Communism and told his colleagues it was time "to fish or cut bait" on the Communist issue. Other ADA members and friends in both Houses joined in to railroad the Communist Control Act through over the objections of the Administration, which claimed that outlawing the Communists would only drive them underground.

The ADA found itself in an embarrassing bind. Its members harbored no illusions about the Communists, but they believed firmly in the constitutional right of freedom of association. Five successive ADA conventions had gone on record against outlawing any political party, even the Communist, and the organization had paid dearly for it. The 1953 convention had dropped this plank from its platform, but the deletion—while seemingly a necessary concession to the political realities of the early 1950's—stuck in the throats of many members. And it certainly did not mean that ADA favored outlawing the Communist party, as some of its most illustrious members had done. ADA leaders, caught between conscience on one hand and a fait accompli on the other, and fearful of undercutting their Congressional colleagues, found a technical way out. Noting that neither the most recent convention nor the national board had taken a stand on the issue, the executive committee asked the President to veto the Communist Control Act, not because it outlawed the Communist party but because of other provisions "so vague and indefinite as to constitute possible danger to individuals in no way involved in the Communist party." During the McCarthy era the price of believing in the Constitution became too high at times, even for ADA.

ADA also paid for "Humphrey's Horror" in other coin. Just prior to the passage of the Communist Control Act it had sent out an appeal for funds to carry on its fight against McCarthy and for civil liberties. Among other pitches, the letter asked: "What would happen to civil liberties if Hubert Humphrey were not in the Senate?" The replies came in, low on money but full of opinions about Hubert Humphrey as a civil libertarian. "I can't imagine anything more satisfying than the Senate without Hubert Humphrey," wrote one member. Another enclosed ten dollars, but with *"terrible reluctance"* because "I can't understand how a 'liberal' Senator is distinguished from a reactionary when the liberals vote 85 to 0 to outlaw the Communist party. A more blind, reactionary and un-American vote was never registered in the U.S. Senate."

Mrs. Roosevelt, ADA's honorary chairman, felt that "if the Democratic liberals do any more things like outlawing the Communist party, I'm not sure I will consider them liberals."

ADA's disillusionment with the Democratic liberals, especially with Humphrey, did not end with their failure of nerve over the Communist Control Act. In 1955 Humphrey, joined by Paul Douglas and Wayne Morse, arose in the Senate to "pay public tribute" to Lyndon Johnson for "his leadership in behalf of an effective Democratic party liberal program." This was an obvious slap at ADA, which the day before had accused Johnson of "affably acquiescing in the Republican assault on liberalism." Humphrey's refusal to fight for an end to the filibuster in 1955 and his failure to push for a strong civil rights plank at the 1956 Democratic convention also irked ADA leaders.

By 1958, however, William Shannon was noting that Humphrey had abandoned his attempt to coexist with the South, had moved back into the filibuster fight, and had taken other steps "which have almost completely mended his broken fences in the liberal community." Almost, but—one suspects—not completely. Even today, although public and private recriminations have ceased and he is again its biggest political name, one senses a residue of suspicion within ADA toward Humphrey and other Congressional liberals. It is perhaps nothing more than the traditional distrust of the reformer, not much given to compromise, for the politician, who must compromise. Humphrey, at least, sees it in this light, and is not much bothered. "ADA gives me hell sometimes," says Humphrey, "but sometimes I need it. I'm a politician. I have to compromise." While there were no serious repercussions, ADA's temporary alienation from the Democratic liberals did provide added evidence that it was winter season for liberalism in Congress during the 1950's.

"Moderation" and Civil Rights in 1956. It was no accident that ADA's differences with the Congressional liberals had arisen primarily over civil rights and civil liberties. These were areas which the New Deal had hardly touched, and ADA still considered the New Deal unfinished business. Since the platform victory in 1948, it had felt a possessive interest in civil rights. One of its major legislative goals had been to abolish the filibuster in the Senate and make possible the enactment of that platform. Its own experiences since 1949 had made it acutely sensitive to the importance of civil liberties. During the 1950's these became ADA's two main issues. Congressional inaction on civil rights, and all too much action of the wrong kind on civil liberties, only added to liberal disenchantment with the legislative branch.

But if Congress was the natural habitat of conservatives, liberals could have their innings elsewhere. The Democratic National Convention, in particular, was a place where Southerners and other conservatives went to nominate liberal candidates, swallow a liberal platform, and go home to sulk. So, at least, it had seemed in 1948 and 1952. In 1956, however, liberals found that this stronghold, too, had been breached, that both the Democratic candidate and the Democratic platform had been infected by the virus of "moderation" and "party unity."

The great debate over "moderation" opened in November, 1955, when Adlai Stevenson told a gathering of Democratic leaders that he "agreed this is an age of abundance as well as anxiety . . . that it is a time for catching our breath . . . that moderation is the spirit of the times." Stevenson's remarks came in the middle of a speech which otherwise was sharply critical of the Eisenhower Administration, but other Democratic hopefuls—now that Eisenhower's illness had made their party's nomination seem worth something—chose to make an issue of them. Governor Averill Harriman of New York announced that " there is no such word as 'moderation' in the Democratic vocabulary," and became a very active "inactive" candidate. Senator Estes Kefauver announced his candidacy, thus forcing a reluctant Stevenson to meet him in a series of bruising primary contests. Former President Truman began to hedge on his earlier—and none too enthusiastic—support for Stevenson.

ADA had some ideas of its own about moderation, breath-catching, and abundance, but it had no desire to be caught in the crossfire which began to rake the Democratic party. While some of its leaders favored Kefauver or Harriman, the rank and file were still madly for Adlai. Despite ADA's official neutrality, the national office, operating on the assumption that he would be the nominee, had already made contact with Stevenson headquarters to discuss cooperation between ADA and the Stevenson for President Clubs. So long as the debate over moderation was limited to semantics, the ADA would stay out of it. Joe Rauh urged the "light horses and the dark horses" of the Democratic party to "quit arguing about 'moderation' and 'immoderation' and take a stand on the real issues of 1956."

In February the debaters finally got down to specifics, and the argument took a turn not to ADA's liking. During a preliminary foray into California, Stevenson came out in opposition to the Powell Amendment, which would deny federal funds to segregated schools, and indicated that as President he would not use federal troops to enforce the Supreme Court's desegregation decision or to crack down on racial violence in the South. Since 1952, long before the Powell Amendment had become a national issue, ADA had opposed granting federal money to segregated schools. (In 1958, after a heated battle, the ADA convention reversed this position and voted to oppose any future Powell Amendments.) And for months it had been deploring Eisenhower's refusal to intervene in Mississippi and other Southern states where Negro rights were being denied.

Stevenson's statement fed a growing fear among ADA leaders that he was preparing to make peace with the South, where serious defections to the Republicans had occurred in 1952, at the expense of a militant liberal platform and campaign on civil rights and other issues. Such a course, they were convinced, not only would damage the Democratic party's moral position but was bad politics as well. It would lose more electoral votes in the North than it would save in the South. Joseph Rauh, at the request of the ADA executive committee, wrote Stevenson "to convey to you the deep concern of the

liberal community with your position on certain key civil rights issues."
Rauh urged Stevenson to make a strong statement in support of the
Court's desegregation decision, to denounce discrimination against the
voting rights of Negroes, and to condemn the recent violence in Mississippi. Stevenson's reply was tart:

"I regret that the ADA people are disturbed about my position on
desegregation. I really feel that I have made it as clear as I can what
I think and that the Court's decision must and will be complied with
given time and patience and a lot more understanding on the part of
some of my Northern friends than I have perceived yet.

"The denials of the right to vote and violence I have denounced
repeatedly anywhere and used the Illinois National Guard to prevent
it in Illinois. I really don't believe I should have to say the obvious
over and over."

ADA's only reaction to Stevenson's rebuff was an oblique warning
by Rauh to all Democratic candidates that "Ike has squatter's rights
on the middle of the road. Let him have it." But the middle of the
road was a crowded avenue in the 1950's, and ADA lacked the leverage
to push either a Republican President or would-be Democratic President to the left of center.

Stevenson's insistence upon a moderate stance toward the South
also boded ill for ADA's hope of repeating its platform victories of
earlier years on civil rights. In 1952 liberal forces in the Democratic
convention had been able to prevent party professionals, led by Governor Paul Dever of Massachusetts and National Chairman Frank Mc-
Kinney, from watering down the 1948 civil rights plank. ADA hailed
the 1952 platform as "the most progressive ever written by a major
political party, including a stronger civil rights program than in
1948."

By 1956, however, the Supreme Court's desegregation decision had
intervened, and the ante was up on civil rights. "The Democratic
platforms of 1948 and 1952 pledged the party to the principle of civil
rights," said ADA in a letter to all Democratic convention delegates,
"but in 1956 a pledge to principle is not enough." Specifically, ADA
was demanding a plank including a statement of "complete and
unequivocal support of the Supreme Court decision on desegregation,
pledging action by the Executive and the Congress to implement and
uphold the decision." The 100-odd ADA members who were delegates or alternates to the Democratic convention were instructed to
coordinate their activities with the Leadership Conference on Civil

Rights, a group composed of the NAACP, ADA, and a few of the more militant trade unions, in working for a strong civil rights plank.

But the national party represented by the Democratic convention, like the Congressional party, was no longer listening to ADA's demands. Its civil rights plank—replete with such fighting phrases as "Our country is founded on the proposition that all men are created equal" and "emphatically reaffirming" the party's support of "the historic principle that ours is a Government of laws and not of men"—read like a chapter from an elementary civics textbook. The Supreme Court's desegregation decision had "brought consequences of vast importance to our nation as a whole and especially to communities directly affected." The Court itself was magnanimously recognized as "one of the three constitutional and coordinate branches of the Federal government," but its decisions were only "*part* of the law of the land." The platform pledged no action by the Democratic party, the executive, or Congress to uphold and implement the Court's decision, and a 1952 provision favoring federal legislation to secure equal employment and voting rights was dropped.

A major factor contributing to the civil rights failure of 1956, in sharp contrast to the victory of 1948, was the indecision and dissension within the liberal bloc, and specifically within ADA. While ADA's nonpolitical leaders, headed by Joe Rauh, wanted a clear-cut fight on the civil rights issue—win, lose, or draw—its major political figures held back. Hubert Humphrey, who had said in 1948 that it was time for the Democratic party "to get out of the shadow of states rights and walk forthrightly in the sunshine of human rights," stayed cautiously in the shadows of the 1956 convention. On July 14th, one month prior to the convention, Humphrey had written Rauh: "I agree that the Democratic platform on civil rights should include everything we had in 1952, plus a declaration in support of the Supreme Court decision on segregation. Count me in on any meetings that are held in Chicago." By convention time, however, Humphrey was engaged in a frantic and futile run for the Vice-Presidential nomination and was hoping for Southern support. On August 13th he called for "understanding of Southern problems on the race issue," and was conspicuously absent from the caucus of the civil rights group. The civil rights issue quickly degenerated into a ploy by which the Harriman forces hoped to stop Stevenson. Mrs. Roosevelt, ADA's honorary chairman and a Stevenson champion, countered by coming out specifically against endorsement of the Supreme Court decision. These plus other defections left ADA with no means to conduct a floor fight. A minority report incorporating part of the stronger 1952 civil rights plank reached the floor but was howled down by voice vote. Rauh and other ADA leaders who were not delegates but had infiltrated to the convention floor saw the Minnesota and Michigan delegations back down on their earlier promise to take the lead in trying to get a roll-call, the tactic that had succeeded so effectively in 1948.

In surveying the final compromise on civil rights, Robert Bendiner noted that "outside amateur groups that for twenty years had occupied a favored and strategic spot at these affairs were isolated and without influence on the one issue that mattered most to them." The Leadership Conference on Civil Rights "might just as well have set up shop in Biloxi."

Despite the differences of some of its leaders with Stevenson over platform, policy, and the conduct of his campaign in 1956, ADA as an organization saw no choice but to endorse him. This time, however, it was done with none of the ebullient enthusiasm of 1952, although most of the rank and file seemed as madly for Adlai as ever. No ADA leader sat close to Stevenson, as Wilson Wyatt had done four years earlier. Republican spokesmen continued to attack ADA, but even this was done halfheartedly.

There was, in fact, an aura of 1948 surrounding ADA's participation in the 1956 election. Its primary contribution to Truman—a sideshow war against Henry Wallace—had been important but essentially negative. Its primary contribution to Stevenson was publication of a pamphlet entitled "The Second Man," which pictured the dire consequences of making Richard Nixon a sick President's Vice-President. Altogether, 105,000 copies were distributed, chiefly in cities along Nixon's campaign itinerary. This was, again, an essentially negative contribution, and this time relatively important. An inside evaluation of ADA's operations in 1956 is provided by national director Ed Hollander's dispirited comment to his predecessor: "As always, ADA is operating on the fringes in this election."

ADA's alienation from the Democratic party did not begin or end with the 1956 convention and election. Since the "Furcolo affair" of 1953, Congressional, state, and local candidates had become increasingly less enamored of ADA's endorsement. In the fall of 1954 several Massachusetts Democrats who had accepted ADA help in earlier races asked to be overlooked this time around. The Massachusetts ADA explained: "These candidates, before endorsements were decided upon, have yielded to threats from various sources and noticeably one source in particular that the support of ADA will make them a target for the sort of vilification and misrepresentation to which ADA itself has long been exposed." The "one source in particular" was reported to be gubernatorial candidate Foster Furcolo.

Shortly, however, there occured a "Harriman affair" in New York paralleling the Furcolo fracas in Massachusetts. In January, 1955, Harriman—elected governor three months earlier with ADA support —refused an invitation from Senator Herbert Lehman to speak at the New York Roosevelt Day Dinner. Joseph Rauh, who had managed Harriman's successful 1952 primary campaign in the District of Columbia, went to Albany to clear up the "misunderstanding." Harriman, according to press reports, ordered Rauh out of his office and later denied that in the heat of argument he had told Rauh "I'm not running out on ADA the way your good friend Mr. Stevenson did." One ADA official reported that the dispute, while finally smoothed over, "has created a near state of chaos in the ADA."

Incidents such as these, repeated in other sections of the country, led to a movement within ADA to cease making endorsements at all. James Patton, head of the National Farmers Union and an ADA national board member, made this proposal to the board in 1955. Patton's suggestion, which would have taken ADA out of politics altogether, was rejected, but there remained an "undercurrent of uneasiness and frustration at the isolation of ADA from some of the politicians we have always considered to be allies."

In addition to its other difficulties during the Ike Age, ADA found itself increasingly alienated from the labor elements which had always played so large a part in its political planning. ADA leaders believed from the beginning that no liberal group would prosper in the United States without substantial labor participation and support. In late 1948 it could claim: "ADA has received an increasing measure of labor support. High-ranking leaders of the CIO, AFL, the Railway Brotherhoods and independent unions are members of the ADA national board. This labor representation might well be strengthened, but it is no exaggeration to say that ADA has a broader labor representation than any similar organization has ever had."

This happy situation ended shortly. By April, 1950, the *New Republic* reported that ADA's labor relations were beginning to show strain. "Labor has not been willing to treat the ADA as an equal partner in liberalism. Aside from Walter Reuther and David Dubinsky, few important union leaders are much concerned with ADA." Jack Kroll, head of the CIO's Political Action Committee, was unenthusiastic about a labor-liberal electioneering alliance. "Whatever understanding PAC and ADA might reach at the top," said Kroll, "on a local level our people should lay off ADA and work through PAC."

Policy differences with labor have been kept to a minimum, primarily because ADA has swallowed hard and looked the other way. Such differences as have arisen, however, have had serious consequences. In 1951 Sol Hoffman pulled his International Upholsterers Union out of ADA because of its China policy. After Philip Murray's death, David McDonald withdrew the Steelworkers' substantial subsidy because ADA was "too socialistic." ADA's concern with consumer interests has led to clashes with labor over questions of wage, price, and credit controls. In 1960 the Massachusetts ADA refused to support a labor effort to obtain unemployment compensation for striking workers, but the close liberal-labor cooperation in state politics had disintegrated years earlier.

Labor's most serious defection, however, came in the withdrawal of financial support. In its early years ADA leaders felt that it would be "unhealthy" for more than one-third of the organization's income to come from labor contributions. They need not have worried. During the 1950's ADA financial reports are replete with complaints about the dearth of labor contributions. In 1954 the "decline in contributions from labor was again cited as accounting for the most part of the deficit." By 1960 labor's subsidy to ADA amounted to only $13,000, about one-tenth of its total income.

ADA leaders attribute their loss of labor support to many factors, primarily to decreasing labor interest in broad social issues outside the "bread and butter" union concerns. They would agree without reservation to the conclusion of labor expert William Kornhauser: "With the rise of the CIO and the New Deal, many individuals expected labor to assume a more ideological role. Increasingly, however, U.S. trade unions have operated within the narrower frames of their market needs, and their political roles are aimed more toward protecting their present positions than in achieving social change."

The merger of the AFL and CIO in 1955, according to ADA, acted as a brake on the historical CIO crusading impulse. "The merger," says one ADA leader flatly, "was a catastrophe for liberalism." Ironically, by serving as a common meeting ground for the more liberal figures in both federations, ADA played some small part in bringing about the merger.

In its first months of operation ADA's political director listed and commented upon four "essential elements" of a liberal movement:

"1. Political leaders—The objective of any political movement is obviously political power, in the best sense of that term. No political program is valid unless it is acceptable to those liberal public servants who must depend on the electorate to win public office.

"2. Organized labor.

"3. Farm groups—There is always optimistic debate in progressive circles about farm groups.

"4. Independent liberals."

By the end of the 1950's ADA could count fully on none of these elements. Most political leaders had wanted no part of ADA, and those who did had found identification with the group and its program a very dubious asset in winning and holding public office. Organized labor had become disorganized, discouraged, and disinterested in an alliance with ADA. There was no longer any optimistic debate about the farmers. The loss of these three elements forced ADA to fall back upon the fourth, its own organization of independent liberals.

In Chapter II we saw what happened to ADA's organization—in terms of members and money—during the decade of the 1950's. There is ample evidence in ADA files of the frustrations encountered during this period. In 1956 the national director frankly admitted:

"The election activities revealed the appalling consequences of several years of organizational neglect. Without overlooking the faults ot omission or commission of the national office, I must recall the warning, which accompanied the presentation of the budget in 1953, that without the means to carry on continuous organizing activities, ADA would tend to contract to a few large Eastern and Midwestern cities. In the face of a reduced budget since mid-1954, exactly this has happened. Not only the many small chapters but some of the larger ones have been seriously weakened.

"All of our major chapters—Massachusetts, New York, New Jersey, Baltimore, Detroit and D.C.—are without full-time executive directors. These are the areas in which we have the bulk of our membership and most ADA activity. Most of these groups plead financial difficulty in connection with hiring adequate staff.

"The lack of a field staff for two years has taken its toll of chapters throughout the country. Except for the West Coast, we have no active chapters west of St. Louis. It will be difficult to revive dormant chapters or organize new ones."

By 1957 the same officer was wondering if "a Fabian Society or a Liberal Party wouldn't be such a bad idea after all."

Even the election of 1958, interpreted by most observers as a sweeping liberal victory, provided no boost for ADA, which played little part in it. Again, ADA's director reported that "relatively few chapters engaged in direct political activity in behalf of candidates, either through the local ADA organization or through campaign committees." James Wechsler noted of that election:

"To judge by nearly all the public evidence, liberalism and independence had carried the day, and most of the liberal communiques had a tone of exultation reminiscent of the dancing in the streets of 1948.

"Yet on the morning after the binge, there appeared good reason to re-examine the premises of the celebration . . . The condition of anything that might be described as a movement of organized liberalism in the U.S.A. was inescapably poor."

Given all the difficulties enumerated, one may well wonder why ADA survived at all. In the author's opinion, it survived for one reason only: because of the selfless dedication of a few top leaders and numbers of other anonymous people scattered across the country.

Many busy individuals with pressing personal and professional interests of their own have given time and effort to ADA which was not and could not be recompensed. Joseph Rauh, one of the nation's leading civil liberties lawyers, probably has devoted more time to ADA than to his own practice. Rauh, accurately described by the *New York Post* as "Mr. ADA," is a friendly bear of a man who is congenitally unable to resist a political fight. During the early years Rauh and James Loeb (who worked for a pittance both for the Union for Democratic Action and ADA) literally carried the organization on their shoulders and in their hats. Vi Gunther, now national director, joined up in 1947. Robert Nathan, a prominent Washington economist, has in recent years joined Rauh as one of the group's unpaid mainstays. Rhodes Scholar David Williams has spent many thankless years editing the *ADA World*. These and many others whose names are scattered throughout this book are responsible for ADA's survival.

Right-wing publicists frequently picture ADA as a lavishly-financed propaganda machine. Recently, Matt Cvetic, one of the numerous "ex-FBI" men roaming the plush pastures of the far right wing, described ADA as a "group of gold-bricking intellectuals" who, "for some substantial salaries, are willing to 'sacrifice themselves' to tell the American people how they should be governed." For the record, the top salary paid to any national ADA official is $9,100 a year. ADA's lobbyist receives $6,500 a year.

An example of the kind of grass-roots faith which saved ADA

appears in a 1957 letter from a Texas woman who wrote that she could not make a contribution because of the expense of sending two children through school: "But it is difficult for me to ignore the plea of an organization which has made a unique and effective contribution to the preservation of the liberal tradition which is our children's priceless inheritance. I have a quantity of Confederate currency which was left me by my father, who was born in 1861 and died last summer in his ninety-fifth year. He believed the currency had some value . . . I can think of no better use to which to put such an heirloom than aiding an organization which is still at work trying to unravel the tangled problems which are our legacy from the War Between the States."

ADA returned the gift reluctantly, explaining, "We had the Confederate paper appraised by dealers here in the Yankee capital, and they have not offered us more than token cash." Apparently, nothing was going right for ADA during the 1950's.

But whatever other explanations may be offered for the failure of liberalism—and the decline of ADA—during the Ike Age, in the end we must return to one primary factor. In 1948 this factor was omitted from ADA's list of "essential elements" for a successful liberal movement. Perhaps Mr. Truman's presence in the White House had something to do with it. But the Ike Age demonstrated that a Strong Liberal Democratic President was the most crucial element of all. As the Eisenhower era drew to a close and the elections of 1960 approached, ADA had more than a passing interest in seeing this void filled.

Part Five

NEW FRONTIER DAYS

Chapter XII

SKIRMISHING ON THE BORDER

"We would warn the Democratic party that if it is to win in 1960, it must nominate in Los Angeles a candidate whose record, whose convictions, and whose fighting capacity as a liberal will offer the American people a clear alternative to the reactionary Republican candidate already selected."

This public statement on political policy released by the national board on January 25, 1960, indicated that ADA, despite its straitened circumstances, still felt itself called upon to perform its usual role of gadfly mentor to the Democratic party. If it could no longer play in the political big leagues, it could sit in the stands and coach. The board's statement seemed to imply, moreover, that ADA was quite willing to help the motley Democratic team pick its captain for the coming season.

ADA was indeed willing to lay out specific qualifications which the Democratic candidate "must fulfill." He must among other things, "believe deeply in the nation's capacity to re-establish the national strength and prestige of the United States by taking the initiative in the fight for peace, by real efforts at disarmament, and by a more imaginative program of foreign economic aid." He must "be committed to a program based on America's capacity for economic growth which can permit the richest nation in the world to meet the basic needs of its people . . ." He must "believe so deeply in human rights that he will use the prestige of the most powerful public office in the world to make a reality of our proclamations of equality before the law." Finally, he must "have the capacity for leadership that he can once more bring together that great coalition of voters which gave the nation Franklin D. Roosevelt and Harry S. Truman." In other words, in addition to the other prerequisites, he must be a winner.

Despite these specifics, any Democrat in search of political guidance must have found ADA's advice somewhat puzzling. The story was, of course, much the same as it had been in previous seasons: pick a liberal candidate or else . . . And the coach was clear enough about what not to do: "ADA believes it of vital importance to point out . . . that if the American people are offered a choice, for instance,

171

between Mr. Nixon and Senator Lyndon Johnson, the Democratic party would be failing in its responsibility to the nation." Lyndon Johnson had played around in right field for so long, and displayed such a propensity for straying into foul territory, that he was obviously not fit to run the team. But if Johnson would not do, what about center-fielder Adlai Stevenson, left-fielder Hubert Humphrey, and the other players who were beginning to make their moves? More to the point, in view of subsequent developments, what about John Fitzgerald Kennedy, the young rookie who seemed to be making quite an impression on the fans?

After warning the Democratic party that it must select a liberal, that it must not choose Lyndon Johnson, after setting out the qualifications its nominee should have, one might have thought that ADA would come up with some hints about the candidate the Democrats should nominate. In its public statement, however, the national board decreed that "Americans for Democratic Action makes no endorsement at this time among the declared and undeclared candidates for the Democratic nomination." The board had, of course, taken precisely the same position in 1952 and 1956.

Since its ill-fated attempt to pinch-hit Eisenhower for Truman in 1948, ADA had been wary about sticking its official neck out too far or too fast. But public professions of neutrality in earlier years had been primarily a tactical maneuver designed to preserve some bargaining power with the candidate eventually nominated. They had not disguised the fact that the great majority of ADA members were for Adlai Stevenson before Chicago in 1952 and 1956. Who, then, were they for before Los Angeles in 1960?

In a private "Political Policy Position," also adopted on January 25th and circulated to ADA chapters, the national board reiterated that "National ADA does not at this time endorse any one candidate for President." In the preconvention period local chapters were directed to "work for the strengthening of liberal forces at the national conventions." In pursuing this policy they were to make public endorsements "only where it shall be in support of the objective of getting maximum cooperation among liberal forces against attempts to nominate conservative candidates for the top national offices." Translated, this meant that if Lyndon Johnson entered any state primaries, ADA in those states would move against him.

These public and private "policy positions," it is evident, added up to no policy at all, except the negative policy of opposing Lyndon Johnson, but they are accurate reflections of the indecision and un-

Knox in Nashville (Tenn.) Banner

Cans, Firecrackers, and a Bowl of Milk

Knox in Columbia (S.C.) State

Mr. Kennedy Seems To Have Surrounded Himself

certainty within ADA as it approached the most crucial Presidential election since its formation.

There were various reasons, compounded of political expediency and political principle, behind ADA's inability to engage in positive thinking about a Presidential candidate in 1960. For one thing, there were no indications that any of the declared and undeclared candidates, except perhaps Hubert Humphrey, were anxious to have ADA's stamp of approval. No representatives from Stevenson, Kennedy, Symington or anyone else were besieging ADA to come out for their man. The time had passed, if there ever was a time, when Presidential hopefuls concerned themselves very much about what ADA would do. In the past, of course, ADA had not concerned itself very much about what Presidential hopefuls—or Presidents—had thought. While not unmindful of the possible negative effects of its embrace, this factor was not responsible for ADA's failure to make a positive endorsement.

ADA's silence stemmed primarily from the fact that it did not know, or could not decide, who it was for. Its bill of particulars for a Democratic nominee was, like most of the requirements the organization made upon itself and others, a rather large order. Looking over the field in 1960, ADA could not make up its collective mind which of the prospective candidates could fill this bill.

In February, 1959, press reports had circulated to the effect that ADA, fearful that Kennedy was getting too big a jump on other candidates, was heading a "stop-Kennedy" movement. ADA's publicity director promptly wrote the Senator: "I am sure it's utterly superfluous for me to tell you that any kind of talk about a stop-Kennedy movement in ADA is absolute baloney."

The message was not superfluous, and the talk was not baloney. Today ADA leaders deny that they ever engaged in a stop-Kennedy drive; activity in behalf of other candidates, they explain, was "for" those candidates and not "against" Kennedy. It is a question of how you slice the cake. One thing is certain. There was no pro-Kennedy movement within ADA in 1959 and little sentiment for Kennedy prior to Los Angeles in 1960. And in Presidential politics, above all else, if you are not for a man you are against him.

Behind the facade of neutral policy statements during the months preceding the Democratic convention, ADA was in fact a house divided against itself. Its members agreed on only two points: neither Lyndon Johnson nor Richard Nixon would do. Both had to be stopped. For some ADA members this was sufficient; they cared little about what happened otherwise. But most proved loyal to the traditional liberal propensity for lost causes and backed Adlai Stevenson or Hubert Humphrey to the bitter end.

Few top leaders worked openly for Stevenson. Of the big names, only Mrs. Roosevelt and James Doyle, former Wisconsin Democratic party chairman and former national ADA co-chairman, became identified with the forlorn effort to draft Adlai again. On the rank and file level, however, pro-Stevenson sentiment was vociferous and unshakable. Many had joined ADA via the Stevenson Clubs of 1952 and they retained the fanatical enthusiasm of that year; to them Kennedy was a Johnny-come-lately trying to usurp a right which Stevenson had earned. It was such devotion to Stevenson, in fact, which immobilized ADA and prevented other leaders from swinging it almost wholly, if unofficially, behind Humphrey.

In January, 1960, Rauh and James Wechsler opened a drive to dent pro-Stevenson support. Speaking to the Baltimore Roosevelt Day Dinner meeting, both men urged liberals "to drop their sentimental loyalty to Adlai E. Stevenson and support a liberal with a chance to win." Continued loyalty to Stevenson, they warned, would deprive Humphrey and Kennedy of badly needed support and lead to a deadlocked convention in which the nomination would go to either Symington or Johnson by default. Rauh complained that big campaign contributors who had invested heavily in Stevenson in 1952 and 1956 were sitting on their pocketbooks. Neither Rauh nor Wechsler, the *ADA World* noted, showed any enthusiasm for Senator Kennedy.

By this time Rauh, Nathan, and virtually the entire ADA national staff were working for Humphrey in preparation for his primary battles with Kennedy. Rauh served as an unofficial campaign manager. David Williams took leave from ADA to write Humphrey's speeches. One official claims today: "Hubert wouldn't have had a campaign but for ADA."

In early May, three days prior to the West Virginia primary, the national board met during the organization's thirteenth annual convention. Many members were restive about ADA's stance of official neutrality, feeling they should pick a candidate and take a stand. Rauh suggested five possible positions they might take:

1. "Endorse Humphrey.
2. "Endorse Humphrey and Stevenson.
3. "Endorse Humphrey among the active candidates.
4. "Commend Humphrey for his articulation of our liberal principles in the press and for having clarified issues, and endorse him as

an active candidate. If a stalemate should develop our candidate would be Adlai Stevenson.

5. "We are against Johnson and Nixon."

There was no mention of Kennedy. The convention compromised between positions four and five, commending Humphrey but not endorsing him, blasting Nixon as the candidate of the "ultra-conservative elements" in the Republican party, and taking an inferential slap at Lyndon Johnson.

Rauh estimates that preferences among ADA convention delegates were divided about 40% for Stevenson, 50% for Humphrey, and "10% or less" for Kennedy. "Kennedy had the Massachusetts people and Monroe Sweetland of Oregon," says Rauh, "and nothing else."

ADA convention delegates are selected in such a manner as to provide a reasonably accurate reflection of overall opinion within the organization. If Rauh's estimate is correct—and there is no reason to doubt it—it is most revealing. If these people could not have Humphrey, they wanted Stevenson. If they could not have Stevenson, they wanted Humphrey. They wanted no part of John F. Kennedy.

Rauh insists that for him the Humphrey campaign, at this time nearing its end, was a serious matter, not just a stop-Kennedy maneuver. He recalls a 1959 discussion with Kennedy, in which Kennedy asked about Humphrey as a possible Vice-Presidential choice. Rauh replied that Humphrey was not interested, that he—Rauh—was for him, but "if it became obvious that Hubert couldn't make it, he would get behind Kennedy."

The West Virginia primary settled the question whether Humphrey could make it. After an all-night row with James Rowe, a former Johnson aide also in Humphrey's camp—who urged Humphrey to stay in the race, hold his delegates, and hope for a deadlock—Rauh finally convinced Humphrey to pull out. "I told him his position as a leader of American liberalism was worth more than a few lousy convention votes which would be used by Johnson." In the end, Rauh drafted Humphrey's statement of withdrawal.

With the Humphrey matter settled, Rauh joined Arthur M. Schlesinger, Jr., in a drive to wean the liberals away from Stevenson. Schlesinger, a Humphrey man in 1959, had switched to Kennedy earlier, saying "I'm nostalgically for Stevenson, ideologically for Humphrey, but realistically for Kennedy." On June 17 both men joined other ADA members and prominent sympathizers in a public letter urging "fellow liberals" to "turn to Senator Kennedy for President." There is little evidence that they had much success within ADA.

During the first half of 1960, while paralyzed by its inability to resolve the Stevenson-Humphrey internal conflict, ADA kept a wary eye on Lyndon Johnson. It was, in fact, very much afraid of him. In January Vi Gunther felt that "as things then stood it was not at all impossible that the Democratic party would nominate a conservative. The candidacy of Senator Johnson has gathered real momentum in the last few months. He has possibly the single most powerful bloc of support, not only in the united South, but also among leading national and state political figures." By March Mrs. Gunther saw "the position of moderation which has dominated the Democratic party in Congress" as "seriously threatening" to dominate the Democratic convention.

In April ADA issued an analysis of Johnson's voting record. Its major conclusion: "A review of Senator Lyndon Johnson's voting record in Congress over the past two decades stamps him as the most conservative of the candidates for the Democratic nomination. If the Democrats are seeking a candidate who will pursue new vigorous domestic and international policies to pull us out of the stagnation of the last eight years, Johnson would be least likely to fill the bill."

The Texan professed to be pleased by ADA's attentions. "We don't want the support of the odd balls on the left or the right," he explained, adding that he didn't like extremism either way—"ADA or KKK."

As the time for the Democratic convention approached, Stevenson sentiment in ADA continued to churn to the surface. The New York chapter forwarded to national headquarters a resolution calling for an endorsement of Stevenson. The executive committee rejected it by a 6-3 vote. "The ADA constitution," Vi Gunther wrote the New York chairman, "authorizes state and local chapters to endorse candidates at the state and local levels. State and local chapters may endorse national candidates only with the specific permission of ADA. The no-endorsement policy adopted at the convention prohibits the executive committee from granting such permission. It also, therefore, precludes the chapters from making national endorsements."

In June Mrs. Roosevelt learned that Kennedy people were using ADA's mailing list and posted a vehement objection to the national office. Nathan explained that the list was made available in January to both Kennedy and Humphrey, but Kennedy had not used it until recently. "This explanation certainly puts Joe Rauh and Art Schlesinger in the clear as far as having brought undue influence to bear on ADA," Nathan wrote Mrs. Roosevelt. The incident also showed that Kennedy had begun a belated repair job on his liberal fences. During the weeks immediately preceding the convention ADA continued its assault on Johnson. On June 30th national chairman Samuel Beer forwarded to all Democratic delegates a letter urging opposition to the "conservative, anti-civil rights, gas-and-oil Senator." His reasons were cogent: "For the first time since 1924, the conservatives have a chance to capture control of a Democratic convention. They mean to do so through Senator Lyndon Johnson's candidacy. The Democratic party has a number of leading figures who can carry the banner of liberalism to the American people and through them to victory this fall. Senator Johnson is not one of them."

An ADA Platform. With its political radar thrown out of focus by Stevenson blips, ADA was turning away from the Presidential contest and looking toward the platform which the Democratic convention would write. As if by unspoken consent, Democratic platforms always had been a special liberal province and the platform committee a place where Southerners and liberals could fight over words while the professionals played for all the marbles.

In 1960 the liberals were well prepared, while the South was far more concerned about nominating one of its own than about the platform on which he might have to run. Chester Bowles, an ADA founder, was named chairman of the full platform committee in April. Philip Perlman, former Solicitor General and a long-time ADA sympathizer, was vice-chairman. Both were members of the Democratic Advisory Council, a liberal stronghold within the party which had tried to act as a counterweight to the Johnson-Rayburn Congressional axis. Bowles set up regional platform hearings at which ADA members testified in Philadelphia, St. Louis, Detroit, and other cities. Rauh and three other ADAers were named to the full committee, and Rauh was on the 20-man drafting committee. In earlier conventions the liberals had been mostly on the outside looking in and had been forced to go to the floor with minority reports to beef up the platform. In this convention they were running the show.

On July 7th Rauh appeared before the platform committee to present ADA's position on "the single most important issue," the question of civil rights:

"We believe the Democratic party must be unmistakably committed to a program of federal action which will result in the eradication of segregation and other forms of discrimination from all aspects of American life.

"Such a program would pledge that the next President, if he is a Democrat, will use the tremendous resources of his office to make desegregation a reality as quickly as possible; will act immediately to end existing federal subsidies to discrimination in education, housing, employment and other fields, and will use all of the means at his command to fulfill his constitutional responsibility to 'take care that the laws be faithfully executed.' "

Specifically, ADA urged the Democratic party to agree to:

"1. Enact Title III to empower the Attorney-General to file civil injunction suits in cases involving denial of civil rights.

"2. Support the Supreme Court's decree in the school desegregation cases and provide assistance for school districts prepared to desegregate.

"3. Declare support for the sit-in demonstrations.

"4. Improve procedures in both Houses of Congress so that the will of the majority shall prevail and Congress will be a more responsive instrument of our national purposes.

"5. Pledge vigorous enforcement of existing voting laws and enact additional legislation to protect the right to vote, including, if necessary, direct federal control and operation of registration and elections.

"6. Promulgate an executive order forbidding segregation and other forms of discrimination based on race, religion, or national origin in all federal or federally-aided programs.

"7. Enact a federal fair employment practices law to establish and enforce equal job opportunity in all employment in or affecting interstate commerce."

The platform actually had been written weeks before the opening of the Los Angeles convention. Rauh's testimony was, in effect, the civil rights section of that platform as it was to be presented to the delegates. Southern objections on civil rights and other provisions were beaten down easily within the platform committee. Two Southern minority reports, one on civil rights, the other on fiscal policy, were howled down on the floor by voice vote.

The final Democratic platform, entitled "The Rights of Man," contained many other planks which had appeared for years in ADA's annual platforms. The party was pledged to a greatly expanded program of foreign economic aid and to closing tax loopholes such as the oil depletion allowance, which had created numerous Texas millionaires.

For the first time in history, the platform contained a strong civil liberties plank and pledged a "full and fair hearing, including confrontation of the accuser, to any person whose public or private employment or reputation is jeopardized by a loyalty or security proceeding." This had been a pet project of Joseph Rauh's, and the civil liberties section could have been lifted from almost any of his speeches of the McCarthy years. The original draft as composed by the committee staff had not contained an FEPC provision, but Rauh and others—working all night to contact other members of the drafting committee—got it put in.

ADA hailed the civil rights plank as "the most far-reaching ever put forward by any American political party," and was well-satisfied with the other planks. "We got everything we asked for," Rauh said later, "and it was so easy." Some ADA leaders insist that the Democratic platform was not quite all that they could ask for, pointing out certain differences between it and their own 1960 document. The differences are noticeable only to the trained eye of a perfectionist liberal. One suspects that if the Democrats had adopted ADA's platform, word for word, several ADA people would have been found leading minority revolts against it. For once, the Southern senator who charged that the Democratic platform was "an ADA platform" was not exaggerating.

Rauh explains the ease with which such a liberal platform was put over simply: "Kennedy did it." Kennedy, it seems, wanted an all-out liberal platform, particularly on civil rights, on which to campaign in the North. Rauh recalls taking the civil rights draft to Robert Kennedy and being told: "Don't change a word of it." Some of the Kennedy staff expressed hope that the civil rights plank would "be strong enough to get some Southern delegates to walk." In a campaign speech in October Rauh explained: "The Democratic civil rights plank did not get into the Democratic platform by accident. It got there by design—the design of one man and his staff and his supporters—and that one man was John F. Kennedy."

If the platform was the South's Gettysburg, the dramatic defeat of Lyndon Johnson's bid for the nomination was its Appomattox. Rauh recalls his thoughts on the day following the Presidential balloting:

"I was sitting in a bar celebrating something liberals had waited for over twenty years. The Democratic party was visibily shifting and changing direction under our eyes. The alliance of Southerners and big-city bosses was smashed. We had the most liberal platform ever. The first serious Southern bid for the Presidency since 1924 had been turned back. I knew we had a winner in Kennedy and a liberal, despite what some of my friends thought. Everything he had done indicated that he wanted to make a race in the North and West on down-the-line liberal issues and was saying to hell with the South. In fact, we had assurances that this was what he wanted to do. We knew that the Vice-President would be Henry Jackson or Stuart Symington or some other Midwesterner, and we didn't much care who he was. We were watching the whole power structure of the Democratic Party being changed, something which even Roosevelt never had been able to do. We had everything we wanted."

A Double Cross of the Liberals. Kennedy's selection of Johnson as his running mate burst over the liberal camp like the political equivalent of a fifty megaton bomb.

"The true story of the choice of Lyndon B. Johnson for the Vice-Presidency of the United States," according to Theodore White, "must remain an exercise for tomorrow's historians, not for today's reporters." Not having any inside information on how or why that choice was made, this author accepts White's account as authoritative. But we are interested here in its effect on ADA and liberals—a facet of the story White does not cover.

The effect of Johnson's selection was, as Robert Nathan put it, "stunning." Many in ADA had reason to be stunned. In persistent efforts to wean liberal delegates away from Stevenson and over to Kennedy, Rauh and other ADA officials had spread assurances all over Los Angeles that "Johnson would not be on the ticket" if Kennedy won. One press report from the convention quoted Rauh as saying that "he and some of his liberal friends agreed to work for Kennedy in the preconvention campaign upon a specific pledge that Kennedy would not take Johnson as his running mate."

White says that Kennedy discussed his choice of Johnson with all three of the "major elements" of the Democratic party—the South, the big-city leaders, and labor. In his press conference on the afternoon of July 14th Kennedy emphasized that Johnson's selection "had been reviewed with all the elements of the party leadership."

Thus put on notice that they were not even worth consulting about the Vice-Presidency, the liberals poured into the convention on the night of July 14th like a bride after the groom who had left her at the church. Forgetting that Roosevelt himself once had plucked a powerful Texan from his Congressional perch and buried him in the obscurity of the Vice-Presidency, they set out to block Johnson's nomination. Rauh, reached by a roving TV reporter in the middle of the angry District of Columbia's delegation, pleaded with Kennedy "not to do it" and charged "it is an absolute double cross of the ADA and the liberals of the United States." Rauh later denied using the term "double cross," but other ADA leaders insist they heard him say it. The *New York Post* quoted Rauh as saying, "I think the nomination of Senator Johnson may spell disaster in November" and describing the ticket as a "monumental blunder."

Rauh and Nathan sparked a revolt within the District of Columbia delegation. At one point they had twelve of the delegation's eighteen half-votes in favor of a protest on the floor, "but the numbers dwindled as pressure was brought to avoid a public fuss." Rauh and the delegation chairman, W. John Kenney, almost came to blows when Kenney attempted to carry the D. C. banner into a demonstration for Johnson. A last-ditch effort to place the name of Orville Freeman of Minnesota in nomination was stopped only by the intervention of Humphrey and Freeman's refusal to give his permission.

Few observers agree in their estimate of the noise which erupted from the floor when convention chairman Leroy Collins called for a voice vote on Johnson. The *New York Times* man found that "the chorus of ayes far exceeded in volume the negative votes." A *Washington Post* reporter felt that "the nays were about as numerous as the ayes." This viewer recalls vividly the memorable television shot of Leroy Collins hesitating before declaring Johnson nominated by acclamation as the camera moved to the floor for a close-up of the late Sam Rayburn pounding an imaginary gavel, obviously using language which could not be printed in a family newspaper. Joe Rauh insists to this day: "We won the decibel vote."

But the decibel vote did not count. In the early morning hours of July 15th Rauh and other ADA leaders paid for their support of Kennedy. Vi and John Gunther distinctly remember Stevenson supporters "pounding on our door at 4 a.m. demanding to know how many pieces of Joe Kennedy's silver we had got for our work." The fallout from the Democratic convention of 1960 is still coming down within ADA.

Rauh unburdened himself of his experience in a letter to a friend shortly after the convention: "The simplest way I can put my feelings is to say that I was misled." In his efforts to get liberal support after West Virginia, Rauh said, Kennedy had indicated that he wanted to be nominated by the North without Southern support "because he

felt this was the way to get elected and the way to put across the
liberal program he had in mind." Rauh had felt he had positive assurances that the Vice-President would be "some Midwestern liberal."
And, in the last days before the nomination, Robert Kennedy had
"knocked down the Johnson thing several times."

"It was against this background of no-compromise-with-Southern-
conservatism that I worked for Jack against the Stevenson movement.
This was no easy thing. I think I received more vilification for supporting Kennedy over Stevenson than I ever got for defending Bill
Remington."

Rauh indicated that he would not volunteer to work in the campaign, but "It's still a great platform. Maybe my best service will be
to spend the next four years reminding President Kennedy through
such forms of communication as remain available that he is obligat-
ed to put it into effect."

"The Lesser of Two Evils". In the weeks following the Democratic
convention, as the country took a brief time out from politics and
Senator Kennedy struggled through the special Congressional session
which was to have been Senator Johnson's stepping-stone to the
Presidency, a strange, agonizing debate began to build up within ADA.
Most ADA debates were agonizing, and some had been strange indeed,
but never had there been one to compare with this. The question
was whether or not ADA should endorse the Democratic ticket selected at Los Angeles. There were a number of things wrong, it seemed,
with John F. Kennedy.

Prior to 1960 ADA's contacts with Kennedy were conducted primarily through its Massachusetts chapter, and the relationship had
been distant, occasionally turbulent. While the state ADA had
endorsed Kennedy in his early House races, its support had not been
wildly enthusiastic. In 1952, moreover, a small cold war broke out between ADA and the Kennedy people, particularly Joseph Kennedy,
over the question of McCarthyism. Kennedy, making his first Senate race against the presumably formidable Henry Cabot Lodge, Jr.,
needed all the help he could get and wanted ADA's endorsement. Gard-
ner Jackson, an old-time New Dealer close to Kennedy, the ADA,
and labor, served as negotiator. ADA agreed to back Kennedy on
condition that he issue a clear statement denouncing McCarthy.
Apparently, Kennedy accepted this condition and asked Jackson to
draft the statement, hoping at the same time to get Representative
John McCormack to sign it with him. When Jackson presented his

draft—a ringing denunciation of McCarthy—to the Kennedy command, he met a cool reception. All versions of the story agree that Joe Kennedy assailed Jackson in abusive terms, accused him of trying to destroy his son's political career, praised McCarthy, and declared that the statement would not be issued. Kennedy himself took neither side in the dispute. The statement was not made public, and Kennedy ignored the McCarthy issue in his campaign.

Kennedy explained to Sam Beer, a Harvard professor active in the Massachusetts ADA and later national chairman, that he "could not run on an anti-McCarthy platform in Massachusetts." Joe Rauh agrees that "Kennedy couldn't be expected to stand up to McCarthy with a Catholic constituency when Humphrey, with a Protestant constituency, didn't stand up to him on the Communist Control Act."

Here was the classic problem of the difference between noncompromising, independent liberals and a politician's assessment of political realities. With the passage of time, some in ADA came around to an appreciation of the politician's difficulties. But most ADA people saw it as a failure of nerve on Kennedy's part, and they did not forget it.

Kennedy's subsequent performance in the Senate was not overly impressive to ADA, despite the high rating he received in its annual assessment of Congressional voting. In the 1956 clash between Kefauver and Kennedy for the Vice-Presidential nomination, "everybody in ADA was for Kefauver," according to one ADA leader. (Kefauver is one of the few politicians for whom ADA members seem to have an almost unreserved admiration. As a Southerner, he is—by definition—a sinner, and the liberals like nothing better than to see a sinner get religion.)

As Kennedy began to take on the coloration of a serious Presidential candidate in 1958 and 1959, the liberals' doubts about him became more acute. In September, 1959, Allen Taylor, director of the New York State ADA, forwarded to Ted Sorensen a long memorandum entitled "Liberals' Doubts About Kennedy and How to Handle Them." Taylor listed "religion," "liberalism," and "youth and inexperience" as the primary reasons for liberal coolness toward Kennedy.

"Religion is the major element in the liberals' doubts about Kennedy," said Taylor, although "it is rarely mentioned out loud." "There is something puzzling about anti-Catholic feeling as it applies to Kennedy." Despite the liberal disenchantment with Mayor Wagner of New York, Taylor noted that "the Catholic issue was not raised against

him by liberals." It was not raised against Frank Hogan, "even though
he was put over by DeSapio, a Catholic, against Finletter, and the
liberals were bitterly disappointed." Then why is it raised against
Kennedy? Perhaps because "the Presidency is different," answered
Taylor, "but I suspect it is because Kennedy is associated in the public
mind with Catholicism to a much greater degree than other prominent
Catholics, in part because his father is frequently identified as a
leading Catholic layman." Taylor's advice was to meet the religious
issue head on. "It is important to get this issue out of the subcon-
scious and on the table for frank discussion."

On the question of Kennedy's liberalism, Taylor noted that "Many
liberals doubt that Kennedy is a real liberal. Mrs. Roosevelt's comments have had an effect. Yet what the liberals are willing to accept
from Stevenson, they criticize in Kennedy." Taylor thought this
was partially due to a lack of knowledge about Kennedy's stand on
issues and was partly an offshoot of the religious question. "A great deal
of missionary work needs to be done in acquainting liberals with
Kennedy's record and public statements on issues."

Kennedy's "youth and inexperience" was a less important issue, but
liberals were aware of the dangers it might pose in foreign policy.

These and other liberal doubts had not been resolved by the primary
campaigns and the Democratic convention. But ADA could not
simply wash its hands of Kennedy and sit out the election, and the
national board was scheduled to meet August 27th to decide the
question of endorsement of the Democratic ticket.

Normally, ADA's staff would have prepared an endorsement to
which the board members would have given perfunctory approval.
This had been the practice in earlier years. But on the eve of the
board meeting Vi Gunther reported that she was not submitting a
draft because "I am rather nervous of having any language emanate
from the staff in view of the fact that there seems to be such a sharp
division of opinion among board members."

In the previous days letters had been coming in to the national
office from board members and plain members expressing very divergent views. Former Senator Herbert Lehman wanted ADA "to
place the stamp of its unreserved approval" upon Kennedy's candidacy: "Senator Kennedy must be elected not only because the
alternative would be tragic for America but also because his election would place in the White House a man clearly and unequivocally
committed to the most liberal program that has ever been presented
to the American public in a major party platform within my memory.'

A New Jersey ADA official had written: "I regard the alternatives to be considered at the board meeting ridiculous. Obviously we must support Kennedy over Nixon. Anything else is nonsense. Not worth debating."

But from another New Jersey chapter came the word: "In our view Senator Kennedy does not measure up to the principles which guide ADA. An endorsement of Kennedy will reinforce the already prevalent belief that ADA is subservient to the Democratic party." Still a third New Jersey member felt that ADA should withhold endorsement of the ticket. "Such endorsement will neither help Kennedy, hurt Nixon, nor do the ADA and American liberalism any good. With so many reservations regarding Kennedy and Johnson, it may be especially prudent for ADA to remain aloof."

A Texas ADA leader also questioned the wisdom of an endorsement so early in the campaign: "I believe there is a lot of truth in what Norman Thomas says in evaluating the two candidates and programs—that to shake them up in a sack and bounce them out without their party labels, that both Kennedy and Nixon might come out fairly close to agreeing on an approach to most every problem that they conceive confronting them." The Texan wanted endorsement withheld until he could see what Lyndon Johnson was going to do: "The South, and it seems to me the nation, is going to be quite interested in whether we have Lyndon Johnson, the Liberal, or Lyndon Johnson, the Conservative, campaigning. If it is Lyndon Johnson, the Conservative, then the next question is how far is Mr. Kennedy going to go with that sort of nonsense."

Two days prior to the meeting of the national board, the New York State ADA board voted to endorse the Kennedy-Johnson ticket by a 16-15 margin.

At the national board meeting only members-at-large and chapter members or their designated alternates had the right to vote. The following excerpts are taken from a typescript of the proceedings:

Massachusetts: "Board agreed to endorse Senator Kennedy, though there was some controversy. Believed ADA should endorse Kennedy and that ADA should take active role. Believed we should accept statement of nominees that they would attempt to put platform into effect."

Pittsburgh: "When Schlesinger came out for Kennedy Pittsburgh people felt he must have something they had not seen before. Chapter earlier had favored Stevenson."

Dallas: "Think ADA has higher duty than endorsing lesser of two evils. Should endorse Democratic platform but no candidate."

D.C. Chapter: "D.C. agreed to endorse Democratic ticket. Endorsement emphasis should be based on content of platform. Should refer to Senator Johnson in constructive way. Should not belabor him for sins of past, but should hope he would support platform pledges."

Chicago: "Before convention Chicago overwhelmingly approved Stevenson first and Humphrey second. Thinks majority would approve Kennedy over Nixon. Doubtful about Johnson."

St. Louis: "Unanimous vote that ADA should endorse Democratic ticket though some hostility expressed."

Youngstown, Ohio: "Voted 80-20 to endorse Kennedy. Those opposing endorsement much more fervent."

Nassau: "9-2 in favor of endorsement. Very little enthusiasm with one exception."

West Side, N.Y.: "Majority for position we don't trust Kennedy and don't like Johnson but Nixon so bad we have to do something."

Brooklyn: "On executive committee three of four members voted for Kennedy. Thought Kennedy far superior person and platform something liberals should seek to put into operation."

East Westchester, N.Y.: Informal poll showed slight majority in favor of no endorsement by ADA at this point. Thought national board should hold off."

Philadelphia: "Board should endorse Kennedy but should say nothing good about Johnson."

Essex County, N.J.: "No feeling for Kennedy. Strong feeling against Nixon. General feeling wait and see."

Middlesex, N.J.: "Board hotbed of Kennedy support. Does not know about membership. Suspects many would oppose endorsement of Kennedy."

Los Angeles: "Those who worked hard for Stevenson in 1952 and 1956 now working hard for Kennedy."

San Francisco: "Took part in crusade for Stevenson. After convention Stevenson urged group in San Francisco that Nixon was simply impossible."

Campus Division: "Division divided. Three proposals, endorsement, no endorsement and endorsement with reservations all defeated."

Each of the following paragraphs is an excerpt of remarks of different members of the board at large:

"Feels ticket should be endorsed. Between two tickets Kennedy is more liberal. What is happening in special Congressional session suggests some things which we have blamed on Johnson have not been his fault."

"No qualms about how he will vote. We cannot vote for Kennedy without voting for Johnson and Bobby Kennedy. We should give gracious endorsement, not one that will do more harm than good. We would be in sorry position if we did not endorse."

"Thinks it would be embarrassing for Kennedy because of work ADA did in preparing platform if we did not endorse him."

"We ought to approach decision strictly from point of view of ADA board members rather than Democratic officials. ADAers different from party people. If there are doubts about ticket as a whole those doubts can only be resolved if liberals work so hard for ticket that they demonstrate in election that it is liberal support that is responsible for election. Therefore let us endorse, if we do endorse, with enthusiasm. But strongly opposes any endorsement. ADA is not in business of choosing lesser of evils . . . Time for ADA to remain enthusiastically silent."

"For endorsement. Thinks everyone has qualms. How often do we have choices when we do not have qualms? We live in a real world where we have doubt. Difference between Kennedy and Nixon is so great, prospects for forward movement with Kennedy are so great it is not a matter of two evils."

"Thinks New York and California could be lost to Nixon and liberals could be responsible for Nixon's election. Qualms of American liberalism Nixon's secret weapon . . . Kennedy could be defeated by a few votes here and there. We would all feel dejected."

"Thinks reaction to Kennedy has no logical basis. He is chilly and ruthless but other great politicians the same. Problem obviously personal. We feel this is a man without conviction even though he has a good voting record. We are afraid he does not believe in anything except ambition. What we have against him is not his record but his political style. Stevenson is a Greek figure, Kennedy Roman. Intellectuals have never liked Romans. But we are not voting on style. We must permit him to grow up. He has traveled from his family. Under Eisenhower we have had conservatism tempered by incompetence. Under Nixon we would not get incompetence. Temper of liberalism is a very bad one. We should not come to grief through a paralysis of perfectionism."

"Cannot believe there is a single member on this board who would not like to see Kennedy elected President against the grim alternative of Nixon. Should we decide here that we don't propose to tell mem-

bers, friends and supporters of ADA that we are going to vote for
Kennedy? Thinks we can endorse Kennedy with no reservations what-
soever. Should say that Johnson does not represent our views. Thinks
Johnson will have something to say about us and we should get in
first lick."

"Not at all certain endorsement can galvanize liberals into active
workers. We should not feel ADA is crucial to campaign. We feel
apathetic because Kennedy follows traditional centrist policies. He
kicked the left in teeth and embraced right wing of party within twelve
hours of nomination. We should let him know he cannot take liberals
for granted."

"Vice-Presidential candidate is not an issue since we have objected
to Vice-Presidential candidates before."

"We are united by contempt for Nixon. Nixon is for scarcity and
against growth. Bad internationally. We must endorse now. Kennedy cannot win election without liberal support."

"It is a choice of evils in this campaign as it always is. Cannot
forgive Kennedy's failure to express himself on McCarthy issue. But
we know what Nixon represents. He is a great menace and more of a
menace than Eisenhower because he has brains. There is tremendous
danger. The evils on one side are negligible and on the other side
tremendous. If we fail to take position we are proclaiming ourselves
a middle-aged organization and spiritually bankrupt."

"Kennedy has not shown leadership. In 1958 liberal Congress killed
by Johnson. Thinks it is up to Kennedy to show us. We can endorse platform. Thinks there should be another meeting of national
board to determine question of endorsement. We have not been
shown leadership, liberalism, or integrity."

"There is no way under the Constitution we can vote for Kennedy
without voting for Johnson. Kennedy was not our first choice but we
cannot help that. He does have liberal record and has shown liberal
leadership in past two or three years. We have to be positive. This
is a chance to demonstrate that a Catholic can be President. Kennedy has subscribed to separation of Church and State."

"Kennedy has the makings of a great President. Consider fact that
many people with same opinion as ours think of Kennedy not as
lesser of two evils but as good man and one who has displayed
character."

Debate was closed after several hours of what the *ADA World*
termed "vigorous discussion" and one staff member called "the biggest
row we ever had." A motion postponing a decision on endorsement

until October was defeated, 29 votes to 10. Rauh moved that the board endorse the Democratic ticket. Another discussion broke out over whether a Schlesinger draft embodying Rauh's motion was not "too fulsome" in its praise of Kennedy, and some of Schlesinger's adjectives went under the axe. One member moved to eliminate reference to "the Democratic ticket" and endorse only "Kennedy for President." This motion drew a 20-20 deadlock, and the Democratic ticket was saved only by chairman Sam Beer's tie-breaking vote.

The board's statement was issued to the press on August 28th. The full text follows:

"Americans for Democratic Action today endorses John F. Kennedy for the Presidency of the United States. We urge all liberal and independent voters to join with us in enthusiastic support of the Democratic platform and the national Democratic ticket. Active liberal participation in this election is essential if liberalism is to play an effective role in the next four years.

"John F. Kennedy is well qualified by record, by ability and by personal commitment for the Presidency. In the critical fields of humane concern—foreign affairs, economic and social policy, minority rights —he stands with conviction. He has displayed the qualities of political skill essential to transform the Democratic platform pledges into national policy.

"The Democratic platform of 1960 deserves the ardent support of all those interested in bringing peace to the world and abundance to the United States. It is the best platform ever adopted by any party in the history of the Republic. To make sure that this platform will be carried out, we call for the election not only of a Democratic President but of liberal majorities in both Houses of Congress. Only a liberal President and a liberal Congress can circumvent the Republican-Dixiecrat coalition which, through vetoes, filibusters, committee chairmanships and other forms of obstruction, has so successfully frustrated the liberal forces in recent years.

"Our belief in the necessity of Senator Kennedy's election is strengthened by a contemplation of the alternative. Vice President Nixon throughout his political career has represented the most depressing forces in American politics. He is the apostle of the tired, unimaginative, resentful, complacent conservatism which clings fearfully to the status quo and automatically recoils from new policies and new ideas. To elevate him to the Presidency would be to condemn our country to four more years of drift, sloth, mediocrity and materialism. At this point in world history, four more such years might well work permanent damage to the safety and welfare of our country. The best way to return to the broad highway of American liberalism is to elect the Democratic ticket."

Thus, through earnest argument, long soul-searching, and fearful contemplation of the grim alternative, ADA pulled itself—kicking and screaming—into the Kennedy camp.

It Does Make a Difference. With the endorsement question settled, ADA set out in the weeks preceding election day to make its endorsement meaningful. In previous Presidential elections its efforts had been directed primarily toward registration of voters, get-out-the-vote drives, and attempts to influence groups and individuals on the fringes of the liberal movement. It had not wasted much time preaching to the converted, its own members and known sympathizers. But in 1960 ADA was forced into an internal missionary campaign to convince liberal apostates that there were meaningful differences between Kennedy and Nixon.

In November national director Vi Gunther reported that "the activities of the national office since the ADA board meeting in August have been almost exclusively concerned with the election campaign. The national staff interpreted ADA's endorsement of the national Democratic ticket as a directive to concentrate on the success of that ticket."

Among other activities, the staff published a weekly Campaign Bulletin which went to editors, reporters, and other opinion formers, and noted proudly a Kennedy aide's description of the Bulletin as "the liveliest of all the campaign material that crossed my desk." In October ADA initiated a round-robin letter signed by prominent liberals—including Mrs. Roosevelt—urging Kennedy's election on the basis of his foreign policy position. The letter, mailed to 50,000 individuals, also appeared as an advertisement in the *Saturday Review.*

At the request of the Democratic National Committee, ADA distributed 10,000 copies of a special "civil rights" edition of the Committee's campaign paper, "New Frontier." William Taylor, then ADA's lobbyist, now Special Assistant to the Staff Director of the Civil Rights Commission, worked with the Civil Rights section of the Democratic National Committee and served as a staff aide to Kennedy's Civil Rights Conference in New York.

The Independent Voters of Illinois, ADA's Chicago affiliate, put 1,-200 workers into 400 precincts in support of the national, state and local Democratic tickets. IVI reported that "the result has been a tremendous quickening of enthusiasm and an all-out determination to help make Jack Kennedy the next President of the United States." Philadelphia reported that ADA people had taken over the area's "Citizens for Kennedy" organization, despite an effort by the Democratic machine to shut out the independent liberals. More than a million pieces of literature had been distributed in the Philadelphia area, and the ADA was succeeding in combating the "I don't care" attitude which had characterized the early days of the campaign. Pittsburgh ADA people were heading the Western Pennsylvania Citizens group and had organized twenty-three counties as compared with five in 1956. ADA chapters in Cleveland, Detroit, St. Louis, Akron, Boston, and other cities also were active.

In September the national office issued a release on Kennedy's voting record showing that his overall average of ADA support was 90% during his fourteen years in Congress. Kennedy had a "liberal quotient" of 100% for the last three years.

ADA speakers—particularly Schlesinger, Nathan, Rauh and Wechsler—made the round of chapters urging their fellow members to forget their Stevenson and Humphrey hangovers and get to work. Rauh, forgetting his earlier pique at Kennedy, told the Cleveland chapter: "Sitting on the sidelines won't get the job done. Senator Kennedy's civil rights task will be hard enough in the years ahead no matter how big his margin of victory. It will be well-nigh impossible if his margin of victory is in the Southern states which oppose that part of his platform."

Arthur Schlesinger's surprisingly successful campaign tract, *Kennedy or Nixon: Does It Make a Difference?*, was aimed squarely at those liberals who still thought it didn't.

The need for such missionary work had been demonstrated in September when Kennedy forces in the New York State ADA convention narrowly beat back a move to repudiate the national board's endorsement by striking all reference to the Kennedy-Johnson ticket. "This would have had the effect of sweeping Kennedy under the rug as the National Board did with Johnson by not mentioning his name." In October the chairman of the New York ADA wrote Kennedy explaining the group's efforts—consisting primarily of a rally billed "Kennedy or Nixon: It *Does* Make a Difference"—to dispel the doubts of independent liberals about him.

James M. Burns, Kennedy's biographer, made a last-minute assault on these doubts in the liberal house organ, the *New Republic*. Burns explained that his own doubts about Kennedy had been dispelled, "but many liberals are in effect still sitting out the 1960 election." Burns thought the main reason was that Kennedy lacked "liberalism's tragic quality . . . By liberalism's tragic quality, I mean that so many of its finest and most passionate causes . . . have been lost causes, that the pursuit of great causes has often been far more rewarding than their realization." For liberals, Burns added, "Kennedy is — or at least has been — too successful. His seems to be a liberalism without tears."

As the campaign progressed, many in ADA became more sanguine. By the end of September Vi Gunther was reporting that the Kennedy campaign obviously had gained momentum: "The hesitations and anxieties of the independent liberals who were antipathetic to Kennedy are being diminished somewhat simply by the passage of time, i.e., by the nearing of election day. The conduct of the candidate himself has won him support among these people."

And as the polls seemed to show Kennedy pulling ahead, the crowds began to swarm after him, and the press began to predict a landslide, some in ADA became too sanguine for their own good. By late October Joe Rauh, ever the enthusiast, was offering four-to-one odds that Kennedy would carry forty states.

Did ADA Make A Difference? What effect did ADA's belated but strenuous work for Kennedy have? ADA leaders admit that they cannot "deliver" a single vote in Presidential elections, as that term is understood by professional politicians. They do feel that ADA's arguments in behalf of Kennedy had a significant impact on the mass of die-hard Stevenson supporters who could not be reached by the professional Democratic machines. They could point to Philadelphia, where ADA's smooth operation had helped to produce an "incredible majority" of 326,000 votes for Kennedy, while he was carrying Pennsylvania as a whole by only 131,000. The Philadelphia ADA had done its most intensive work in the suburban counties surrounding the city, and here Eisenhower's 175,000-vote margin of 1956 had been cut to 91,000 for Nixon. Allegheny County, where the Pittsburgh ADA focused its main effort, had gone for Eisenhower by a 70,000 margin but was carried for Kennedy by 110,000 votes. In other areas ADA could make similar if less dramatic claims.

But, measured against the vast expenditure of time, money, and sweat which goes into a Presidential campaign in the United States, ADA's work for Kennedy was negligible. It could not begin to claim that it had supplied the margin of victory. For that matter, no group

—or perhaps every group—could make that claim in 1960. For the margin was so close that Kennedy could reject all such claims, or —conversely—any group of people numerous enough to fill a small room with the President could claim that they elected him.

One suspects, moreover, that ADA's efforts may very well have been unnecessary. The history of American liberalism in the 1950's offers strong support for the suspicion that not a single member of ADA—and very few liberals holding similar beliefs—would have voted against Kennedy or stayed at home when faced with the "grim alternative" of a "dangerous, menacing, competent, and brainy" Richard Nixon.

Chapter XIII

KENNEDY, THE ADA, AND AMERICAN LIBERALISM

The Ike Age ended with the election of 1960. The eight years of stagnation and sloth, bluff and blunder, had passed. The President-elect—while he might be sunburned—was no Coolidge, and he had promised to get the country moving again. The missing link in ADA's list of essential elements for a successful liberalism presumably had been forged. ADA could look forward to the now unaccustomed sight of the unparalled power of the Presidency being brought to bear to realize the bright promises of the platform and campaign and to help solve the problems it had been pointing to for a decade. So, at least, it seemed in January of 1961 when the *ADA World* hailed the Kennedy Inaugural: "In every line of his thought-packed Address, the passionate commitment and deep ardor of the youngest President the Republic has ever elected shone through."

The beginning was auspicious. The interim between election and inauguration had been taken up primarily with selection of the men who were to fill high posts in the Administration, men who would—in effect—act as ball bearings and oil to the great engine of the Presidency. ADA, which had originated as a "New-Deal-in-exile" and quarelled continually with Truman over the matter of appointments, had some interest in this process of selection. Within three weeks after election day Sam Beer, a personal friend of the President, tendered his congratulations, then added:

"I am writing now to convey to you the strong hope within ADA that your first acts as President will demonstrate to the nation and to the world that your goal of a New Frontier for America will be fashioned with the help of men identified in the public mind as forward-looking, imaginative and courageous public servants. ADA has no interest in individuals as such; however, we feel that the appointment to high public office of such men as Chester Bowles, Orville Freeman, Adlai Stevenson, and G. Mennen Williams will signify to the world your determination to shape your Administration in the image of your eloquently liberal campaign."

All the men named—and many others—were appointed to high and low posts in the Administration.

Six months earlier William S. White had hailed the Johnson nomination as signifying an end to the influence of "the quivering crackpots of the left wing" of the Democratic party. "Farewell to the knee-jerk liberals, like Americans for Democratic Action." Now the liberals had returned, in force, and the exile was over.

As we saw in Chapter I, the appointment of numerous members of ADA to positions in the Kennedy Administration has agitated right-wing publicists considerably. Neither Kennedy nor the ADA has heard the last of their complaints by any means. To them, these appointments are political payoffs to people who really do harbor dark designs on the future of the Republic.

The facts are otherwise, although reasonable men may disagree over details. Responsible Republican conservatives on Capitol Hill—who until recently had some small hand in arranging political *quid pro quos*—profess to see certain elements of the payoff in the ADA appointments but manage to view the situation with equanimity. But these men do not claim to be completely impartial observers. Moreover, they know a good stick when they see one and consider it only proper performance of their duty to use anything they can lay hands upon to beat a Democratic Administration.

So far as the public and private evidence indicates, however, not one of the appointments was due to the appointee's association with ADA. Bowles, Freeman, Stevenson, Williams, and all the others had many things to recommend them to the President other than their rather tenuous ties with ADA. Some of these men did hold valid political checks which had to be cashed, but the debt was not run up on an ADA account book.

There is evidence that some of the appointments were made in spite of the ADA association, or in ignorance of it. The appointment of Jim Loeb might, at first glance, seem the most suspicious. While he had been active in liberal politics from the early 1940's onward, Loeb was no big name. He was virtually unknown outside the narrow circle of liberal and labor groups, and he had spent the years since 1953 in semi-retirement as editor of a small newspaper in upstate New York. His political reputation, such as it was, had been made as national director of ADA.

In previous Administrations, heavy contributions to campaign funds had been considered as uniquely qualifying the giver for an ambassadorial post. Loeb admits to contributing twenty-five dollars to the Kennedy campaign, then asking for a refund when the candidate said something he didn't like. He tells of a brief visit to the Oval Room, during which the President congratulated his new ambassador to Peru and remarked: "The last time we worked together was in Wisconsin, wasn't it, Jim?" Loeb had been in Wisconsin, but on the Humphrey side of the barricades.

Loeb's appointment can be traced primarily to two factors. As a former Spanish teacher, he spoke the language of the Peruvians. He had been closely associated with the anti-Communist, anti-Franco exiles in Latin America and thus had contacts with the democratic liberals who would play a large part in operating the Alliance for Progress program in their countries. Loeb suspects also that a highly-placed friend in Washington had something to do with his appointment, but if this was a political payoff it was a rather unique one in the history of such affairs.

There are, in fact, many more ADA members or former members in the Administration than have been named publicly. One such case is that of Lawrence O'Brien, the President's key liasion man with Congress. O'Brien usually is identified as a member of the "Irish Mafia" group in the White House, an informal clique of professionals who came up through the rough and ready school of Massachusetts politics and who are seen as something of a counterweight to the liberal advisers surrounding the President. O'Brien is no longer a member of ADA, but he was very active in its early formation in Massachusetts. The extent of "infiltration" is greater than Senator Goldwater dreams.

It is difficult for an outsider to evaluate the significance of these appointments. Executive advisers, particularly those close to the President, operate in an aura of anonymity. They are the President's men, and their relationship with him is privileged even from the scrutiny of Congress.

Several things seem clear, however. The ADA appointments are not political payoffs, and the appointees are not running the government. It is ridiculous to point to a specific Administration policy and say that that policy was written in the ADA office and put across with the President by his ADA advisers. The advice which they give him, assuming that it is not contradictory, is only part of a wide stream of advice which flows up to the President from many sources. The picture of a passive, captive President being manipulated by ADA underlings is merely an extension of the caricature which conservatives have painted since 1950.

On the other hand, these appointments are not wholly without significance. The fact remains that President Kennedy has surrounded himself with many individuals who were associated, through membership or through a community of belief, with Americans for Democratic Action. And in most cases, his choices were free of political claims. The explanation seems to be simply that the President wanted these men.

In a 1959 speech to the Philadelphia Roosevelt Day Dinner, Senator Kennedy addressed himself to what he apparently saw as the major facet of ADA:

"I am particularly happy to be addressing the members of this organization tonight. For you have demonstrated, on the local and national levels, that you have the creative talent, the energy and the know-how to play a major role in the formulation of new programs and policies. A political party cannot always objectively reexamine our nation's policies with respect to any important group in the electorate — whether they be taxpayers, farmers, union members or any others. Your organization, on the other hand, can be free of such restraints. Practicing politicians are too often caught up in the urgent and the immediate, instead of finding time to think about the important and the long-range. Your wealth of talented minds, on the other hand, has no such handicap."

As President, Kennedy was looking for talented minds and took them wherever he found them, whether in the State Department of a former Republican Administration, the state offices of Midwestern capitals, or the other side of the fence in Wisconsin. It was inevitable that he would find a good many in ADA.

There is, moreover, another side to these appointments. The President—in effect—holds hostages which could be used against ADA if he wished. There is no doubt about where the primary allegiance of Freeman, Goldberg, Ribicoff, Schlesinger, Weaver, Williams, *et al.*, would lie in such a case.

ADA leaders insist that no such case has arisen, that they would not be intimidated if it did, and that Hubert Humphrey as Assistant Majority Leader of the Senate is an even better hostage. There is little evidence that ADA has been intimidated, except perhaps in the Bowles case. For when Chester Bowles was buffeted about in the State Department and finally eased out, ADA said nothing in public. Privately, some of the group's leaders profess to believe that the President had good reason to be dissatisfied with Bowles' performance in the State Department. Perhaps, but during the Truman and Eisenhower Administrations ADA's reaction to similar cases was blistering.

Despite gratification that some of its leading figures had found places in the Administration, ADA was not interested solely—or pri-

marily—in patronage. National chairman Sam Beer wrote Kenneth
O'Donnell, the President's appointments secretary, just prior to the
Kennedy-ADA conference: "We would like to pay our respects.
More particularly, we should like to ask what we can do to help his
program. I want to make it clear that it is program, not jobs, in
which we are interested."

Beer later reported that the conference dealt chiefly with questions
of economic policy and civil rights. The ADA officers "felt that in
both fields the President's objectives were ours, and that he was attempting and would continue to attempt to pursue them just as far
as he thought he politically could. We came away with heightened
admiration and respect for Kennedy and convinced that he is a man
of extraordinary integrity and a liberal."

Leap-Year Liberalism. Very shortly, however, ADA was beginning
to wonder if the great promises of the Democratic platform and
campaign were to be part of the Kennedy program, whether they had
been taken in by the "leap-year liberalism" which Presidential candidates exhibited every four years, and if the New Frontier was not to
prove a rhetorical facade behind which the business of government
would be carried on as usual.

The wondering actually began before the White House conference
even before President Kennedy took office, during the traditional
effort to change the Congressional ground rules which so frustrated
liberals. At the opening of every Congress since 1948, ADA had
pushed for two major changes: modification or abolition of the filibuster rule in the Senate and curbing of the power of the Rules Committee in the House. The Democratic platform and candidate
Kennedy had pledged both.

In the 86th Congress liberals succeeded in modifying Senate Rule
Twenty-Two to provide for termination of debate by two-thirds of
the Senators present and voting, rather than two-thirds of all members.
The victory was meaningless, since a filibuster would bring every
Senator able to walk to the floor to vote. As the 87th Congress opened, Senator Clinton Anderson of New Mexico offered a resolution
which would permit cloture to be invoked by three-fifths of the members present. The Democratic and Republican whips, Senators
Humphrey and Kuchel, joined in a substitute motion to allow cloture
by a simple majority. Vice-President Nixon, ironically cast in the
role of the liberals' ally, cleared the way for a vote on both resolutions by holding that the Senate was not bound by previous rules,

therefore the rules changes themselves were not subject to a filibuster. Preliminary debate indicated that the Humphrey-Kuchel resolution would fall short of a majority, but the Anderson motion had a good chance of passage. The liberals awaited word from President-elect Kennedy, who would take office shortly and whose legislative program could be enhanced by modification of the filibuster.

The word which came was that if Mr. Kennedy were a Senator he would vote for majority rule as he had in the past, but he would not make the filibuster an Administration issue. Here, for the first time, was the solicitous concern for Congressional *amour propre* which remains today a constant frustration for the President's liberal supporters. With no Administration pressure on, Senate Majority Leader Mike Mansfield succeeded—by the narrow margin of 50-46—in referring both proposals to the Rules Committee, thus preserving the filibuster. The ADA *Legislative Newsletter* noted that Kennedy could have altered the result without becoming embroiled in a public fight and charged him with "maintaining an attitude of inertia while his policies received a setback and his liberal supporters an almost humiliating defeat."

In the House ADA wanted reinstatement of the so-called "21-day" rule, which would prevent the Rules Committee from blocking legislation indefinitely while it forced compromises to suit its conservative membership. Liberals had put across this rule in 1949 following Truman's victory only to lose it promptly at the beginning of the 82nd Congress. After several weeks of maneuvering in the 87th Congress, Speaker Rayburn—backed by vigorous White House pressure—succeeded only in enlarging the committee by adding two new Democratic and one new Republican member. ADA noted that the change was unlikely to loosen the grip of the conservative coalition over legislation.

With the 87th Congress only three weeks old, and President Kennedy in office only four days, liberals thought events were beginning to bear a suspicious resemblance to the early days of the 81st Congress, when the last Democratic President found that his writ did not run up to Capitol Hill. In the liberal book Presidents were supposed to manipulate Congress, as Woodrow Wilson and F.D.R. had done, or— if that proved impossible—go to the country and give it hell in the Truman style. President Kennedy was doing neither. To ADA, Washington was "a place of suspended animation and suspended judgment." In his Inaugural Address the President had said: "Now the trumpet summons us again." ADA asked, in words once applied to Eisenhower: "But who can say what the result will be if the trumpet give forth an uncertain sound?"

But the ADA itself was uncertain; despite the ill omens, it was not yet passing judgment on the Kennedy Administration. "Most observers have a healthy respect for the power of a strong President to move a recalcitrant Congress," the *Newsletter* noted, "and they believe Mr. Kennedy has both the will and the ability to alter the political climate through the exercise of determined leadership."

As the Kennedy program began to unfold, ADA remained sympathetic but uncertain and puzzled. It hailed the State of the Union and Economic Messages to Congress; in these the President "did his best to instil a sense of urgency in Congress." He was "apparently listening to the advice of his liberal advisers and implementing it very vigorously."

Two weeks later ADA was questioning "the wisdom of major strategy decisions made by the Kennedy Administration in placing its economic recovery and social welfare programs before Congress" and bewailing the "absence of any sense of urgency in a closely divided Congress." The Administration was placing primary emphasis upon quick passage of its unemployment compensation and aid to depressed areas legislation. The first bill differed from Eisenhower's 1958 proposal in only one minor respect; Congress had passed a depressed areas bill by an overwhelming majority in 1959 only to face an Eisenhower veto. ADA argued that in these and other proposals—aid to education, medical care for the aged, housing—the Administration had been "guided by a penchant to keep the budget from going very far out of balance in the first two years." Kennedy was asking for too little and would get less, because "it will be virtually impossible to strengthen the recommendations of the Administration in Congress, and if the usual whittling-down process takes place in committee, on the floor, and in conference, the legislation may emerge as a pale shadow of the original program."

Many observers record that President Kennedy's obvious determination to get a depressed areas bill passed stemmed from experiences in the primary campaigns, when he had been shocked by the poverty he saw in the hills of West Virginia. In the early months of 1961, some liberals were wondering if it might be possible to find a West Virginia to fit other issues.

ADA was equally ambivalent about the Administration's education bill, which called for a three-year, $2.3 billion program of aid to public elementary and secondary schools. While a "reasonable start," the bill fell "far short" of what was needed and was only a "scaled-down version" of earlier proposals. In this case, moreover, ADA was unhappy about the work of one of the President's liberal advisers. In an effort to neutralize Southern opposition, HEW Secretary Abraham Ribicoff stated that he did not believe the executive branch had authority to withhold aid to racially segregated areas without Congressional authorization and that he opposed such action by Congress or the executive as a matter of policy. ADA assailed its former member for endangering school aid and other programs and accused him of making "insensitive and imprudent remarks."

On all the issues mentioned, it should be noted that ADA was not in opposition to the Administration, nor was it finding fault with the direction the Kennedy program was taking. Its criticism was that the President was not taking the bold initiative he had promised in the campaign, was not asking enough of Congress, was not pushing vigorously enough for what he did ask, and was tailoring his program in advance to meet conservative opposition.

By May, 1961, it was obvious that, as one ADA leader put it, "Kennedy is trying to take the country to the left, but not to the ADA frontier." The liberals were puzzled and confused. They had a President whose rhetoric could not be faulted, and rhetoric was a strong point with them. They brushed aside the contention that Kennedy's narrow victory over Nixon precluded any striking initiatives; he was President and should act like they thought a President should act. From one week to the next, they could not make up their minds whether to cheer or boo. On May 21st, T.R.B., the *New Republic* columnist, complained: "We get awfully sick of this 'moderation.' All during the Eisenhower Administration there was moderation. And again during the Johnson-Rayburn control of the 86th Congress. And now instead of Kennedy urgency there is some more moderation." In the next issue, however, T.R.B. was noting: "Kennedy is not flamboyant. The theatrics and emotion which liberal reformers adore he detests. They love an all-out, no compromise fight for principle and think it worth the cost even if they lose. Maybe it is. Kennedy isn't like that, he wants to win. He probably will win."

Gathering in Washington for their fourteenth annual convention, ADA members were—as usual—frustrated. Joe Rauh summed up the First Hundred Days of the Kennedy Administration as "100 days of caution." Delegates drew understanding laughs when, upon being asked "How's your wife?," replied "Compared to what?" National chairman Sam Beer, speaking to the press on the eve of the convention, expressed moderate criticism of some parts of the Kennedy program but hailed his Administration as "a brilliant and progressive one." Arthur Schlesinger, Jr., urged the delegates to go easy on criticism of Kennedy and told them no President could go faster in formulating new policies than public opinion would allow.

But it was obvious that neither Beer nor Schlesinger, but *New York Post* editor James Wechsler, spoke for the majority in ADA. In a speech punctuated by applause, Wechsler paid tribute to the Kennedy of 1960:

"Mr. Kennedy exhibited during most of the campaign qualities of human compassion and rough-minded intelligence that disarmed and captured us.

"To put last things first, he met the so-called 'Catholic issue' with gallantry and dignity.

"He spoke courageously of new beginnings in foreign policy.

"He identified himself with the longings of the under-privileged at home and abroad.

"At almost every point he reflected both the spirit and the substance of positions fashioned in the smoke-filled backrooms where ADA eggheads had gathered through so many long convention nights.

"He even dared to suggest that Quemoy and Matsu might not be worth atomic war.

"When Martin Luther King got into trouble in Georgia, Mr. Kennedy did not simply issue a pious remark; he and his brother did something about it.

"I do not mean to romanticize these matters. I merely suggest that John F. Kennedy found himself running for President on a platform that bore suspicious resemblance to the program and, perhaps more important, the attitudes of the movement assembled here."

Then Wechsler began to lay out the liberal bill of particulars against the Kennedy of 1961:

"I believe the essential question to which we should address ourselves is the gap between the great expectations of November, 1960, and the rough reality of May, 1961.

"Even more seriously, it is the gap between the liberalism that flourishes in so many bipartisan backyards during campaign autumns and withers between election seasons."

Wechsler felt the change in the Washington climate was due partly to the shock over the Cuban debacle, but it had begun much earlier:

"It began when Mr. Kennedy, in the first House vote on the wage-hour bill, suddenly confronted the ancient alliance between Southern Democrats and conservative Republicans.

"It began when the 'realists' started explaining to him that he was hardly President at all, that he survived by sufferance of the Southern contingent, that his margin of both electoral victory and Congressional rule was so narrow that he would have to abandon any great dreams."

Such a conception of the Presidential role would not solve the problems which candidate Kennedy had outlined so eloquently in the fall:

"Mr. Kennedy has proposed a series of moderate domestic legislative measures. They represent, I am sure, his own best judgment of what is 'practical' in the real political world. Yet in wide areas of the press they are branded 'extremist' or 'radical.'

"Too many newspapers in too many places are faithful echoes of the vested-interest lobbies now engaged in a massive assault on the very modest economic and social reforms advanced by the President.

"Too many have rallied to the offensive against all welfare programs now being unleashed by Mr. Nixon and the GOP Congressional leadership under that historic war-cry of reaction: 'Guns, not butter.'

"The battalions of the American Medical Association are still warning the sick and the enfeebled against the fatal potion of 'socialized medicine,' and imploring them to rise from their beds as one with the cry: 'Give me that old-time medicine.' The real estate lobby thunders its reminder to the slum-dweller: yours is the house beautiful if it was privately built; let no federal subsidy invade your castle. The opponents of federal aid to education tell the kiddies: pray, children, that no federally-constructed building replace that structure lest your teacher lose his freedom and your humble place of learning become a bright red schoolhouse.

"And so it goes in every area of distress. The most depressing thing about American political debate is its primitive level. Twenty-nine years after Franklin Delano Roosevelt's election, we are still arguing about whether the use of government funds to build a classroom in Oshkosh would cause the founding fathers to rise from their graves."

Wechsler noted that some would claim that any critical appraisal of the President at this time was ill-advised and ill-considered, a liberal luxury the country could not afford:

"I disagree.

"He has, I am sure, our sympathy, our prayers, and, yes, our confidence in a very fundamental sense. He commands our respect even when we differ with him.

"But he would be poorly served by us if we assembled here simply to hail his good works, rationalize his errors, ratify his retreats and pledge blind allegiance to his leadership.

"That is not our function.

"ADA is an independent liberal organization, or it is nothing.

"It is the conscience of the political community, or it is nothing.

"If ADA does nothing else, it must cut through the fog and absurdity and lift the level of our national discussion. If that requires our saying out loud that the President has proposed too little, not too much, let us say so. If that means we shall be damned as extremist by those who define a moderate as one who favors reduction of the oil depletion allowance from 27½ to 19¼ per cent, we shall survive the slur. If that means we must raise our voices against the kind of unholy compromises involved in the minimum wage bill, let no one tell us we are out of order.

"We must provide a thunder on the left that will not be mistaken for querulous lament.

"We must fight hardest on the most neglected areas of the new and old frontier."

Wechsler's speech was given in May, 1961, but it could be repeated today and still provide an accurate reflection of ADA's attitude toward the Kennedy Administration. As of this writing, nothing has happened to bridge the basic differences between Kennedy and the liberals which appeared in the first weeks of his term. An examination of these differences, issue by issue, shows—if anything—that liberal frustration has deepened and hardened into a suspicion that the New Frontier was, literally, only a *promised* land.

It should be noted that these differences are tactical rather than substantive. On only two issues has ADA come out in direct opposition to the Administration. In July, 1961, it spoke against a Justice Department bill which would permit federal and state law enforcement officials to gather evidence by wiretapping. ADA had all along been concerned about Kennedy's general civil liberties position, particularly when Robert Kennedy became Attorney-General. Despite vast respect for his abilities, ADA feels, as one member put it, that "Bobby just has no conception of the civil liberties problem. He thinks this game of catching crooks is like football, played without a referee and no rules." In recent weeks ADA has come out against the Administration's proposal for a privately owned space communications satellite system, urging instead that the system be owned and controlled by the government.

On other issues ADA's view is that the Kennedy program is all right so far as it goes, but it does not go far enough. Civil rights may be an exception. As noted earlier, civil rights became the number one liberal issue during the 1950's. Here the liberals felt they had an unequivocal commitment, both in the Democratic platform and from candidate Kennedy, that the new Administration would move quickly and vigorously in this area. This belief was heightened in the fall of 1960 when Kennedy commissioned Senator Joseph Clark and Representative Emanuel Celler to write a bill embodying the platform pledges. This legislation remained on the shelf in the early months of the 87th Congress and was ignored by the Administration when Clark and Celler introduced it.

According to one official who attended the Kennedy-ADA conference of February, 1961, the President indicated that he "did not want to be pushed" on civil rights. In the early months ADA honored this request by rejecting NAACP urging that it oppose the possible nomination of Senator William Fulbright of Arkansas as Secretary of State and by turning down a move by other civil rights organizations to set up an emergency conference to protest Kennedy's attitude on the Clark-Celler bill. In subsequent months, however, ADA became increasingly restive over the President's inaction on the legislative front. While pleased with such actions as vigorous Justice Department prosecution of voting rights violations and the Interstate Commerce Commission's strong measures against segregation in transportation, it disagrees with Kennedy's apparent belief that the civil rights problem must be kept out of Congress and be dealt with only through use of existing executive powers.

This difference over civil rights is closely related to the tactical differences between Kennedy and the ADA referred to above. In ADA's view the President committed a major blunder by trimming his entire legislative program to fit the Congressional obstacle course. It maintains, moreover, that he has not been successful even then. In summing up the Administration record in the first session of the 87th Congress, the *ADA World* noted:

"The legislative formula of the Democratic majority under a Democratic Administration has varied little from the formula developed when the Republican party controlled the White House. It is a formula of accommodation and compromise with the same coalition of Southerners and Republicans which had dominated the last several Congresses. It is a pattern of legislation by least common denominator which might have—but not certainly—been upset by strong Administration pushing for legislative goals. For whatever reason—the rapid acceleration of the international crisis, the slimness of his electoral victory, or simply a concept of Presidential posture—the President chose not to seek more than the barely possible from Congress. By and large that is what he got—or less.

"The President gave the Southern bloc in Congress exactly what it wanted—no civil rights legislation and no aid to the anti-filibuster fight. In return, they voted against him most of the time on the really significant issues."

Many observers have written about the "realism" of the Kennedy Administration and its masterful manipulation of political techniques in its dealings with Congress. The ADA feels otherwise, and an examination of its voting record for the first session of the 87th Congress offers some evidence for its contention. This record was analyzed in the manner explained in Chapter IX. In Senate and House a "liberal support percentage" was figured for Northern Democrats, Republicans, and Southern Democrats. Of ten Senate votes selected by ADA, nine were on issues in which the Administration took the same position as ADA. In the House, eight of the ten ADA positions also represented Administration positions. The other three votes were on issues on which the Administration took no public position. Thus, the figures given below can be said to measure support or opposition to Kennedy, not just to the ADA.

The results of this analysis show a support record for Southern Democrats in the Senate of 33 per cent, seven points less than their average over the previous six Congresses. (See Tables 2 and 3 on page 120 for the figures on the 81st through the 86th Congresses.) Republican Senators had approximately 27 per cent record, exactly the same as their average in previous Congresses. The Northern Democrats, on the other hand, were up to 89 per cent, higher than in any other Congress and ten points above their average.

In the House Southern Democratic Congressmen showed a liberal support record of 33 per cent, three points below their average. The Republican figure was 14 per cent, the lowest of any Congress and down twelve points from the average. The Northern Democratic record was 93 per cent, again higher than in any previous Congress and up five points from the average.

On the basis of this analysis, despite the qualifications which must be made, it can be argued that Kennedy's success, such as it was, was made possible by increased support among the Northern Democrats. Despite his conciliatory stance toward the Southern Democrats and

Republicans, on these issues the Kennedy approach succeeded only in pulling these two groups closer together in opposition to liberal legislation.

This whole argument can be reversed, of course. It can be maintained that without conciliation the record would have been worse. Here is the crux of the difference between Kennedy and liberals over the problem of the correct approach to Congress, and the matter cannot be settled by a few figures.

Kennedy has opted for the conciliatory approach. The liberals recognize that he has a real problem with Congress, but they want a wholesale assault on that obstacle, not the cloakroom give and take which was patented by Lyndon Johnson.

When asked to assess the future prospects of American liberalism under the Kennedy Administration, most ADA leaders are not sanguine about the short term. They are not placing bets on the long run, either, but in talking of the "second Kennedy Administration" they tend to fall back on what might be called a hopeful historical syllogism which goes something like this:

"Major premise: There is an historical correlation between liberalism and Great Presidents, at least in the 20th century United States.

"Minor premise: Kennedy wants very badly to go down in history as a Great President.

"Conclusion: Kennedy will—sooner or later—drop his conciliatory approach to Congress and go to the country with a fighting liberal program."

Even granting the history of the major premise and the psychology of the minor premise, at least two questions may be raised about the conclusion. The time may very well have come when the yardstick for measuring Presidents is fashioned on an international rather than a domestic scale. The Great President of the present and future may not be the one who found jobs for the unemployed, provided medical care for the aged, or saved the family farm, but the one who contained international Communism while keeping us out of war—assuming that even the greatest could no longer be expected to wage war successfully. Such a President presumably would devote more time, and money, to issues and problems of defense and foreign policy than to domestic policy. Even if successful, he would not be the President of the liberal syllogism, for liberals have not made their peace with foreign policy. Their scale for measuring Presidents still is calibrated largely on how they perform internally.

Secondly, there is a catastrophe syndrome lurking in the back-

ground of the liberal syllogism. Most liberals deny it, and their policies are designed to avert such an eventuality, but one senses an unspoken assumption that the Great President will respond as Franklin
Roosevelt did and turn left in reaction to an internal economic catastrophe. But the internal catastrophes of the present and future may
be of the creeping variety, not easily recognized. Also, the big catastrophes may be external, not internal, and the direction taken in
response to them may well be the opposite of what the liberals desire.

In the meantime, the pattern of suspicious toleration which has
existed between Kennedy and the liberals for two years is likely to continue. In its early days the ADA adopted a slogan which said, in part,
"Liberalism is a demanding faith." It was meant to be an inspirational
exhortation to the membership, but the words can have another mean-
ing. In its sixteen-year history ADA has demanded much of others
in the name of liberalism. It has seldom pulled its punches when
dealing with public personages, high or low, and its criticism often has
seemed extreme or misdirected. Its never-ending and vocal suspicion
of all politicians brings to mind the old story of the Quaker lady who
said to her sister: "I have doubts about everyone but me and thee,
and sometimes, sister, I wonder about thee." One suspects that if
"Mr. ADA" himself, Joe Rauh, were President, some faction in ADA,
at some time, over some issue, would accuse him of dragging anchor,
and at least one member would suggest the desirability of instituting
impeachment proceedings.

Perhaps Senator Kennedy had this in mind when, in his 1959 speech
to the Philadelphia Roosevelt Day Dinner, he reviewed FDR's accom-
plishments, then said:

"Contrast this image of Franklin Roosevelt's dynamic leadership
with another Presidential image more familiar to us today—the man
described by the *New Republic* as one "who, despite his excellent
intentions, lacks great intellectual force or supreme moral stamina'—
the man who *Nation* magazine sums up as failing to offer this country
either 'boldness in grasping issues and problems, or courage and origin-
ality in finding solutions'."

The Senator added: "You all know, of course, whom these words
were used to describe—the answer is Franklin Roosevelt in 1932.
Whether this demonstrates the chronic discontent of the liberal movement or the subsequent conversion of Franklin Roosevelt, I leave for
you to decide. But it should, in any event, cause us all to temper our
judgments of men and events."

But the differences between the President and ADA, as noted above, are more tactical than substantive. To Presidents, politics is the art of the possible. To liberals, on the other hand, it is the pursuit of the impossible.

The point can be made, moreover, that each needs the other. Without the power of the Presidency behind them, for liberals progress is almost literally impossible. The need on the other side is less easily demonstrated. President Kennedy has wide latitude to take the liberals or leave them, except perhaps for his rendezvous of November, 1964. But Presidents, despite their great power, are by no means free agents. They must react to great pressures boiling up from their huge and heterogeneous constituency. Given the structure and nature of American society, the balance of these pressures comes from conservative or status quo forces. If the President wants to move in a liberal direction—and there are ample indications that Kennedy does want to—he needs to feel countervailing forces rising up from the liberal sector of his constituency. There is evidence that President Kennedy is disturbed by the weakness of the countervailing forces on the left. In the conference with ADA leaders, Kennedy indicated that he wanted to be "pushed from the left" on economic and other issues. And in a recent column in the *New York Times,* James Reston quoted Presidential complaints to associates that "the major pressures are coming from the Right."

The "Roosevelt coalition" of labor, farmers, minorities, and independent liberals was such a countervailing force. This coalition broke up in the late Thirties and early Forties, however, and ADA's efforts to rebuild it were unsuccessful. It is doubtful that the same coalition could be refashioned today, at least with the same elements. It is certain that the liberals alone cannot put together a similarly powerful force. Pungent press releases, ADA's stock in trade, often make good reading, but they have little effect on events. If the job is to be done at all, it must be done by the President. And here we come to the vicious circle. The liberals can do little without the President. The President can move only painfully and slowly without a potent liberal force behind him. But that force will not come into being unless the President first moves forcefully in a liberal direction and begins to build it under him, and very likely not even then.

All indications are that the circle will not be broken during the Kennedy Presidency, that Kennedy will continue to move haltingly toward his modest goals by the manipulation of political techniques which the liberals despise. He will not break out of the circle with the surge of reform and progress which the liberals demand. And the liberals will continue to be querulous and discontented.

The Demon ADA Again. Despite the visible differences between Kennedy and the ADA, there are many indications that ADA will be used by conservative spokesmen to belabor the Administration and all its works during the 1962 Congressional elections. In recent months there have been definite signs of a move to resurrect "the demon ADA" among those groups and individuals to the right of Senator Barry Goldwater.

During the 1960 campaign virtually nothing was heard of the ADA, "socialistic" or otherwise. In a 1261-page compilation of Nixon's campaign speeches between August 1st and election day, not a single mention of ADA can be found. The same is true of the 1290-page compilation of Kennedy's speeches. For once, a Presidential campaign approached a true political dialogue over issues, and there was no point to dragging in such extraneous matter.

But ADA had not quite disappeared from the conservative demonology. As usual, the issue was raised against Senator Humphrey in his bid for re-election. But in Minnesota ADA is not a good stick. As Humphrey says, "the voters thought the opposition was accusing me of being a member of the American Dairy Association, and we didn't attempt to correct that impression." In his bitter primary battle in Tennessee, however, Senator Kefauver was "a favorite of the ADA, a pro-Russian, anti-American Communist outfit headed by Humphrey of Minnesota, the black widow of Hyde Park, and a few other equally known Communists."

ADA also became an issue in the 1959 Kentucky gubernatorial primary. There was no ADA organization in Kentucky waiting in the wings to take over the state government, but Wilson Wyatt, who had severed his ties with ADA years before, was running for lieutenant-governor on a ticket opposed to the candidate backed by Governor A. B. "Happy" Chandler. A newspaper quoted Chandler as describing ADA as "an organization devoted to using its influence in the Democratic party for a socialistic-type government. They are not Democrats. One of them is a Communist." Upon inquiries from ADA demanding to know who the Communist was, Chandler wrote that he had made "no such statement in the precise form as quoted. I do not know personally whether any member of ADA is a Communist, but, on the other hand, I do not know that you bar Communists from membership." A Kentucky paper picked up Chandler's charge and improved upon it, calling ADA "a defunct and outlawed Communist front organization." The paper printed a retraction after ADA threatened legal action.

There are many reasons why Republican conservatives are tempted to make ADA the whipping boy of the 1962 campaign, as it was in 1954. Perhaps the primary reason is that they need some counterbalance to Democratic attacks on the John Birch Society and allied groups on the far right.

In a November, 1961, speech in Los Angeles, President Kennedy warned against the "discordant voices of extremism which are convinced that the real danger comes from within" rather than from the Soviet Union and international Communism. Such people, said the President, "call for a 'man on horseback' because they do not trust the people. They find treason in our churches, in our highest court, in our treatment of water. They equate the Democratic party with the welfare state, the welfare state with socialism, and socialism with communism."

Senator Goldwater saw the handle and seized it within hours. Speaking the following day on "Meet the Press," Goldwater charged that "the real extremists are the people to the left, the socialists in the Kennedy Administration." When asked to give the names of leading socialists in the Administration, the Senator did not "have time to go clear through them," but mentioned three: Arthur Schlesinger, Jr., Ted Sorensen, and one other ADA member in the White House whose name "slips my mind for the moment." Goldwater pointed out that no members of the John Birch Society were in the government, but "some thirty" ADA people were.

Mr. Spivack: "Are you suggesting they are running the government rather than President Kennedy?"

Senator Goldwater: "I am suggesting that they have a mighty strong hand in it because what they have advocated all down through the history of ADA seems to be coming—the parts that haven't been accepted seem to be coming to be accepted by the Kennedy Administration."

In an earlier speech in Atlanta the Senator charged that the President was "surrounded by ADA extremists of the left" who were "far more dangerous than those of the right."

Shortly after the Goldwater opening, there appeared on the newsstands a paperback book, *America; Listen!,* which purported to be "an honest report to the nation which reveals that the threat to our survival is greater than most Americans have been permitted to realize." One chapter of the book deals with the ADA, listing thirty-five of its members in high Administration posts. ADA is described as "the left-wing counterpart of some of the right-wing groups which have been so publicly attacked lately." It is "probably the most influential single element in Jack Kennedy's government."

In January of this year the Michigan Republican State Central Committee adopted a resolution denouncing the "ultra-conservative John Birch Society" and called upon the Democratic party to "repudiate immediately and fully the Americans for Democratic Action and other organizations of the extreme Left."

It is evident that the Republican strategy this fall and perhaps in future elections will be to equate ADA with the Birchites, the Christian Anti-Communist Crusaders, and other far right groups. In recent weeks ADA's publicity director has reported an enormous increase in press clippings, most of them reflecting speeches—or editorials based on speeches—by Goldwater, Senator Strom Thurmond of South Carolina, and various Republican Congressmen, in which such an equation is made. The comparison is, of course, as absurd as the older "ADA= Communism" equation. Joe Rauh points out that "it is saying that Mrs. Roosevelt is the equivalent of Robert Welch." Somewhat surprisingly to ADA, several newspapers not deemed particularly friendly in the past have countered this equation. In an editorial of January 30th, for instance, the *Toledo Blade* said:

"The ADA is not a semi-secret organization whose thinking is shaped by little blue books and would-be superpatriots. It is not going around charging that past and present Presidents of the United States are traitors. It is not calling for the abolition of the income tax and impeachment of the Chief Justice of the U.S. Supreme Court.

"There is room in this nation for the ADA, with its liberalism, just as there is for the National Association of Manufacturers, with their conservatism. For the Republicans to try to equate the ADA with the John Birch Society is an attempt to divert attention from their own extremists and is patently unfair."

But if past experience is any guide, ADA can expect an increasingly vigorous buildup against it as election day approaches. As in 1954, the most vicious charges first made by fringe groups may be taken over by more respectable Republicans. An example of the possibilities appeared in an article in the July, 1961, issue of *Christian Crusade,* an organ of the rightist group headed by evangelist Billy James Hargis. The author was Matt Cvetic, billed as a former FBI infiltrator among Communist groups. Entitled "A Counterspy Views Communist Subversion," the article charged that "for the past decade the ADA has been in the forefront demanding the recognition of Red China, and a seat for this murderous Red government in the United Nations." The ADA was "the political action arm of the Fabian Socialist movement in America." Cvetic claimed to have been a member of the Political Commission of the Communist Party in 1947-48: "One of my Red Party assignments is those days was to meet with these starry-eyed ADA daydreamers in secret Progressive Party meetings to plan strategy."

Cvetic apparently had been reading the decade-old articles of John T. Flynn, Fulton Lewis, Jr., and the material inserted into the *Congressional Record* in 1950 by Senator Homer Capehart. He had added some of his own "experiences," but these adventures presumably came as an afterthought. Following the article there appeared an advertisement for Cvetic's book, *The Big Decision*, "the amazing story of his nine years as a counterspy for the FBI." The book appeared in 1959, and it contains no mention of ADA or of Cvetic's "secret meetings" with ADA people in the Progressive Party.

In his article Cvetic referred "the ADAers" to his sworn testimony before the Senate Internal Security Subcommittee and other Congressional committees on "the Kremlin strategy for Red China." This sworn testimony contains no mention of ADA.

Since charges of "Communists in ADA" will be heard again, it might be well to call attention—at the risk of tediousness—to what appear to be some salient facts. During the years from 1947 through 1961, various subcommittees of the Senate Judiciary Committee held numerous hearings on the subject of communism. These hearings comprise 7,035 pages of sworn testimony by experts and professed experts on Communist infiltration of American life. In all this, there is one reference to ADA. In a 1952 hearing a witness—an employee of the anti-Communist magazine *Counterattack*—cited the ADA as a "non-Communist organization."

During the years from 1947 to 1955, the House Un-American Activities Committee listened to 18,928 pages of sworn testimony on the same subject. There are six references to ADA. Five of these are innocuous. The sixth is testimony by Adolph Menjou, a Hollywood personality now backing several right-wing groups, to the effect that ADA was an anti-Communist group which "does not permit" Communists as members.

If, after all this, there really are Communists in the ADA, the conclusion would seem inescapable that the President should fire J. Edgar

Hoover and his boss, Attorney-General Robert Kennedy, and rebuild the FBI.

Since no hearings have been held on socialist infiltration of American life, the question of "ADA socialism" cannot be resolved quite so unequivocally. The Union for Democratic Action, ADA's predecessor organization, was a splinter group spun off the Socialist party. Very few UDA members remain in ADA today, and none in positions of leadership. There are, however, a few lower-case "socialists" in ADA. The author saw one in person at the 1961 ADA convention. During a heated debate before the Foreign Policy Commission, an old gentleman got the floor, announced that he had been a member of the Fabian Society in Britain, denounced the ADA for its lack of militancy, and accused it of senility. He was welcomed as "an old antagonist" by a member of the Commission, listened to politely by the delegates, and ignored.

In his newspaper column of January 25, 1962, Senator Goldwater backed up his charges that ADA was socialistic by referring to a 1952 *Saturday Evening Post* editorial which reported that the ADA convention of that year voted down a resolution in favor of "free private enterprise." ADA has no transcript of the proceedings of that convention, and its leaders disagree in their recollections of it. Some say no such vote was taken; others contend that the delegates did reject one resolution on private enterprise while accepting another. But the platform finally adopted by the 1952 convention contains a plank on monopoly which reads, in part: "We affirm our belief in the principle of free and private competitive enterprise."

The question whether ADA "advocates socialism" perhaps could be settled—for reasonable men—by an exhaustive comparison of ADA platforms with those of the Socialist party. Such a comparison was made, but will not be inflicted upon the reader. Put briefly, ADA people are liberals in a hurry, but not socialists. Experts agree that the chief distinguishing characteristic of a socialist movement or party is its advocacy of public ownership or "nationalization" of major industries. The ADA has never advocated this.

But rational arguments are not likely to convince the right-wing groups operating in the United States today. Any individual or group which sees former President Eisenhower as a "dedicated, conscious agent of the Communist conspiracy" is beyond reach of rational argument. At this writing, there are ample signs of a renewed attack on ADA building up among these groups. And the circumstances are far different from what they were in 1954. Then, no ADA members held any post in the Administration. Many do today. Thus the weapon is at hand, and conservatives will need and use all the weapons they can find in 1962. We are likely to see a rerun of the morality play of 1954 entitled "The Demon ADA." The script will be only slightly altered, but there will be sharp competition for the star role once filled by Vice-President Nixon. Senator Goldwater has taken the early lead, but he will have to perform well if he is not to be upstaged by the many haunted and demon-ridden minds who ride the banquet and television circuits of the far right wing.

Conclusion. But it must be admitted that ADA people themselves were not quite normal, according to the standards of postwar America. They, too, were restless and frustrated, and they had a facility for being in the "wrong" place at the "wrong" time and on the "wrong" side of many issues.

When the Communists made an undercover bid for power, they insisted that a Communist by any other name was still a Communist and had no place in American life. When others began to conjure up imaginary Communists for use as political tackling dummies, they tried to blow the whistle. When the Neanderthal men began to roam the land and Presidents, politicians, and plain citizens began to seek cover, they stood almost alone against them. None of them took the Fifth Amendment, but they insisted that those who did take it still were entitled to the guarantees of the First and Sixth Amendments.

Their faith was demanding, and they demanded too much of others, but no less of themselves. They stood up for the middledogs and the persistent pockets of underdogs in a decade of private abundance and public parsimony. Most of them lived in comfortable homes, had adequate incomes, went to good schools, voted, and sat where they pleased when they rode on a bus; but they showed concern for those who had none of these rights and privileges. They sought what they conceived to be best for their country, and they seldom asked what their country could do for them.

Some considered such things queer and called them "Communists," "socialists," and "quivering crackpots." They looked foolish at times, and at times they were foolish. But President Roosevelt—and long before him the immortal Dante—held that the sins of the coldblooded and the sins of the warmhearted should be weighed in different scales.

BIBLIOGRAPHY

The primary source materials for this book were the records of the Americans for Democratic Action, located in ADA's national headquarters in Washington. These consist of letters, memoranda, transcripts and summaries of executive committee and national board meetings, staff reports, press clippings, ADA publications, and a mass of other material. Although these files, particularly for the early years, are not in the order a researcher might wish, the author spent several weeks combing through them and believes that nothing significant was overlooked. He had unrestricted access to these records and full cooperation of ADA leaders, without which the book could not have been written. Other primary sources were the *New York Times*, the *Congressional Record*, and other government publications. The two major liberal weeklies, the *New Republic* and *Nation*, provided valuable background for the period covered. The major secondary sources are listed below.

Books

Abels, Jules. *Out of the Jaws of Victory.* New York: Henry Holt, 1959.

Bailey, Stephen K. and Samuel, Howard D. *Congress at Work.* New York: Henry Holt, 1952.

Bentley, Arthur F. *The Process of Government.* Chicago: University of Chicago Press, 1908.

Blaisdell, Donald C. *American Democracy Under Pressure.* New York: Ronald Press, 1957.

Buckley, William F. *Up From Liberalism.* New York: McDowell, Oblensky, 1959.

Burnham, James, *Congress and the American Political Tradition.* Chicago: Henry Regnery Co., 1959.

Burns, James M. *Congress on Trial.* New York: Harpers, 1949.

Burns, James M. *John Kennedy: A Political Profile.* New York: Harcourt, Brace, 1960.

Calkins, Fay. *The CIO and the Democratic Party.* Chicago: University of Chicago Press, 1952.

Campbell, Angus and Kahn, Robert L. *The People Elect a President.* Ann Arbor: Survey Research Center, University of Michigan, 1952.

Crown, James T. and George Penty. *Kennedy in Power.* New York: Ballantine, 1962.

Ehrmann, Henry W., (ed.). *Interest Groups on Four Continents.* Pittsburgh: University of Pittsburgh Press, 1958.

Flynn, John T. *The Road Ahead.* New York: Devin-Adair, 1949.

Garceau, Oliver. *The Political Life of the American Medical Association.* Cambridge: Harvard University Press, 1941.

Goldman, Eric F. *Rendezvous with Destiny.* New York: Alfred A. Knopf, 1952.

Greer, Thomas H. *American Social Reform Movements.* New York: Prentice-Hall, 1949.

Griffith, Ernest S. *Congress, Its Contemporary Role.* 2nd ed. revised. New York: New York University Press, 1956.

Hesseltine, William B. *Rise and Fall of Third Parties.* Washington, D.C.: Public
    Affairs Press. 1948.
Hicks, Granville. *Where We Came Out.* New York: Viking Press, 1954.
Howe, Irving and Coser, Lewis. *The American Communist Party.* Boston: Bea-
    con Press, 1957.
Irish, Marian D. and Prothro, James W. *The Politics of American Democracy.* Engle-
    wood Cliffs, N.J.: Prentice-Hall, 1959.
Kampelman, Max W. *The Communist Party vs. the CIO.* New York: Praeger, 1957.
Kluckhohn, Frank L. *America, Listen!* Derby, Conn: Monarch Books, 1961.
Lasky, Victor. *John F. Kennedy: What's Behind the Image?* Washington: Free
    World Press, 1960.
Latham, Earl. *The Group Basis of Politics: A Study in Basing-point Legislation.*
    Ithaca, N.Y.: Cornell University Press, 1952.
Lerner, Max, *Actions and Passions; Notes on the Multiple Revolution of Our Time.*
    New York: Simon and Shuster, 1949.
Lubell, Samuel. *The Future of American Politics.* New York: Harper, 1952.
McCoy, Donald R. *Angry Voices; Left-of-Center Politics in the New Deal Era.*
    Lawrence, Kansas: University of Kansas Press, 1958.
MacDonald, Dwight. *Henry Wallace; the Man and the Myth.* New York:
    Vanguard Press, 1947.
Nash, Howard P. *Third Parties in American Politics.* Washington, D.C.: Public
    Affairs Press, 1958.
Peterson, Lorin W. *The Day of the Mugwump.* New York: Random House, 1961.
Redding, Jack. *Inside the Democratic Party.* Indianapolis: Bobbs-Merrill, 1958.
Saposs, David J. *Communism in American Politics.* Washington: Public Affairs Press,
    1960.
Schlesinger, Arthur, Jr. *The Vital Center.* Boston: Houghton Mifflin, 1949.
Schmidt, Karl M. *Henry A. Wallace; Quixotic Crusade: 1948.* Syracuse, N.Y.: Syra-
    cuse University Press, 1960.
Shannon, David A. *The Decline of American Communism.* New York: Harcourt,
    Brace, 1960.
Truman, David B. *The Governmental Process.* New York: Alfred A. Knopf, 1951.
Viereck, Peter. *The Unadjusted Man.* Boston, Beacon Press, 1956.
Voss, Earl, and others. *New Frontiersmen.* Washington, D.C.: Public Affairs Press,
    1961.
Wechsler, James A. *The Age of Suspicion.* New York: Random House, 1953.
Wechsler, James A. *Reflections of An Angry Middle-Aged Editor.* New York: Random
    House, 1960.
White, Theodore H. *The Making of the President.* New York: Atheneum, 1961.
White, Williams S. *Citadel: The Story of the U.S. Senate.* New York: Harpers, 1956.
Wilson, Woodrow. *Congressional Government.* 15th ed. Boston: Houghton Mifflin, 1913.
————. *The New Freedom.* New York: Doubleday, 1913.
Young, Roland. *The American Congress.* New York: Harper, 1958.
————. *Approaches to the Study of Politics.* Evanston, Illinois: Northwestern
    University Press, 1958.

Articles

"ADA, a Snark in Political Clothing," *Business Week,* No. 1201 (September 6, 1952),
    30-32.

"The ADA Can Take McCarthyism or Leave it Alone," *Saturday Evening Post,* CCXXVIII (May 5, 1956), 10.

"ADA Convention," *New Republic,* CXXII (April 17, 1950), 15.

"ADA Convention," *New Republic,* CXIV (March 5, 1951), 6.

"ADA in the Next Two Years," *New Republic,* CXIX (December 20, 1948), 6-7.

"ADA on the Record," *New Republic,* CXXIII (July 24, 1950), 8.

"ADA Policy Statement," *New Republic,* CXVII (December 22, 1947), 10-11.

"Adlai May Find ADA Albatross Hard to Handle," *Saturday Evening Post,* CCXXV (September 20, 1952), 10.

Akers, Milhous P. "The PCA Convention," *Nation,* CLXVI (January 24, 1948), 92.

Alexander, Robert J. "Splinter Groups in American Radical Politics," *Social Research,* XX (October, 1953), 282-310.

Alsop, Joseph and Alsop, Stewart. "Tragedy of Liberalism," *Life,* XX (May 20, 1946), 68-70.

"Americans for Democratic Action," *Congressional Quarterly Weekly Report,* XIII (December 30, 1955), 1347-49.

"Back to Truman by Default," *Newsweek,* XXXII (July 19, 1948), 17

Baldwin, C. B. "The PCA's Position on Henry Wallace," *Nation,* CLXVI (January 24, 1948), 110.

Bendiner, Robert. "ADA and the Democrats," *Nation,* CLXVIII (April 23, 1949), 461-62.

————. "The Compromise on Civil Rights—I," *Reporter,* XVI (Sept. 6, 1956).

————. "CIO Tightrope Act," *Nation,* CLXIII (November 30, 1946), 601.

————. "Has the American Voter Swung Right?" *Commentary,* XI (January, 1951), 27-35.

————. "Politics and People," *Nation,* CLXVI (April 24, 1948), 430.

————. "Revolt of the Middle," *Nation,* CLXIV (January 18, 1947), 65.

————. "Rout of the Bourbons," *Nation,* CLXVIII (July 24, 1948), 92.

————. "Wallace; the Incomplete Angler," *Nation,* CLXV (December 20, 1947), 668.

————. "What Kind of Liberal Are You; A Classification of the Species," *Commentary,* VIII (September, 1949), 238-42.

Bolte, Charles. "A Democratic Assembly," *Nation,* CLXV (April 12, 1947), 424.

Burns, James M. "John F. Kennedy; Candidate on the Eve," *New Republic,* CXLIII (October 31, 1960)

Carleton, William G. "The Dilemma of the Democrats," *Virginia Quarterly Review* XXIV (July, 1948), 336-53.

————. "The Promise of American Liberalism," *Antioch Review,* VIII (Fall, 1948), 331-45.

Cater, Douglas. "How the Democrats Got Together," *Reporter,* VII (August 19, 1952), 6-8.

"Comintern's Challenge to Liberals," *New Republic,* CXVII (October 20, 1947), 2.

Corey, Lewis. "Toward a Liberal Program for Prosperity and Peace," *Antioch Review,* VII (June, 1947), 291-304.

Davenport, Walter. "Ruddy Rodeo," *Collier's,* CXVII (June 1, 1946), 14-15.

"Democrats Boom Eisenhower," *New Republic,* CXVIII (April 12, 1948), 136.

Filler, Louis. "The Dilemma, So-Called, of the American Liberal," *Antioch Review,* VIII (Summer, 1948), 131-51.

Fischer, John. "The Lost Liberals; Can They Find a New Road Map?" *Harper's,* CXCIV (May, 1947), 385-95.

"Five Days that Shook the Democrats," *Newsweek,* XXXI (March 1, 1948), 15.

Flynn, John T. "The Soviet's Second Front," *American Mercury,* LXXVIII (May, 1954), 47.

Flynn, John T. "Fifty Million Americans in Search of a Party," *American Mercury,* LXXX (February, 1955)

Freeman, Howard and Showel, Morris. "Differential Political Influence of Voluntary Associations," *Public Opinion Quarterly,* XV (Winter, 1952), 703-14.

"Glamour Pusses," *Time,* XLVIII (September 9, 1946), 35.

Glaser, William A. "The Units of Political Action," *Southwestern Social Science Quarterly,* XXXV (June, 1954), 25-35.

Goldman, Eric F. "The American Liberal: After the Fair Deal, What?" *Reporter,* VIII (June 23, 1953), 25-28.

Hale, William Harlan. "What Makes Wallace Run?" *Harper's,* CXCVI (March, 1948), 244.

Harrington, Michael. "Myths of U.S. Liberalism," *Commonweal,* LXI (September 17, 1954), 303-06.

Harsch, Joseph C. "Are Liberals Obsolete?" *Reporter,* VII (September 30, 1952), 13-16.

Hennessy, Bernard. "A Case Study of Intra-Pressure Group Conflicts; The United World Federalists," *Journal of Politics,* XVI (February, 1954), 76-95.

Hicks, Granville. "Liberalism in the Fifties," *American Scholar,* XXV (Spring, 1956), 283-96.

"If Not ADA, Then Who?" *New Republic,* CXX (April 18, 1949), 8.

Kirchwey, Freda. "The Challenge of Henry Wallace," *Nation,* CLXIII (September 28, 1946), 338.

————. "Manifest Destiny, 1947," *Nation,* CLXIV (March 22, 1947), 317.

————. "Mugwumps in Action," *Nation,* CLXIV (January 18, 1947), 61-62.

————. "To the Greeks, Bearing Gifts," *Nation,* CLXIV (March 29, 1947), 349.

————. "Toward a New Beginning," *Nation,* CLXIII (November 16, 1946), 544.

Kramer, Dale. "Must it be Truman," *Nation,* CLXVI (March 13, 1948), 296.

Latham, Earl. "The Group Basis of Politics: Notes for a Theory," *American Political Science Review,* XLVI (June, 1952), 376-97.

Lerner, Max. "The Outlook for Party Realignment," *Virginia Quarterly Review,* XXV (Spring, 1949), 179-93.

"Liberals and the Labor Crisis," *New Republic,* CXIV (June 10, 1946), 830-31.

"Liberals, Disband!" *Time,* LXII (December 21, 1953), 21.

"The Line Squall," *Time,* LII (July 26, 1948), 12.

Loeb, James, Jr. "Progressives and Communists," *New Republic,* CXIV (May 13, 1946), 699.

Lowry, W. McNeil. "Wanderer's Return," *Antioch Review,* VIII (Winter, 1948), 463-68.

Mackenzie, Norman. "Dilemma for Liberals," *New Statesman and Nation,* XII (March 6, 1948), 187-88.

Mackenzie, W. J. M. "Pressure Groups; the 'Conceptual Framework'," *Political Studies,* III (October, 1955), 247-55.

"The Marshall Plan," *New Republic,* CXVI (June 16, 1947), 5.

"The Marshall Program," *New Republic,* CXVI (June 16, 1947), 5.

Mathews, J. B. "Communists and the New Deal," *American Mercury*, LXXVI (June, 1953), 33-40.

Moley, Raymond. "Republican Advance and the ADA," *Newsweek*, XXXVI (July 31, 1950), 84.

Moneypenny, Philip. "Political Science and the Study of Groups; Notes to Guide a Research Project," *Western Political Quarterly*, VII (June, 1954), 183-201.

"The Mutineers and the Firm Hand," *Newsweek*, XXXII (July 26, 1948), 17-21.

Nathan, Robert. "The Value of ADA," *Progressive* (September, 1954), pp. 12-13.

Newman, James R. "Reexamination of Freedom," *New Republic*, CXVII (November 17, 1947), 24-27.

Newman, William J. "The President and the Professors," *Twentieth Century*, CLIV (July, 1953)

"Next Steps in the Fair Deal," *New Republic*, CXX (March 7, 1949), 1-31.

Odegard, Peter H. "A Group Basis of Politics; a New Name for an Ancient Myth," *Western Political Quarterly*, XI (September, 1958), 689-702.

"Our Third Party Critics," *Nation*, CLXVI (February 21, 1948), 200-02.

Pattee, Allen, "Attitude Groups," *Political Quarterly*, XXIX (January-March, 1958), 73-82.

"PCA Domestic and Foreign Program," *New Republic*, CXVII (October 13, 1947), 8.

Phillips, Cabell. "That Baffling Personality, Mr. Wallace," *New York Times Magazine*, (February 8, 1948), 14.

"Political Roundup," *New Republic*, CXV (September 9, 1946), 281.

"Progressives' Last Stand," *Newsweek*, XXV (March 6, 1950), 25.

Pye, Lucien W. "Effects of Legislative and Administrative Accessibility on Interest Group Politics," *PROD*, I (January, 1958), 11-13.

"Revolt Against Truman," *Nation*, CLXVI (April 3, 1948), 367.

Riddick, Floyd M. "The Eighty-first Congress," *Western Political Quarterly*, IV (March, 1951), 48-62.

Sancton, Thomas. "Second Chance for the New Deal?" *Nation*. CLXVIII (January 15, 1949), 59-61.

Schlesinger, Arthur M., Jr. "Stevenson and the American Liberal Dilemma," *Twentieth Century*, CLIII (January, 1953), 24-29.

———— and Ascoli, Max. "The Future of Liberalism; A Debate," *Reporter*, XIV (May 3, 1956), 8-16.

————. "The Future of Liberalism—II," *Reporter*, XIV (May 31, 1956), 15-23.

Sevareid, Eric. "Demon ADA," *Reporter*, XI (November 4, 1954), 17.

Shannon, William V. "Hubert Humphrey in Mid-Passage," *Progressive*, XXII (December, 1958)

Shelton, Willard. "The ADA's Dilemma: HST or GOP," *New Republic*, CXVIII (March 1, 1948), 9-10.

————. "Third Party Splits CIO Board," *New Republic*, CXVIII (February 2, 1948), 31.

"Should We Fight Dirty, Too?" *Reporter*, XI (October 21, 1954)

Stedman, Murray S., Jr. "A Group Interpretation of Politics," *Public Opinion Quarterly*, XVII (Summer, 1953), 218-29.

T.R.B. "Neanderthal Men," *New Republic*, CXVII (August 4, 1947), 3.

————. "Washington Wire," *New Republic*, CXIX (November 15, 1948), 3.

"The Third Party Beginnings," *New Republic*, CXVIII (January 19, 1948), 10-11.

Thomas, Norman, "The Trouble with ADA," *Progressive* (September, 1954), 9-11.

Titus, Charles H. "The Two Major Conventions in 1948," *Western Political Quarterly*,
     I (September, 1948), 252-60.
"Truman and the Stop Truman Revolt," *Newsweek*, XXXII (July 12, 1948), 19-21.
"The Truman Doctrine," *New Republic*, CXVI (March 24, 1947), 6.
"Unity on the Left," *New Republic*, CXIV (May 13, 1946), 681.
"Wagner Act, 1949 Model," *New Republic*, CXX (February 14, 1949), 7.
Wallace, Henry. "Bevin Muddies the Waters," *New Republic*, CXVI (June 30, 1947),
     11-12.
————. "Jobs, Peace, Freedom," *New Republic*, CXV (December 16, 1946), 783-85.
————. "My Alternative to the Marshall Plan," *New Republic*, CXVIII (January
     17, 1948), 13-14.
————. "Too Little, Too Late," *New Republic*, CXVII (October 6, 1947), 11-12.
"War Among the Democrats," *New Republic*, CXIV (June 3, 1946), 793.
"We Reject," *Time*, XLIX (January 13, 1947), 26.
Wechsler, James A. "Did Truman Scuttle Liberalism?" *Commentary*, III (March,
     1947), 229-37.
————. "The Liberals' Vote and '48: What Price Third Party?" *Commentary*, IV
     (September, 1947), 216-25.
Wyatt, Wilson. "Creed for Liberals," *New York Times Magazine*, July 27, 1947, p. 38.

Public Documents

U.S. House of Representatives. *Hearings Before the Committee to Investigate
     Campaign Expenditures*. 78th Cong., 2d Sess., Pt. 3, "Union for Democratic
     Action."
U.S. House of Representatives. Select Committee on Lobbying Activities. *Lobbying,
     Direct and Indirect*. 81st Cong., 2d Sess., "Americans for Democratic Action."

Unpublished Material

Clymer, Adam. "Union for Democratic Action: Key to the Non-Communist Left"
     Unpublished Senior Honors Thesis, Harvard Uniuversity, 1958.
Senate Republican Policy Committee, "Americans for Democratic Action," 1958.

INDEX

Abt, John, 62
American Civil Liberties Union, 147
American Federation of Labor, 78, 118-119, 139, 164
American League Against War and Fascism, 44
American Medical Association, 113
American Mercury, 147
American Peace Mobilization, 45
American Youth Congress, 44
Americans for Democratic Action (ADA): members in Kennedy Administration, 11-16, 196, 199-201; conference with Kennedy, 11, 202; and Democratic party, 17, 20, 23-30, 51, 83, 147, 148, 158-159, 162-163, 171; and Republican party, 20-23; "nonpartisanship," 17, 20, 22, 25; in Illinois, *See* Independent Voters of Illinois; in Pennsylvania, 27-28; in New York, 28; in Minnesota, 28; lobbying, 31; exclusion of Communists, 33, 52, 55, 56, 58, 60, 150, 217; membership, 33, 165; finances, 34, 165; founding, 51-52; opposition to Progressive Citizens of America, 56-60, 63-67, 68; opposition to Wallace and Progressive Party, 69-72, 74-81; opposition to Truman in 1948, 87-95; influence on election of 1948, 100-103; and "stop-Kennedy" movement, 175; criticism of Kennedy Administration, 202, 203, 206; "socialism" in, 216
Anderson, Clinton, 200
Arvey, Jake, 92, 94, 95
Atlantic Treaty, 114
Barkley, Alben, 97-98
Beer, Samuel, 179, 185, 191, 196, 200, 203
Bendiner, Robert, 44, 57, 92
Benton, William, 146
Biddle, Francis, 42, 137, 145-146
Biemiller, Andrew, 98

Bingham, Barry, 52
Bingham, Jonathan, 12
Bolling, Richard, 102
Bolte, Charles, 64
Bowles, Chester, 12, 42, 51, 83, 119, 196, 199, 201
Brannan Plan, 113, 137
Brooks, Wayland, 79
Brotherhood of Railroad Trainmen, 53, 73
Browder, Earl, 61
Brownell, Herbert, 145
Buckley, William, 146
Burns, James M., 127, 129, 193, 194
Business Week: on ADA, 29
Byrd, Harry, 92
Cagney, James, 44
Capehart, Homer: attack on ADA, 136-137, 217
Carey, Archibald, 21
Celler, Emmanuel, 207
Chandler, A.B., 212
Chiang Kai-shek, 147
Chicago Conference of Progressives, 53-54
Childs, Marquis, 51
China, Communist, 141, 143-144
Christian Anti-Communist Crusade, 216
Christian Crusade, 214
Civil rights issue, 158; at 1948 Democratic convention, 95-99; in 1948 election, 103; in 81st Congress, 111; at 1956 Democratic convention, 160-162; at 1960 Democratic convention, 179-181.
Clark, Joseph, 17, 27
Clark-Celler bill, 207
Cohen,Wilbur, 12
Collins, Leroy, 183
Columbia Valley Authority, 113
Committee for Constitutional Government, 135
Communist Control Act, 156-157, 185
Communists, 43, 142; and disruption of